MW01448638

Dancer Wellness

M. Virginia Wilmerding, PhD

Donna H. Krasnow, PhD

EDITORS

IADMS
International Association for
Dance Medicine & Science

HUMAN
KINETICS

Library of Congress Cataloging-in-Publication Data

Names: Wilmerding, M. Virginia, editor. | Krasnow, Donna H., editor.
Title: Dancer wellness / edited by M. Virginia Wilmerding, PhD, University of
  New Mexico, Donna H. Krasnow, PhD, York University, Toronto, Canada,
  Professor Emerita.
Description: Champaign, IL : Human Kinetics, [2017] | Includes
  bibliographical references and index.
Identifiers: LCCN 2016004374 | ISBN 9781492515814 (print)
Subjects: LCSH: Dance. | Dancers. | Physical fitness. | Dance--Physiological
  aspects. | Dance--Psychological aspects. | Dancing injuries--Prevention.
Classification: LCC GV1588 .D355 2017 | DDC 792.8--dc23 LC record available at https://lccn.loc.gov/2016004374

ISBN: 978-1-4925-1581-4 (print)
Copyright © 2017 by M. Virginia Wilmerding and Donna H. Krasnow

All rights reserved. Except for use in a review, the reproduction or utilization of this work in any form or by any electronic, mechanical, or other means, now known or hereafter invented, including xerography, photocopying, and recording, and in any information storage and retrieval system, is forbidden without the written permission of the publisher.

The web addresses cited in this text were current as of July 2016, unless otherwise noted.

Acquisitions Editor: Gayle Kassing, PhD
Senior Developmental Editor: Bethany J. Bentley
Managing Editor: Anne E. Mrozek
Copyeditor: Joanna Hatzopoulos Portman
Indexer: Laurel Plotzke
Permissions Manager: Dalene Reeder
Senior Graphic Designer: Nancy Rasmus
Cover Designer: Keith Blomberg
Photograph (cover): © Jake Pett
Photographs (interior): © Human Kinetics, unless otherwise noted
Photo Production Manager: Jason Allen
Senior Art Manager: Kelly Hendren
Illustrations: © Human Kinetics, unless otherwise noted
Printer: Premier Print Group

Printed in the United States of America   10 9 8 7 6 5 4 3 2 1

Human Kinetics
Website: www.HumanKinetics.com

United States: Human Kinetics
P.O. Box 5076
Champaign, IL 61825-5076
800-747-4457
e-mail: info@hkusa.com

Canada: Human Kinetics
475 Devonshire Road Unit 100
Windsor, ON N8Y 2L5
800-465-7301 (in Canada only)
e-mail: info@hkcanada.com

Europe: Human Kinetics
107 Bradford Road
Stanningley
Leeds LS28 6AT, United Kingdom
+44 (0) 113 255 5665
e-mail: hk@hkeurope.com

Australia: Human Kinetics
57A Price Avenue
Lower Mitcham, South Australia 5062
08 8372 0999
e-mail: info@hkaustralia.com

New Zealand: Human Kinetics
P.O. Box 80
Mitcham Shopping Centre, South Australia 5062
0800 222 062
e-mail: info@hknewzealand.com

E6649

Contents

Part I   Foundations of Dancer Wellness

1   The Dance Environment

3

Luke Hopper, PhD, and Alycia Fong Yan, PhD

2   Dance Training and Technique

13

Donna H. Krasnow, PhD, M. Virginia Wilmerding, PhD,
Arleen Sugano, MFA, and Kenneth Laws, PhD

3   Cross-Training and Conditioning

37

Emma Redding, PhD, MSc, and Pamela Geber Handman, MFA

Part II   **Mental Components of Dancer Wellness**

Part III   **Physical Components of Dancer Wellness**

Preface

Donna H. Krasnow, PhD, and M. Virginia Wilmerding, PhD

As a dancer in the modern era, you are likely to be far more inquisitive about how to care for your body than previous generations of dancers were. In addition, you may have some or all of these experiences:

You ask questions about how your body works when you dance, and you are beginning to understand problems with floors that are not sprung and shoes that fit poorly. You wonder whether additional exercises or classes can enhance your technique. You question how the atmosphere and teaching style affect your emotions in class, and you rely more on imagery to influence your training. You think about what to eat before class or a performance and how to remain lean while getting all the nutrients you need. You are concerned about injuries. You question how you can discern good pains from bad pains (i.e., when you have sore muscles as opposed to an actual injury). You think about whether you are getting enough rest. At times you are concerned that you do not know whom to see for your injuries, and you fear that injuries might end your career.

All of these thoughts and concerns fall under the umbrella of health and wellness for dancers. *Health* is the general condition of both the body and mind in terms of vitality, energy, and ability to adapt to challenges. *Wellness* defines the state of being healthy in both mind and body through conscious and intentional choices and efforts. Although dancer wellness has several components, it generally refers to overall health and well-being.

This book is for dancers and dance students in any setting, including colleges or universities, high schools, local dance studios, preprofessional training programs, or dance companies. Regardless of previous training or level of expertise, anyone interested in the health and wellness of dancers can benefit from this book. The book covers each aspect of dancer wellness, whether environmental, physical, or psychological. Well-known experts in the field of dance present each topic in the book. The authors were selected based on their research and writings in dance and their reputations as leaders in the field. In addition to theoretical concepts, this book provides practical applications that you can use to enhance your health and wellness as part of your dance practice.

Dimensions of Wellness

The National Wellness Institute (NWI) and leaders in the field of health have generally agreed on these ideas about wellness:

> Wellness is a conscious, self-directed, and evolving process of achieving full potential.

> Wellness is multidimensional and holistic, encompassing lifestyle, mental and spiritual well-being, and the environment.

> Wellness is positive and affirming.

In addition, the NWI defines these six dimensions of wellness, seen in figure 1, which can be applied to almost any activity, including dance:

1. **Occupational wellness** suggests that you should have satisfaction and enrichment through your work, whether as a performer, a teacher, a choreographer, or a proprietor of a dance studio. It implies success and contentment with a chosen occupation and knowing how to plan for the future. In dance, part of occupational wellness relates to the environment in which you train; in other words, the physical space and the emotional climate affect occupational wellness. Factors such as improper floors and negative teaching strategies can affect your environment.

2. **Physical wellness** means that you should strive to achieve fitness (physical strength, flexibility, and endurance) while taking care of your body to ensure safety. It involves

overall health, but in particular it relates to dancers' technique, injury prevention, and physical conditioning. This approach implies taking personal responsibility and care for minor injuries and knowing when professional medical assistance is required.

3. **Social wellness** suggests that you should contribute to the common welfare of your community and not think only of yourself; in other words, it describes how you interact with others and whether or not you receive support. If the dance environment is too competitive, a climate can develop that pits dancers against each other and creates tension.

4. **Intellectual wellness** embraces challenging the mind through dance practice, stimulating creativity, and identifying potential problems. It includes the ideas of mind–body connection, learning how to pay attention, and exploring information that must be learned, such as dance terminology.

5. **Spiritual wellness** implies that you will have greater satisfaction if you live in a way that is consistent with your values and beliefs. It implies an understanding of your beliefs and developing a purpose in your chosen work in dance.

6. **Emotional wellness** recognizes awareness and acceptance of your feelings as well as the feelings of others and emphasizes being optimistic in your approach to dancing. It embraces psychological issues, such as self-esteem, perfectionism, body image, and stress.

Figure 1   Six dimensions of wellness.

Based on National Wellness Institute. Available: www.nationalwellness.org/?page-Six_Dimensions

Dance writers and researchers have taken these ideas of the six dimensions of wellness and expanded them to relate in specific terms to dance practice. Since the 1990s, dance researchers and educators have started designing dance training programs in educational settings that incorporate aspects of wellness, drawing from fields of dance medicine, dance science, somatics, and information about wellness and self-help for the general population. In attempting to develop a balanced and interdisciplinary approach, they proposed that these aspects should be included in a curriculum for dancers: anatomy, injury prevention, nutrition, psychology, and motor learning.

How This Book Is Organized

The new model of dancer wellness has three main categories, which correspond with the first three parts of this book:

1. Foundations of dancer wellness (part I)
2. Mental components of dancer wellness (part II)
3. Physical components of dancer wellness (part III)

Recognizing the importance of these components in health and wellness, in this book, researchers, teachers, and medical practitioners from the International Association for Dance Medicine & Science (IADMS) discuss their areas of specialization in thorough investigations of all aspects of dancer wellness. The foundations of dancer wellness lay the groundwork for dance training. The mental components of dancer wellness include all of the tools that focus on the mind and that accompany dance experience. Physical components of dancer wellness explore all of the additional areas that affect the body beyond the foundations. Each of these three categories in the model has subtopics that are essential for anyone participating in dance today. They are discussed in the chapters of this book.

Part I: Foundations of Dancer Wellness

Foundations begin with the physical environment, including appropriate dance attire and the studio space, which are presented in chapter 1. Also fundamental is the body, how you train and learn, and the sciences that support training (chapter 2). In today's dance training, supplementary conditioning (such as strength training) has also become a foundation of dance training (chapter 3). The three chapters that make up part I cover foundations of dancer wellness: dance environment, scientific foundations of dance training and technique (such as anatomy, motor learning, and physics), and conditioning for dancers. Each of these three components has a major influence on health and well-being.

Part II: Mental Components of Dancer Wellness

Part II helps you understand how to maintain solid mental and psychological health. When you think of dance, your first images are of the physical beauty and elegance of the body moving through space. However, many mental factors come into play in training the dancer; they are discussed in chapter 4. You can learn about the human brain and how it controls and directs movement. To assist this process and to develop mental strategies that enhance technique, you can use imagery and somatic practices. The psychological side of the dancer is also covered (chapter 5). Psychology is the science that studies the mind and its functions, particularly those affecting behavior. Dance psychology is the study of aspects of psychology that are specific to dancers, including self-esteem, perfectionism, body image, stress, anxiety, competition, and social pressures. Chapter 6 examines a third mental component, how rest, fatigue, and burnout affect learning, technique, and injury. Mental aspects of dance can dramatically affect health and wellness.

Part III: Physical Components of Dancer Wellness

Part III addresses physical aspects of dancer wellness. Nutrition for dancers is not only about the content of what you eat, but also about timing of the intake of various foods, challenges in achieving good nutrition, and issues concerning weight (chapter 7). Bone health (chapter 8) is so important across your lifetime that it has been given its own chapter. Injury risks in dance are high, and you must include injury prevention in your wellness toolbox. In case you do get injured, you need to know about immediate treatment; chapter 9 covers injury prevention and first aid.

Part IV: Assessments for Dancer Wellness

Finally, part IV considers ways to assess your current state of dancer wellness and how to set goals for improvement. Screenings are often available to

dancers, and how these screenings are conducted and archived (stored), is covered in chapter 10. With the knowledge you have gained in the three categories of dancer wellness presented in the first nine chapters, you can examine and assess your personal abilities, then design a realistic wellness plan for your long-term health as a dancer (chapter 11). Motivation in terms of wellness comes from seeing progress and knowing that you are doing what is best for your mind and body.

Benefits and Features of This Book

This book includes not only information but also exercises and activities to keep you active in the learning process. The knowledge that you will gain can enhance and complement your daily training and practice. In addition, the book provides you with many strategies that will actively support what you are already doing to develop yourself as a dancer. Your individual capabilities and needs will become clear to you, allowing you to design unique programs for self-improvement. Finally, the special elements in each chapter will guide you in creating your personalized dancer wellness plan.

Special elements are placed at the beginning and end of the chapter. At the start, you can read the Learning Objectives, which offer a snapshot of the chapter. At the end of each chapter is a series of review questions, allowing you to test what you have read and remember from the chapter. These questions encourage you to go back and re-read anything you may have missed that is important to you.

In addition, each chapter contains valuable sidebars that cover four ideas: self-awareness, empowerment, goal setting, and diversity. *Self-awareness* is the ability for introspection and the skill to recognize oneself as an individual separate from others. *Empowerment* refers to measures designed to increase the degree of independence and self-determination in your life in order to enable you to support your interests in a responsible and self-determined way. *Goal setting* is an important method of deciding what you want to achieve in your life, determining what is important versus what is a distraction, and learning how to motivate yourself. *Diversity* is the quality or state of having many different forms, types, ideas, and even personalities. Each of the sidebars provides activities that you can do as you read the book to help you develop personal approaches to the material. The final chapter will help you put all of these sidebar activities together to develop your dancer wellness plan.

After you read each chapter, visit **www.HumanKinetics.com/DancerWellness** to find supplemental activities, worksheets, study aids, and web links for further information. As time goes on, continue to study dancer wellness and reevaluate your wellness plan, then modify it according to your changing needs. Dancer wellness is a lifelong project that can be a rewarding source of enjoyment and learning in your dance practice.

eBook
available at
HumanKinetics.com

How to Access the Web Resource

Throughout *Dancer Wellness*, you will notice references to a web resource. This online content is available to you free of charge when you purchase a new print or electronic version of the book. The web resource offers supplemental learning activities, study aids, web links, and more. To access the online content, simply register with the Human Kinetics website. Here's how:

1. Visit www.HumanKinetics.com/DancerWellness.
2. Click the first edition link next to the corresponding first edition book cover.
3. Click the Sign In link on the left or at the top of the page. If you do not have an account with Human Kinetics, you will be prompted to create one.
4. Once you have registered, if the online product does not appear in the Ancillary Items box at the left, click the Enter Pass Code option in that box. Enter the following pass code exactly as it is printed here, including any capitalization and hyphens: **WILMERDING-7TU49-WR**.
5. Click the Submit button to unlock your online product.
6. After you have entered your pass code for the first time, you will never have to enter it again in order to access this online product. Once you have unlocked your product, a link to the product will appear permanently in the menu on the left. All you need to do to access your online content on subsequent visits is sign in to **www.HumanKinetics.com/DancerWellness** and follow the link!

If you need assistance along the way, click the Need Help? button on the book's website.

Acknowledgments

We would like to recognize the many dance educators, medical practitioners, researchers, and scientists who have contributed to the body of knowledge in the field of dancer wellness. We are grateful for their ongoing efforts to move the dance community forward in this important journey. The authors of this book hope that the members of these disciplines will continue to collaborate on projects and outreach for the benefit of all dancers.

Part I

Foundations of Dancer Wellness

The first three chapters of this book discuss the foundations of dancer wellness. Dancer wellness begins with the physical environment, including appropriate dance attire and the studio space (chapter 1). Also fundamental are the sciences that support training and technique, such as anatomy, motor learning, and physics (chapter 2). In recent years conditioning (such as strength training) has become another essential tool in dancer wellness (chapter 3). These three components of dancer wellness have a bigger influence on health and well-being than you might think.

Chapter 1 discusses the dance environment. Dancers might take for granted many of the aspects of the physical environment. The studio or stage floor, equipment, temperature, ventilation, lighting, and even apparel and grooming are such familiar aspects of the physical environment that you usually don't think about them as factors in your well-being. However, each factor has a unique impact on your life and can influence health.

Chapter 2 explains how dance training and technique influence dancer wellness. The scientific foundations that are most influential for you (whether you recognize them or not) are anatomy, alignment, technique, motor learning, and physics. They each provide a unique and important contribution to your daily routine. Anatomy is the branch of science dealing with the structures of plants and animals; human anatomy focuses on body structures such as bones and muscles in humans. As you go from class to class, you will discover that teachers talk about alignment in very different ways. Alignment for dance practice defines how the parts of the body organize in stance and movement. You will hear in class some of the important issues that underlie all technique. You might wonder why certain dancers learn best from watching demonstration and others

want to hear explanations of how to do steps. This difference has to do with different learning styles. Motor learning refers to changes that occur with practice or experience that determine a person's capability for producing a motor skill. Physics is the science of matter, motion, and energy. Gravity and momentum play a large role in defining how you move, whether you are doing turns, jumps, partnering lifts, or balances. When you apply these scientific principles, you can enhance technique and cause less wear on the body.

Chapter 3 discusses cross-training and conditioning. Conditioning for dancers involves many aspects of fitness, including muscular strength, flexibility, and aerobic training. In past years, dancers and dance teachers believed that dance class covered every area of conditioning for dance. With today's deeper understanding of the physical demands of dance and the increasing difficulty and complexity of choreography, dancers and teachers are recognizing the need for supplementary training beyond dance class. Some of the dance-specific conditioning work in this chapter might be more interesting and useful for dance practice than the traditional methods, because these methods address various components of fitness in ways that use dance and dance-related movements.

With awareness of the dance environment and the training needs of the body, you can enhance your technique. It is also possible to minimize injury risks by setting goals for fitness that create a strong, flexible body. Often you are not aware of the ongoing stress to the body caused by poor fitness, faulty alignment, and bad movement habits. A better understanding of all of the foundations of dancer wellness can raise awareness and empower you to take responsibility for your long-term artistic success and health.

The Dance Environment

Luke Hopper, PhD, and Alycia Fong Yan, PhD

Key Terms

area deformation
bite
decibels (dB)
energy return
force reduction
friction
insole
midsole
outsole
rosin
sprung floor
upper
vertical deformation

Photo courtesy of Jake Pett.

LEARNING OBJECTIVES

After reading this chapter, you will be able to do the following:

> Understand how to recognize a sprung floor, and recognize how the floor affects your dancing.

> Be aware of the temperature and ventilation needs of the space in which you dance.

> Realize the benefits and limitations of working with barres and mirrors.

> Determine whether the lighting in your dance space is adequate for your learning needs.

> Select the best apparel and footwear for the style of dance you are doing.

The essence of dance is human movement through space. In the dance space, many factors can influence a dancer's movement, performance, and well-being. These factors include floors, barres, mirrors, and the general ambience and dimensions of the environment. Dance apparel often provides the connection between a dancer and the environment. Shoes and costumes can greatly influence the way a dancer moves and the forces a dancer experiences in connection with the environment. This chapter outlines these important environmental considerations for dance and provides suggestions for how you can adapt the dance environment, dance training, and performance to ensure safe and effective dance practice.

Dance Space and Facilities

Dancers perform the art of human movement in various types of spaces, including studios and stages. The space that dancers use to train, rehearse, and perform can have direct influence on their performance, injury risk, and general well-being. Therefore, dancers, teachers, and choreographers must consider whether the dance space is appropriate for the dancer, what facilities are available in the studio or theater, and how to conduct safe dance practice.

Dance Floors

Dancers spend hours training and perfecting their art form on dance floors. The dance floor provides a direct connection between the dancer and the physical environment. Most dance movements are produced through an interaction between the dancer and the floor. Therefore, the floor can have a large impact on your body. For optimal dance performance and well-being, you should have a sound knowledge of what to expect in a suitable dance floor.

Sprung Floors

A **sprung floor** absorbs shock, improves performance, and may prevent dance injuries. Often when people hear the word "sprung" referring to a dance floor, they assume it is appropriate for dance. However, this term generalizes the several characteristics of a floor that can influence dance training and performance. Many different aspects of a floor can contribute to a dancer's opinion of what is or is not a sprung floor. In order to be classified as a suitable floor for dance, dance floor manufacturers must have their floors tested to ensure they meet certain standards. This section outlines the key properties of a dance floor that are tested by industry standards.

Sprung floors that are made specifically for dance are typically made from a wooden surface that sits on foam pads or a basket weave structure (see figure 1.1). The structures of both of these designs enable the floor to move up and down as the dancer jumps from and lands on the floor. This up-and-down movement is referred to as the floor's **vertical deformation**. The vertical deformation of the floor provides two important properties for the dancer, namely, force reduction and energy return.

Force reduction refers to the impact-absorbing properties of the floor. When a dancer lands on a sprung floor, the floor moves downward, thus absorbing energy. A floor with high force reduction will absorb more energy than a floor with low force reduction. This energy absorption can reduce the

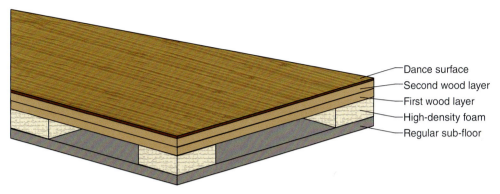

Dance surface
Second wood layer
First wood layer
High-density foam
Regular sub-floor

Figure 1.1 Sprung floor.

amount of energy being absorbed by the muscles, bones, and soft tissues of the dancer's legs, reducing fatigue and injury risk. **Energy return** of a floor relates to the upward vertical movement of a floor when a dancer jumps from the floor. This upward movement can release stored energy from the floor to the dancer. A floor that has trampoline-like elastic properties can store energy. The landing impact of a dancer can store energy in a floor, which is released when a dancer rebound jumps from the floor. Like a trampoline, which has a very high return of energy, a sprung floor's energy return can assist a dancer in jumping higher. Too much force reduction or energy return can be problematic, because the floor can become unstable due to too much vertical deformation, which makes balancing movements difficult. For example, performing a pirouette or an arabesque on a floor with too much force reduction or energy return could be difficult if the floor moves too much underfoot. This movement means the floor is not providing the stability needed for balance. The levels of force reduction and energy return are particularly important when the dancer makes first contact with the floor, because quickly gaining balance and maintaining it are necessary for successful movement.

Because dance floors are typically made with wood, a certain surface area of the floor that surrounds a dancer will vertically deform when a dancer lands on the floor, much like a trampoline does. This is called the **area deformation** of a floor. Low area deformation is an important property of a dance floor. A wide area deformation can cause the floor to become unstable for dancers standing or moving around another dancer and also can destabilize any sets that are sitting on the floor during performance. For example, a group of dancers moving together in a close group will each be contacting the floor, causing vertical deformation underfoot. If this

deformation is large, it can cause the floor to wobble and become unstable for all of the dancers moving close to one another, which may increase the risk of injuries such as ankle sprains. Similarly, if the group of dancers moves close to a set, the floor underneath the set can also wobble, become unstable, and, in the worst case, the set might fall over.

The final important property of a sprung floor is the force reduction consistency across the floor. If the force reduction is inconsistent in a floor, landing becomes difficult; the dancer must make constant adjustments when moving across the floor, which can result in not landing correctly and therefore increase risk of injury. When landing from a jump, the leg muscles must absorb energy to perform a successful landing. An inconsistent floor makes coordinating this energy absorption between the leg and the floor very difficult. If a dancer is expecting the floor to have high force reduction and energy absorption but instead lands on a part of the floor that is hard and has low force reduction, it can cause unexpected and large impacts to the leg muscles, bones, and soft tissues, and increase the risk of injury.

Vinyl Surfaces

Often a vinyl surface is laid on top of the dance floor. Other common terms for this type of floor are Marley and linoleum. Some vinyl surfaces have a foam underlay to provide vertical deformation, force reduction, and energy return to the dancer. However, the primary function of these surfaces for a dancer is to provide friction from the floor. **Friction** refers to the horizontal forces that occur between a dancer's foot and the floor. Balancing the amount of friction between a dancer and the floor is an important and often difficult task; both too much and too little friction can have adverse consequences for a dancer's well-being.

Too little friction essentially means that the floor is too slippery. A slippery floor means that dancers have to be cautious not to fall through fast turns, running, and jumping movements. Falling while dancing can be a painful experience and can cause serious impact injuries. A floor with too much friction is also not ideal for dance. If the friction is too high, the dancer's feet and body can stick to the floor, potentially causing abrasions to the skin and excessive twisting force through the legs that can lead to sprains and fractures. Depending on the style of dance and dance shoes, different dancers may require different levels of friction from the same floor. For example, dancing en pointe has unique requirements for vinyl surfaces. Female dancers en pointe can also have different requirements for vinyls compared to male dancers. Female dancers en pointe will often like to be able to get some **bite** out of the floor with the shoes in order to increase the friction between the shoe and the floor during movements such as balances. Bite means that the outside edge of the toe box can dig into the vinyl, which increases the resistance of the vinyl and stops the shoe slipping along the floor. If a floor is too slippery, some dancers use **rosin**, a sticky material that can be crushed up under the soles of shoes to increase the friction and minimize the risk of falls and slips.

SAFETY TIP

Watch Your Step

Always take caution when performing on stages or taking class in studios where an uneven spread of rosin has built up on sections of the floor. These areas of rosin can create places where the feet can stick, and you can trip or twist your ankle. Further, you can come off an area of rosin to a smoother surface and slip, causing injury by falling.

Maintenance

You can help at your dance studio to maintain a safe and clean floor. Keep food and beverages out of the dance space, except for clear water, preferably in bottles made of shatterproof material. Glass is always dangerous in a dance space; avoid bringing it into your studio or theater. Street shoes should never be worn in the studio, because excess dirt makes floor surfaces sticky and hazardous. Even your dance shoes should be cleaned regularly to maintain clean floors. All garbage should be removed as often as possible, and clutter that can cause accidents should remain outside the dance

area. If you observe a spill or a sharp object on the floor, be responsible to remove it or tell someone. Don't wait for an accident or injury to occur. In addition to maintaining a clean floor, during flu season it is a good idea to wipe down barres and other common surfaces with a disinfectant cleanser. Everyone can contribute to a healthy environment.

GOAL SETTING

Make the Most of Your Dance Environment

Use the following prompts to set some goals for making the most of your dance environment:

> How can you prepare to dance in the dance studio or other performance areas that accommodate your needs?

> Do you need to bring along water or a snack?

> Do you need to take allergy medication before you come to the dance studio or outdoor performance area?

> If the dance studio is always hot, do you need to bring a towel?

> Do you need to bring a journal or notebook to keep track of your daily needs in the studio?

Barres

The barre is another important aspect of the dance environment that can affect your body and training in various ways. The barre is essentially a training tool that can help you practice and develop advanced exercises before attempting them in the center. Barre height is the first consideration. If you are unusually short or tall, you may have difficulty finding a studio with barres that serve your personal height needs. A barre that is too high can result in lifting your shoulder and causing neck tension. A barre that is too low may affect your posture if you have to reach down toward the barre. However, many commercially available barres can be fixed to the wall at two different heights to accommodate a greater range of dancers, and movable barres often have adjustable heights. Ask if your studio can use these options, or find a dance studio that accommodates your needs. As a general guide, adults require a 42-inch (106.7-cm) barre height and children require a 36-inch (91.4-cm) height. When doing exercises at the barre, make sure that you leave ample room between you and the barre so that you are able to move freely without kicking the barre during battements and turns. After barre

The dancer is working at a barre of appropriate height.
Photo courtesy of Jake Pett.

work, you can help to create a safer dance space by placing movable barres well off to the side so that they do not impede on exercises in the center.

In the dance environment, floors and barres are the obvious physical factors that can directly impact dancer well-being, training, and performance. Several other factors, such as dimensions, mirrors, light, sound, and ambient air quality, can also have an impact. These factors are often not acknowledged unless they become problematic.

Raked Stages

Historically, many dance stages and studios were purposely built on an angle to face the stage toward the audience instead of being built at a consistent height relative to the ground. This type of angled floor is referred to as a *rake*. Raked stages are measured as a ratio. The rake ratio is calculated as how much the floor increases in height relative to how much the floor travels away from the audience. That is, if the height of a raked floor is 1 foot (about 30 cm) higher than the front of the stage at a point 10 feet (about 3 m) away from the front of the stage, this floor is considered to be a 1:10 rake. When moving

on a raked floor, you should be wary of the effect of the floor depending on the direction of travel. For example, when performing a grand jeté on a downstage diagonal, you will jump from the floor at a height that is greater than where you will land. This effectively increases the jump height and can therefore increase the landing impact forces. When traveling across the stage, you will experience a slope that is across the body, which can particularly impact the angle of the ankle and knee of the standing leg, which may have complications for ankle sprains and impact on your joints. Choreography that involves lots of movement upstage essentially makes you dance uphill, which can elicit fatigue faster than on a flat floor. For more information on problems caused by fatigue, see chapter 6.

Mirrors

Mirrors can be useful as tools for gaining an understanding of body alignment and learning movement sequences and spacing of dancers in a group routine. However, a risk is that you can become overly reliant on mirrors, therefore the place and use of mirrors in dance is a subject of debate. Mirrors do not actually provide a perfect representation of the body. A difference can occur between the true position and angle of your body when observed from a different line of sight in the mirror, causing you to misinterpret your alignment and posture. You should make sure that you spend as much time dancing without looking in the mirror as you do using the mirror. If your dance space is equipped with curtains that can cover the mirrors, ask your teacher if these curtains can be closed for some of your classes. Alternatively, if you think you are becoming too reliant on the mirror for feedback, try standing in an area of the studio where you cannot see yourself in the mirror.

EMPOWERMENT

Speak Up if You See Problems in the Space

Do you speak up when certain factors in your studio are not supporting your wellness? Do you ask to close the curtains or open windows to alter the lighting and ventilation in your studio? Do you help to keep your studio clean and free of clutter? Do you speak to other dancers about pitching in to make a better dance environment? You have the power to make positive influences in your dance environment. Do not be afraid to speak up respectfully when needed.

Light and Sound

Dancers can perform in a variety of lighting conditions, particularly when moving from the studio to the stage. The studio is usually well lit; onstage, you may be looking out into a completely dark space, as well as dealing with spotlights, different colored lights, and lighting from different angles. Changes in lighting can have a disorienting effect on you, causing your balance to be impaired. Balance requires a combination of input from the eyes, sensors in the skin to give the brain information about movement of the body in relation to the supporting surface, sensors for proprioception, and the inner ear. Dancers have been found to be heavily reliant on their sight to maintain their balance. You can find time to practice balances with your eyes closed, which can increase the contribution of the other components of balance. This practice can result in more stability when your eyes are open. Therefore, working in a variety of lighting conditions can help you prepare for the changes you may experience between locations. However, in everyday practice it is best to maintain a balanced amount of light in the environment that does not impede your dance training. For example, if your studio windows have curtains, remember to close the curtains before class starts to avoid issues with sunlight shining directly into your eyes or at angles that can reflect off mirrors.

Various sources of sound emanate from the dance environment. Just as the legs can become injured as a result of too much impact from the floor, the human hearing apparatus can be injured from too much exposure to noise. Dancers hear sounds from pianos, stereos, the human voice, and contact with the floor (such as in tap dance). All of these sounds can contribute to your overall exposure to noise levels. Excessive noise can occur in the studio but it is more likely to be a problem during performances involving large numbers of musicians or amplified music. Studies have determined the safe exposure of sound levels to prevent hearing damage. The intensity of sound is measured in **decibels (dB)**. Various mobile and online applications are available in order to assess sound levels in the dance environment. Below 85 dB is considered the safe level of sound for continuous everyday exposure. If greater than 85 dB of sound is present in the dance environment, it is recommended that either the sound levels be reduced or time of exposure to the dance environment be reduced. You are responsible to make sure that you do not have exceedingly high sound levels when you are rehearsing by yourself or with other dancers.

Ventilation, Temperature, and Airflow

Dance is often referred to as intermittent exercise that is characterized by short bursts of intense movements followed by short periods of rest. Breathing clean, fresh air is essential in enabling you to both perform at the necessary intensities and recover in between these intermittent activities. Therefore, the dance environment should have a constant flow of air entering and leaving the space. In the same way dancers exhale expired air and inhale fresh air, the dance environment should continually refresh the ambient air, preventing it from becoming stale. If you think that you are struggling to breathe in your studio due to poor ventilation, speak to your teacher or the studio owner, and see if the space can be aired out on a regular basis.

A regular flow of air can also prevent you from overheating during training and performance. If your core body temperature overheats by even a few degrees, it can have serious effects on well-being. Although the dance community agrees that a proper warm-up is essential for safe dance practice, preventing overheating is of equal importance. Heat is generated in the body through the muscles using energy to produce movement. The ambient temperature of the dance environment can have a big influence on body temperature. If the body overheats, many systems of the body, including the circulatory system and the nervous system, can be severely affected. On hot days, be especially vigilant about hydrating regularly and asking that windows allow for good ventilation.

SELF-AWARENESS

Environmental Inventory

Take an inventory of your dance environment. What are your floors and floor surfaces like? How is your space in terms of temperature, ventilation, lighting, and sound? Does your space have mirrors and barres? Become aware of all the elements in your dance space and how you can best use them.

This section has outlined the dance space and facilities that can influence dance performance and dancer well-being. It considered factors such as dance floors, mirrors, barres, dimensions, and ambient environment. These factors will directly impact your body and ability to move. You should be aware of the influence that these environmental factors can have on your training and performance so that modifications can be made where possible. Some factors, such as floor surfaces, are often not immediately modifiable, so you may have to adapt your behavior to the environment. For example, when dancing on a new floor that may be harder than the floor previously used, you should start moving at a lower intensity and gradually build intensity. Other factors, such as temperature, can be more easily modified. With greater insight into the environmental factors that influence dancer well-being, you will be able to take more responsibility for ensuring your own well-being in your dance environment.

Dance Apparel

Footwear and clothing both have the potential to influence dance performance and dancer health. The footwear, practice clothing, and costumes vary considerably depending on the genre and theme of the dance. The following sections discuss aspects to be aware of when selecting footwear and clothing for class or performance. The goal of this awareness is to help minimize the risk of injury and potentially improve dance performance.

Footwear

The design and construction of dance shoes can provide protection and support for dancers' feet, but in some cases the shoes can be a contributing factor for injury risk. Footwear design includes a toe cap (box) that covers the toes, a shank that runs along the bottom of the foot, a heel cup that surrounds the whole heel bone up to the ankle, and the **upper**, which is all the material that lies on the top and sides of the foot. The shank can have one or several layers depending on the design and purpose of the shoe. Conventional shoes have an **outsole** (in contact with the ground), **insole** (in contact with the foot), and **midsole** (lies between the outsole and insole).

Depending on the dance style, dancers can choose from a vast array of footwear designs for class and performance. At one extreme are the thin, barre shoes for contemporary and modern dance that have a strip of suede under the ball of the foot secured with elastic straps or fine mesh material. This minimalist design allows the dancer to move almost barefoot, getting the grip and dexterity of the toes while protecting the ball of the foot from wear during turns. If you opt to wear socks to improve slide and turn performance, you can increase your risk for slips and falls depending on the friction of the dance floor. At the other extreme are high-heeled character shoes, pointe shoes, and jazz sneakers. These shoes are constructed of various materials that meet the unique aesthetic requirements for each genre, but they have design drawbacks in their functionality and injury risk. Given the increasing research on shoe design and safety, and the large variety of shoe designs available, today's dancer needs to think carefully about choosing the right shoe.

Heels

Many dance styles require you to wear shoes with a heel. However, high-heeled shoes pose certain risks to dancer well-being. Changing the height of the heel alters the position of the foot and the ankle bones. Altering the foot position causes you to shift your body weight forward over the balls of the feet in order to maintain upright posture and balance. In order to achieve this posture, further changes must occur higher up in the body. You can use a variety of strategies to alter your alignment in the knees and spine, putting increased pressure on these regions of the body.

Examples of nonheeled dance shoes.
© Alycia Fong Yan.

The knee joint also bears more of the load when landing from jumps in high heels compared to landing barefoot. The elevated position of the heel reduces the capacity for the ankle to absorb impact during the demi-plié, so the knee is required to bend farther. Because of the elevated heel position and the fact that the ankle cannot produce as much power as it can in flat shoes, jump height is reduced. When dance combinations involving jumps are practiced in flats and then performed in high heels, the performance can feel heavy because of the change in footwear. Therefore, in order to optimize the timing and height of jumps, you should rehearse dance sequences in the shoes you will wear for performance.

If you are required to wear high heels for a performance, use caution. For dancing in high heels, ankle strength needs to be increased and the muscles around the knee joint should also be trained. You should aim for a gradual increase in strength training for the ankles and knees, followed by the gradual increase of time dancing in high heels to allow for adaptations in the body to occur, hence minimizing the risk of injury. You can also build up your strength and proficiency dancing in heels by starting with lower heel heights and gradually increasing the heel height as your strength progresses.

Sole Thickness

Dancers spend a large portion of their time in class and rehearsal performing various types of jumps. The repeated impact on the lower limbs can equate to almost two to three times the body weight. Innovations in footwear design have led to the development of materials used to reduce the amount of force that is transmitted to the body in order to reduce the risk of injury. This aspect of shoe design is the same as the force reduction property seen in dance floor design. Ballet shoe design has not changed much since the late 1700s; however, jazz shoe design appears to be driven by fashion and music trends. With the rise in popularity of street dance styles in the 1980s, the need for shoes that looked like sneakers but provided dance performance benefits of dance shoes, such as slides, spins, and toe stands, increased. One might think that the shoes with the thickest outsole and the most cushioning would be the best at reducing impact. A recent study found that two designs of dance sneaker were better at reducing impact compared to flats and high-heeled shoes. Although the older model of dance sneaker appeared to have more cushioning and a thicker outsole, the newer model of the dance sneaker, with less cushioning and a thinner outsole, was actually the most shock absorbing. The large leap forward in materials technology has made way for thinner materials with more shock absorption used in the midsole and less bulky material in the outsole.

Pointe Shoes

Pointe shoes are made from tightly packed layers of paper, fabric, and glue, plus cardboard to reinforce and flatten the tip of the toe box. Without all the stiff and heavy materials, the foot would not be able to support the entire weight of the body en pointe. Then again, the stiffness of the shoe does not allow the foot to roll through and spread during landings to absorb impact.

The toe box is a source of injury for dancers because of the alignment of toes within. Dancers aiming for a sleeker profile of the foot may select a narrower toe box to the detriment of the toes. Narrowing the toes this way can lead to the development of bunions, calluses on knuckles from overlapping toes, and stress fractures from poorly distributed forces across the toes. If the pointe shoe is narrower than the dancer's foot, the crowded position of the toes may cause problems for the dancer when standing flat, transferring weight, lowering from pointe, and landing from jumps. The foot naturally wants to spread wider to maintain balance, distribute weight, and absorb impact. A shoe that is too narrow will not only be uncomfortable, but without appropriate weight distribution the impact must be absorbed by other regions of the lower limb, increasing the risk of chronic injury.

Examples of heeled dance shoes.
© Alycia Fong Yan.

If the structure of the shoe limits foot and ankle motion the audience and teacher will not see a properly pointed foot. Research has shown that wearing different designs of jazz shoes produces a less pointed foot than when the same foot is barefoot. When you select dance shoes, there will be a trade-off between the style that fits the genre of dance and the overall aesthetic of the foot that the audience will see.

Practice Clothing

Depending on the genre of dance, the style and components of the dance apparel for class can affect movement performance and may increase the risk of injury. Dancers must be aware of any restrictions or alterations to movement quality and performance as a result of clothing choices.

DIVERSITY IN DANCE

Dress for Cultural Dance Styles

If you know particular clothing elements are worn in a certain dance style, such as the wrapped skirts in African dance classes or the baggy pants in street dance, you should become familiar with these items as early as possible so that moving in them is familiar to you.

Dance apparel can be made from various materials, which may affect the body's ability to maintain adequate body temperature, may limit the range of movement available, and may present slip or trip risks. Jewelry can become caught on clothing or tangled with your own or someone else's hair or costume. You should avoid wearing jewelry during dance class, particularly when doing partner work, and be mindful of costume design and choreography when selecting jewelry for performance.

Although dance apparel can directly impact your ability to move, footwear and clothing are easily modifiable. Here are some ways you can directly control the dance environment to improve performance and minimize injuries:

› Select the best shoe for the style of dance while maintaining a good fit and ensuring the shoe will function as desired.

› When you must wear a certain type of shoe for performance, make a gradual transition between shoes and gradually increase the time you wear them.

› Perform additional exercises to increase strength and endurance in regions of the body that may be put under greater stress from apparel choices.

› As soon as possible after knowing about apparel choices for a performance, wear elements of the costume or items of similar design during rehearsal.

Dance apparel can have a direct impact on how you move and on your wellness in your dance environment. Select clothing and shoes that fit well, support your body, and function in the dance space; for example, select the sole of the shoe relative to the floor surface. When you select the best apparel, you ensure your best performance.

Summary

The dance environment is one of many factors that can influence dancer wellness in a variety of ways. Your facility should have sprung floors and a surface that is neither too slippery nor too sticky. Barres should be of appropriate height for safe alignment, and mirrors should be used sparingly. Light and sound are important elements in your training. You should be able to see adequately, and sound should be clear and at a reasonable volume. Dance apparel is also part of the environment. Clothing and footwear are determined by your dance genre, but they must fit properly and not impede your movement. Understanding the factors of the dance environment can help you enhance your training experience.

Consider the environment that you most often dance in, such as the local studio, theater, or your living room. No dance environment is ever going to be perfectly safe. An important focus of safe dance practice is acknowledging and minimizing risks to dancer well-being. For this activity, perform a risk assessment of your dance environment, considering the various environmental factors that are described in this chapter. A simple method is to give each environmental factor a ranking of high, medium, or low risk. For high and medium risk factors, write a brief statement of why they present a risk to the dancer. Then, suggest ways to minimize these risk factors.

Review Questions

1. What is a sprung floor, and what are the benefits of working on a sprung floor?

2. How do you know if the temperature and ventilation in your studio are best for your wellness, and what can you do to improve these aspects of your space?

3. What are the benefits and disadvantages of working with barres and mirrors?

4. Is the lighting and sound in your dance studio best for your training needs, and do you work with a good variety of these elements?

5. How can you select the best apparel and footwear for the dance style you are doing, and how can you make sure the fit of these elements does not impede your training?

 For chapter-specific supplemental learning activities, study aids, suggested readings, web links, and more, visit the web resource at www.HumanKinetics.com/DancerWellness.

Dance Training and Technique

Donna H. Krasnow, PhD, M. Virginia Wilmerding, PhD, Arleen Sugano, MFA, and Kenneth Laws, PhD

Photo courtesy of Jake Pett.

Key Terms

alignment
anatomy
center of gravity (COG)
concentric contraction
eccentric contraction
fascia
fibrocartilage
frontal (coronal) plane
hyaline cartilage
hyperextended knees
joint
kinesthetic
ligaments
motor learning
neutral pelvis
perceptual skills
plumb line
proprioception
replication
sagittal plane
synovial joints
synovial membrane
technique
tendons
tibial torsion
torque
transfer of training
transverse plane
variables

LEARNING OBJECTIVES

After reading this chapter, you will be able to do the following:

› Understand the function of bones, joints, ligaments, muscles, and tendons in the body.

› Describe the main muscles that dancers need to know, and describe the various movements at all of the joints.

› Realize the importance of proper alignment, and correct alignment problems in your own body in dance class.

› Explain the main concepts in dance technique, including core support, the spine, turnout, and use of the arms and legs.

› Determine the aspects of motor learning for your age and level, and improve your learning strategies.

› Apply ideas from physics to enhance your balances, turns, and jumps.

As a dancer, you live in an environment of studio space, dance floors, lighting, mirrors, barres, music, temperature, clothing, and shoes. Probably the most important environment for you is the body. Without sound knowledge of how the body works, dance technique is mysterious and injuries are more likely to occur. While you may embrace this need to know about the body, you may be unaware of the many ways to explore the body. Anatomy can explain how muscles work, what groups of muscles work together to create the beautiful and coordinated movements in dance, and how the various structures of the body can give you both control and freedom. Understanding the principles of alignment can contribute to the elegant look of a dancer, help you attain a body that works with ease (sometimes called movement efficiency), and minimize injuries. Science can also provide information that you can use to improve your dance technique, including understanding turnout, having good core support, and using the feet properly when jumping and moving through space. One of the more recent additions to the scientific foundations of dance is the field of motor learning, which can help you to develop good strategies for acquiring new skills and to realize how the brain and the body function in harmony. Finally, physics can teach you about the laws of nature and how these laws play a role in your dance practice. This chapter explores the scientific foundations of training and technique in dance. When you understand the universal principles and ideas that govern the human body, you can gain an accurate and healthy perspective on your individual needs and goals.

Basic Anatomy

When audiences watch dancers perform, they see the elegant coordination of many parts of the body moving in harmony. For this harmony to occur, many areas of the human skeleton are organized to work simultaneously. **Anatomy** is the branch of science dealing with the structures of plants and animals; human anatomy looks at body structures such as bones and muscles in humans. All movement is caused by muscles moving bones, with the exception of movement that is caused by simply letting gravity take over part of the body; in dance this movement is called *fall* or *release of weight*. Where two bones come together, they form a joint, and structures called **ligaments** connect the bones. **Tendons** are made of similar tissue as ligaments but attach muscles to bones. Because the skeletal system is the foundation of the human body (see figure 2.1), this section begins with a discussion of the main bones and joints in use when dancing, then moves on to discuss the muscles and ligaments.

Bones and Joints

The human body has 206 bones, but only 177 of those bones can move. The skeleton is symmetrical, so each of the bones and joints exists on both sides of the body. A **joint** is the articulation of two or

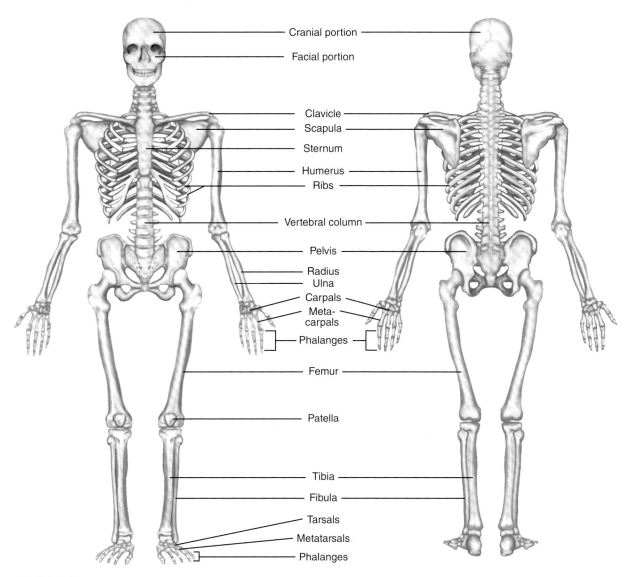

Figure 2.1 Skeletal system.

more bones, that is, where they come together. For simplicity, only the main joints involved when you dance are listed here:

> › Upper extremities: wrist, radioulnar joint, elbow, shoulder joint, and shoulder girdle
> › Lower extremities: foot, ankle, knee, and hip
> › Trunk (vertebrae of the spine): 7 cervical, 12 thoracic, 5 lumbar, and the sacrum/coccyx complex

Types of Joints

The body has six types of **synovial joints** (also known as movable joints), which are the joints with the greatest range of motion:

1. *Gliding joints* have only small movements accessible to them; one bone glides or slides over another (e.g., joints in the foot).

2. *Hinge joints* move in one plane, like the hinge of a door (e.g., elbow joint).

3. *Pivot joints* have rotary movement; one bone rolls over another (e.g., forearm or radioulnar joint).

4. *Saddle joints* are named for their saddle-like shape, and they move only in one plane (e.g., thumb joint).

5. *Condyloid joints* move in two planes; they move front and back, and side to side (e.g., wrist joint).

6. *Ball-and-socket joints* are the most versatile; they move in all three planes—front and back, side to side, and rotational movements (e.g., hip joint).

Upper Extremities

The upper extremities include the wrist, radioulnar joint, elbow, shoulder joint, and shoulder girdle (see figure 2.2). All of the gestures of the arms in dance require movements of several joints in the upper extremities. The elegant coordination of multiple joints makes possible the expressive gestures of the arms, such as the port de bras in ballet or the floreo in flamenco.

The wrist is a condyloid joint between the radius of the forearm and the carpal bones of the hand. The radioulnar joint exists at the two ends of the ulna and radius of the forearm. The proximal junction (where connection occurs closer to the elbow) is a pivot joint, and the distal junction (where connection occurs closer to the hand) is a gliding joint. The elbow joint is where the ulna meets the humerus

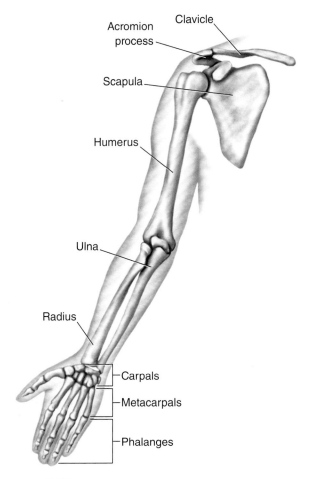

Figure 2.2   Joints of the upper extremities.

(upper arm), and it is a hinge. The shoulder joint is a ball-and-socket joint, so it can move in three planes. The head of the humerus fits into the socket, which is part of the scapula (shoulder blade). Movements of the shoulder joint are apparent when the arms are in motion. The shoulder girdle is most easily understood through observing movements of the scapula. The two articulations of the shoulder girdle are where the scapula attaches to the clavicle (collarbone), and the clavicle to the sternum of the rib cage. However, when the shoulder girdle is moving, what you see is the scapula going up or down, or forward and back. A noteworthy landmark on each scapula is the acromion process, which you can feel as a flat plateau at the very top.

Almost every movement of the upper extremities in dance, whether gesture or weight bearing, involves movement of all of the joints described. In the simple gesture of moving the arms from a low position to overhead, the primary movement seen is that of the shoulder joint, but activity occurs in the wrist, radioulnar joint, elbow, and shoulder girdle as well.

Lower Extremities

The lower extremities include the foot, ankle, knee, and hip (see figure 2.3). All of the gestures of the legs in dance are movements of several joints of the lower extremities. Whether doing a développé in ballet or modern, a kick in street dance, or a layout in jazz, all of the joints must coordinate together to create the movement as well as the dance aesthetic.

The foot has these 26 bones: 7 tarsals in the rear of the foot, 5 metatarsals in the midfoot, and 14 phalanges (toe bones). Because the foot has so many bones, it also has many joints, and they are primarily gliding joints. The ankle joint is where the top tarsal bone (the talus) fits up into the space between the two lower leg bones (the tibia and fibula). It functions as a hinge. The knee is also functionally a hinge, although it allows for some rotation. The knee joint is the meeting of the tibia with the femur (thighbone). The hip joint is a ball-and-socket joint, where the head of the femur fits into the socket on the pelvis, called the acetabulum.

The Trunk: Head, Spine, and Pelvis

The skull sits on the top of the spine, at the first cervical vertebra. The rib cage attaches to the 12 thoracic vertebrae; at the bottom of the 5 lumbar vertebrae is the sacrum, which is both the bottom of the spine and the back of the pelvis. The very bottom of the sacrum is the coccyx (tailbone). Because the pelvis is so important in dance, you should know

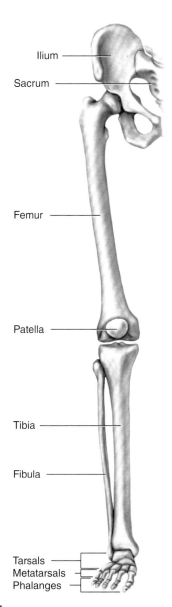

Ilium

Sacrum

Femur

Patella

Tibia

Fibula

Tarsals
Metatarsals
Phalanges

Figure 2.3 Joints of the lower extremities.

some of the bony landmarks. Each side of the pelvis is made of three parts: the ilium is the flaring fan with a crest along the side and the anterior superior iliac spine (ASIS) bones in the front, the pubic bone is in the front and low, and the third portion is called the ischium, which has the ischial tuberosities (sitting bones) at the bottom.

Other Structures in the Joints

Two types of cartilage exist that help with joint function. **Hyaline cartilage** lines all of the ends of bones where they come together to form joints. **Fibrocartilage** functions as a spacer, creating shock absorption, most notably in the spine and knee. Every joint also has a **synovial membrane**, which

secretes fluid that lubricates the joint for smooth action. Bursae are pads in and around the joints that help tendons glide smoothly as the muscles move the bones.

Ligaments

Every joint of the body has ligaments that connect the bones together. In most cases, the ligaments are named for the two bones that they connect. For example, the calcaneofibular ligament connects the calcaneus (heel bone) of the foot and the fibula (lower leg bone). It is not necessary for you to know every ligament in the body; this book discusses some of the more important ones for dance function and wellness.

The shoulder joint is shallow compared to the deeper fit of the hip joint. In the shoulder joint are numerous ligaments, which are not as strong as the ones around the hip joint. These structural aspects demonstrate the focus on mobility for the upper extremities as opposed to stability for the lower extremities. In spite of the extreme range of motion that you desire in the hip joints, the lower extremities are essentially designed for weight bearing.

One of the strongest ligaments in the body is the iliofemoral ligament in the hip joint, also called the Y-ligament because it looks like an upside-down Y. Because this ligament is so taut, it greatly restricts arabesque, which is why you must compensate with spine movement to create the line.

The knee is a particularly unstable joint, considering its role in weight bearing. The four primary ligaments in the knee are the anterior and posterior cruciates, which form an X in the sagittal plane inside the knee joint, and the medial (on the inner side) and lateral (on the outer side) collateral ligaments, which give support to the sides of the knee joint. In full extension, these ligaments are taut, contributing to stability.

Along the outer aspect of the femur is the iliotibial (IT) band, a strong band of ligamentous tissue that adds stability to the outer knee. It also serves as the attachment for two important hip muscles that are described later.

The ankle joint ligaments are lateral and medial to provide stability to the ankle. At the ankle are three lateral ligaments and the deltoid ligament on the medial aspect of the ankle joint. These lateral and medial ligaments provide important support; the feet must not only act in weight bearing, they are critical in ankle support during locomotion, such as jump landings. As part of the foot, the calcaneonavicular ligament is called the medial spring ligament, because it lies on the medial (inner) side of the foot, and it is one of the rare elastic ligaments in the body. It is designed to elongate and shorten during locomotion. Another important structure in the foot is the plantar fascia, which lies over the small muscles on the bottom of the foot. **Fascia**, like ligament, is made of tough connective tissue, and it adds additional stability to the area.

Some ligaments provide a great deal of support to the joint, such as the iliofemoral (Y-) ligament at the hip, and other ligaments are not as effective in that role. These joints rely more on their muscles for support and integrity. The next section discusses the role of muscles in stabilization and how they produce movement.

Muscles

Muscular tissue makes up 35 to 40 percent of body weight (see figure 2.4). The body has three muscle types, but in the context of dance, this text focuses on skeletal muscle—the muscles that move your joints.

The muscles that are most obvious to the observer are on the surface, such as the biceps, pectorals, quadriceps, and gluteals. These visible muscles are the voluntary skeletal muscles; their movements are controlled consciously by the planning areas in the brain. Most skeletal muscles are voluntary, but some, such as those used for swallowing and breathing, are involuntary (controlled without conscious thought). While you can actively and consciously affect these involuntary movements, you do not do so under normal conditions. As with the bones, only the most important muscles for dance function and wellness are described.

Planes of Movement and Movement Terms

To begin the study of muscles, you need to understand the planes of movement and the movement terminology. For an in-depth description of both, see figure 2.5 and table 2.1.

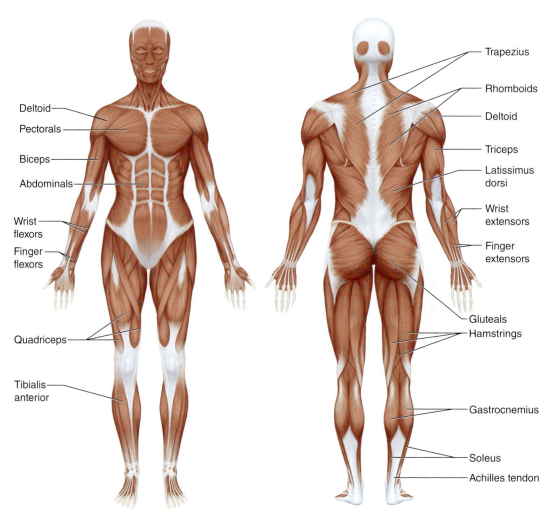

Figure 2.4   Muscular system.

Planes of movement are as follows (see figure 2.5):

The **sagittal plane** is the vertical plane that divides the body into right and left sides; it is sometimes called the *wheel plane*.

The **frontal (coronal) plane** is the vertical plane that divides the body into front and back portions; it is sometimes called the *door plane*.

The **transverse plane** is the horizontal plane that divides the body into upper and lower portions; it is sometimes called the *table plane*.

All of the movements in the joints of the body can be described in terms of the muscles that produce these movements. Sometimes muscles act as the prime movers; other times they are only assisting. However, this text does not go to that level of detail.

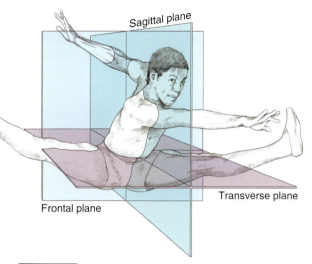

Figure 2.5   Planes of the body.

Table 2.1   Movement Terms

Movement	Definition	Dance example
Flexion	The decrease in the angle of two articulating bones, in the sagittal plane	From standing position, lifting one leg to a parallel passé involves flexion of both the hip and the knee joints. Curving forward is flexion of the spine.
Extension	The increase in the angle of two articulating bones, in the sagittal plane, the return to neutral from the flexed position	Bringing the leg from parallel passé back to standing position is extension of the hip and the knee.
Hyperextension	Continuing of extension beyond anatomical neutral	Arabesque involves hyperextension of the hip and the low back, which arches to achieve the full range of motion.
Abduction	The movement of a bone in the frontal plane away from the midline of the body	Lifting the arms out to second position, or moving the leg directly to the side away from the body are examples of abduction.
Adduction	The movement of a bone in the frontal plane toward the midline of the body	Lowering the arms from second position to straight down, or moving the leg from side to neutral standing position are examples of adduction.
Outward rotation	The movement of a bone around its own axis, away from the midline of the body; also called lateral or external rotation	Standing in classical first is a position of outward rotation at the hip joint. In the arms, Graham second position with the palms facing up involves outward rotation at the shoulder joint.
Inward rotation	The movement of a bone around its own axis, toward the midline of the body; also called medial or internal rotation	Standing with the toes pointing toward each other is a position of inward rotation at the hip joint. In the arms, classical second position involves inward rotation at the shoulder joint.
Pronation	A movement term used for both the forearm (radioulnar joint) and for the foot. In the forearm, the palm is turned to face backward. In the foot, the outside edge moves toward the lateral ankle bone.	When standing, the foot rolls inward, placing most of the weight onto the inside of the foot and lowering the arch. In gesture, when the foot is "winged," it is pronated and everted (moving the sole of the foot away from the midline).

> *continued*

Table 2.1 > *continued*

Movement	Definition	Dance example
Supination	A movement term used for both the forearm (radioulnar joint) and for the foot. In the forearm, the palm is turned to face forward. In the foot, the inner edge moves toward the medial ankle bone.	When standing, the foot rolls outward, placing most of the weight onto the outside of the foot and raising the arch. In gesture, when the foot is "sickled" it is supinated and inverted (moving the sole of the foot towards the midline).
Plantar flexion	Bending at the ankle joint in the sagittal plane so that the toes move away from the front of the shinbone.	Pointing the foot and relevé are examples of plantar flexion.
Dorsiflexion	Bending at the ankle joint in the sagittal plane so that the toes move toward the front of the shinbone	Flexing the foot and pliés are examples of dorsiflexion.
Horizontal flexion	Movement of the arm that starts in 90 degrees of abduction and moves forward in the transverse plane	Moving the arm from second position to first arabesque uses horizontal flexion.
Horizontal extension	Movement of the arm that starts in 90 degrees of flexion and moves backward in the transverse plane	Moving the arm from first arabesque out to second position uses horizontal extension.
Elevation	Upward movement of the scapula (shoulder blade)	Shrugging the shoulders is elevation.
Depression	Downward movement of the scapula	Dropping the shoulders back to neutral is depression.
Upward rotation	Rotary movement of the scapula involving moving the inferior angle (bottom) of scapula laterally and upward; only occurs when the arms are lifting	The scapulae revolve to allow for greater range of motion of the arm, such as from second position to fifth position.
Downward rotation	Rotary movement of the scapula involving moving the inferior angle (bottom) of scapula medially and downward; only occurs when the arms are lowering	The return of the scapulae as the arms move from fifth position to second position and back down to neutral is downward rotation.
Protraction	Moving the scapula away from the spine and toward the front of the rib cage; sometimes called abduction of the scapula because it is movement away from the body's midline	When the shoulders appear to be rounding forward, the scapulae are protracting.
Retraction	Moving the scapula toward the spine and away from the front of the rib cage (returning to neutral from the protracted position); sometimes called adduction of the scapula because it is movement toward the body's midline	When the shoulders appear to be opening wide from a rounded position, the scapulae are retracting.
Lateral flexion	Movement of the spine in the frontal plane to the left or to the right	Side bending is lateral flexion.
Spine rotation	Done left and right, turning of the spine on its vertical axis, sometimes called spiraling the spine	Spotting for turns requires fast rotation of the cervical spine.
Circumduction	Movement that creates a complete circle; occurs as a result of a continuous sequence of flexion, abduction, extension, and adduction	Rond de jambe is circumduction at the hip.

Upper Extremities

When you consider the movements of the upper extremities, like most people you probably think of the arms. When the arms move, they do not move alone; your body coordinates multijoint movement in the upper body. In fact, you learned this coordination in simple tasks such as reaching and grasping, which require multijoint movement in the hands, wrists, elbows, shoulder joint, and shoulder girdle, with some movement in all three planes. Each of these areas can be described separately in terms of specific movements and muscles.

Radioulnar Joint and Elbow   When you move the lower arm, the joint actions occurring are the rotary action (such as turning a doorknob) and the hinging action (such as lifting a glass). In scientific terms, these two prominent movements of the radioulnar joint are in the transverse plane: *supination,* caused by a muscle called the supinator and assisted by the biceps, and *pronation,* caused by the pronator quadratus and pronator teres. The elbow also has only two movements, which are in the sagittal plane. The first is *flexion,* caused by the biceps, the brachialis, and the brachioradialis. The other is *extension,* caused by the triceps. The biceps and triceps are considered the larger power muscles of the elbow joint. Push-ups involve the triceps, and chin-ups involve the biceps.

Shoulder Joint   The shoulder joint is more complex; it moves in all three planes. Three groups of muscles are considered the power muscles of the shoulder joint—the pectoralis major, the deltoid group, and the latissimus dorsi—and they are superficial (closest to the skin). In addition, four small muscles are known as the rotator cuff—supraspinatus, teres minor, infraspinatus, and subscapularis—and they are deep (closest to the bone; see figure 2.6). The primary function of this group of muscles is stabilization of the joint. From this general overview, movements in each plane can be described in terms of the specific muscles that produce these movements.

Flexion is produced by anterior muscles—the upper portion of the pectoralis major (also called the clavicular portion) and the anterior deltoid. The muscles of *extension* are posterior—the latissimus dorsi (and the smaller muscle that always works with it, called the teres major) and the posterior deltoid. *Abduction* is caused by the middle deltoid and the supraspinatus. *Adduction* is caused by the latissimus dorsi, teres major, posterior deltoid, and pectoralis major. *Outward rotation* is produced by the teres minor, infraspinatus, and posterior deltoid. *Inward rotation* is produced by the subscapularis, pectoralis major, anterior deltoid, latissimus dorsi, and teres major. *Horizontal flexion* is caused by the pectoralis major, the anterior deltoid, the subscapularis,

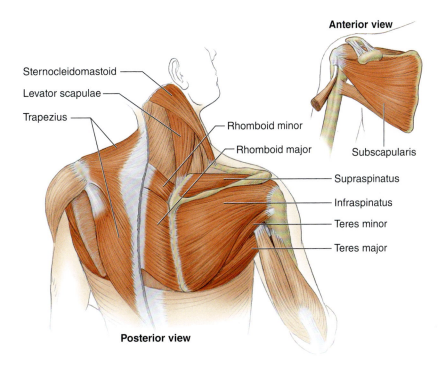

Anterior view

Sternocleidomastoid

Levator scapulae

Trapezius

Rhomboid minor

Rhomboid major

Subscapularis

Supraspinatus

Infraspinatus

Teres minor

Teres major

Posterior view

Figure 2.6   Muscles of the rotator cuff.

and the coracobrachialis. *Horizontal extension* is caused by the posterior deltoid, latissimus dorsi, teres major, infraspinatus, and teres minor. In broad terms, anterior muscles move the humerus toward the front of the body (flexion, inward rotation, horizontal flexion), and posterior muscles move the humerus toward the back of the body (extension, outward rotation, horizontal extension). While all of these muscles might seem a bit overwhelming, the easy way to remember the muscles of the shoulder joint (see figure 2.7) is to think in terms of planes and directions.

Shoulder Girdle   When the humerus is moving (when the arm is in motion), the scapula is also moving to accommodate these actions. This relationship is sometimes called scapulohumeral rhythm. The shoulder girdle has three pairs of movements: elevation/depression, protraction/retraction (also

called abduction/adduction), and upward and downward rotation. *Elevation* is produced by the levator scapulae, the rhomboids (deep to the trapezius), and the upper portions of the trapezius (a large triangular muscle in the back). *Depression* is produced by the pectoralis minor in the front and the lower portion of the trapezius in the back. *Protraction* is caused by the serratus anterior (which connects the scapula to the front of the ribs) and the pectoralis minor, deep to the pectoralis major. *Retraction* is caused by the middle trapezius and the rhomboids. *Upward rotation* is produced by three muscles working together—the upper and lower trapezius, and the serratus anterior. *Downward rotation* is produced by the rhomboids and the pectoralis minor.

Note that in terms of movement function, you can perform elevation/depression and protraction/retraction with your arms hanging at the sides of your body. The shoulder roll done in jazz dance class is actually combining those four movements of the shoulder girdle. However, upward and downward rotation can only occur when the humerus is moving; that is, when the arm moves forward or to the side (the humerus flexing or abducting), the shoulder girdle must rotate upward to accommodate the arm height. Similarly, as the humerus returns to neutral, the shoulder girdle rotates downward.

Lower Extremities

The multijoint coordination of the lower extremities is so common to humans because they have been walking since about 1 year of age. In fact, even simple walking must organize the joints of the feet, ankles, knees, and hips with some movement in all three planes. Each of these areas can be described separately in terms of specific movements and muscles.

Foot and Ankle   Consider the foot and ankle muscles from the perspective of these four quadrants: anterior, posterior, medial, and lateral. The anterior muscles *dorsiflex* the ankle; they are the tibialis anterior, peroneus tertius, extensor digitorum longus, and extensor hallucis longus. The posterior muscles *plantar flex* the ankle; they are the gastrocnemius (superficial) and the soleus (deep). These two muscles have a conjoined tendon, called the Achilles tendon, at the back of the ankle. Activities such as jumping and relevé are examples of movements that use plantar flexion. The ankle does not move medially and laterally, and the muscles in these two quadrants cause movement at the foot. The medial quadrant comprises the tibialis posterior, flexor

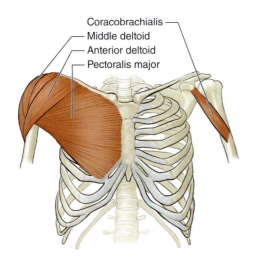

Coracobrachialis
Middle deltoid
Anterior deltoid
Pectoralis major

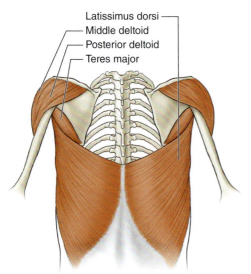

Latissimus dorsi
Middle deltoid
Posterior deltoid
Teres major

Figure 2.7   Muscles of the shoulder joint.

digitorum longus, and flexor hallucis longus, and these muscles *supinate* ("sickle") the foot. In addition, the tibialis anterior contributes to supination. The lateral quadrant comprises the peroneus longus and brevis. These two muscles, along with the peroneus tertius and extensor digitorum longus, *pronate* ("wing") the foot. The three peroneals are also called the fibularis muscles, because they all attach to the fibula on the lateral calf.

In general, the muscles in the foot fall into two main groups. One group is intrinsic to the foot itself, meaning that both attachments lie within the foot. The other group is extrinsic, meaning that the proximal attachment is in the lower leg with the distal attachment in the foot. The simplest guideline for understanding what a foot muscle does is to break down its name; many of the muscles of the foot have three words in the name. You have already encountered some of these muscles in the description of the four quadrants. The first word in the name tells you what the muscle does. The second word tells you whether it affects the big toe (hallucis) or the remaining four toes (digits). The third name tells you whether it is intrinsic (brevis or minimi) or extrinsic (longus). For example, the flexor hallucis longus is a muscle that flexes the big toe and has its upper attachment on the posterior calf. The extensor digitorum longus is a muscle that extends (or hyperextends) the other four toes and attaches laterally on the calf. An important muscle group in the foot is called the deep intrinsic muscles.

These are small muscles on the bottom of the foot that are important arch supports, and they are active in locomotion and elevation work (see figure 2.8).

Knee Because the knee only moves in the sagittal plane, the muscles can be described as either extensors or flexors. *Extension* is produced by anterior muscles, which as a group are called the quadriceps. The three vasti (lateralis, intermedius, and medialis) only affect the knee. The fourth, the rectus femoris, also causes movement at the hip. All four merge into a conjoined tendon, with the patella embedded, that attaches at the top of the tibia. *Flexion* is caused by numerous muscles, and several also affect the hip. These actions are described in the following section on the hip. First, the hamstrings are posterior muscles that cross the knee laterally (biceps femoris) and medially (semitendinosus and semimembranosus). The sartorius wraps around the back part of the distal femur and attaches to the anterior tibia; it is the longest muscle in the body. The gracilis is a thin muscle on the inner thigh that assists in knee flexion. In addition, when the knee fully extends in stance, the femur moves into a position of inward rotation relative to the tibia; this is called the screw-home mechanism. A small muscle called the popliteus initiates knee flexion from full extension, and it brings the femur back into alignment with the lower leg.

Hip Like the shoulder joint, the hip (figure 2.9) moves in all three planes. The five hip muscles that create *flexion* are the sartorius, tensor fasciae latae

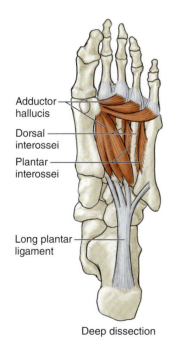 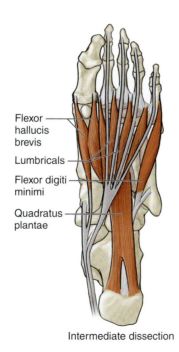 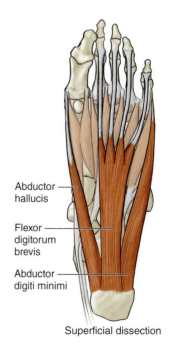

Adductor hallucis, Dorsal interossei, Plantar interossei, Long plantar ligament — Deep dissection

Flexor hallucis brevis, Lumbricals, Flexor digiti minimi, Quadratus plantae — Intermediate dissection

Abductor hallucis, Flexor digitorum brevis, Abductor digiti minimi — Superficial dissection

Figure 2.8 Intrinsic layers of the foot.

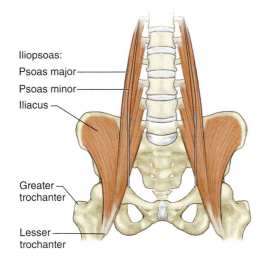

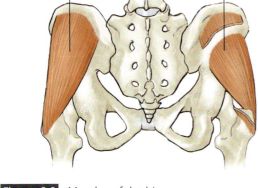

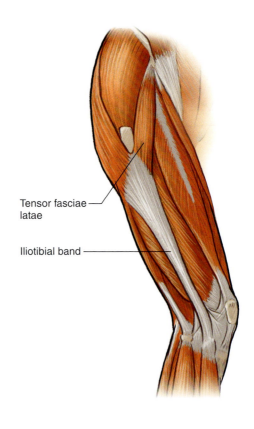

Figure 2.9 Muscles of the hip.

(TFL), rectus femoris, iliopsoas, and pectineus. The TFL assists in abduction and stabilizes the lateral knee due to its attachment onto the IT band. The iliopsoas is actually two muscles, the psoas and the iliacus. The psoas starts on the spine; its effects on the spine will be discussed in that section. It meets the iliacus, and their conjoined tendon attaches to the medial femur. The iliopsoas is the only hip flexor that is deep to the abdominal viscera. The pectineus assists in adduction. The muscles of *extension* are the hamstrings, named in the knee section, and they attach to the ischial tuberosities (sitting bones). The other hip extensor is the gluteus maximus, which is very active in hyperextension of the hip, such as arabesque. *Abduction* of the hip is produced by the gluteus medius and minimus. The medius is important in walking and standing on one leg. *Adduction* is

produced by a group of muscles on the inner thigh: adductor magnus, longus, brevis, and minimus; in addition, the gracilis assists. The six deep *outward rotators* in the hip are piriformis (most superior), gemellus inferior and superior, obturator internus and externus, and the quadratus femoris (most inferior). These six small muscles can contribute to outward rotation in just about any movement of the femur, whereas the gluteus maximus, also an outward rotator, is mainly active in extension/hyperextension. Similarly, the sartorius will contribute to outward rotation in hip flexion. The *inward rotators* are the same as the abductors: gluteus medius and minimus with help from the TFL. Some people say that the iliopsoas contributes to outward rotation, and others say it contributes to inward rotation; no conclusive evidence exists to support either theory.

Trunk: Head, Spine, and Pelvis

The trunk can be viewed simply as having anterior and posterior muscles. The muscles that cause thoracic and lumbar spine *flexion* are in layers. The superficial muscle known as the "six-pack" is the rectus abdominis (figure 2.10). The external and internal obliques run diagonally and essentially lie on the sides of the torso, not underneath the rectus abdominis. Deep to all of these muscles is the transverse abdominis, which does not move the spine at all. It is a stabilizer and not a spine flexor. Flexion of the cervical spine (neck) is caused by the sternocleidomastoid and the deeper scalenes, which are primarily stabilizers. The spinal muscles that cause *extension* fall into two main groups. The superficial group is called the erector spinae, and it is in three portions. These muscles are also known as global, because the fibers run across several vertebrae. Beneath the erector spinae lie the deep extensors; again, these muscles are in several groups, such as the multifidi and the rotatores. These muscles are sometimes called segmental, because they only go across two or at most three vertebrae.

A muscle that is on the side of the body, just posterior to the plumb line is the quadratus lumborum (QL). While it does contribute to extension, its main function is stabilizing the ribs on the pelvis, especially in locomotion. *Lateral flexion* (side bending) is caused by all of the anterior and posterior muscles on one side. Spinal *rotation* involves muscles in all four quadrants (anterior right, anterior left, posterior right, and posterior left). For example, rotating to the left involves the right external obliques, the left internal obliques, the right deep extensors, and

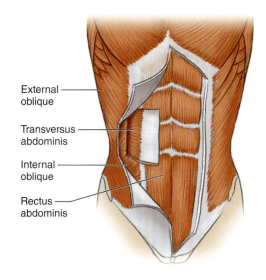

External oblique

Transversus abdominis

Internal oblique

Rectus abdominis

Figure 2.10   Abdominal muscles.

An excellent example of the external oblique abdominals.

© Herb Ritts / Trunk Archive

the left erector spinae. In the neck, the sternocleido-mastoid serves to create opposite-side rotation; that is, the left one rotates the neck to the right.

EMPOWERMENT

Take Charge of Your Training

Understanding the planes of movement and movement terms gives you a clear insight into what is happening in dance movement, and it provides tools for learning clarity in line and action. While you do not want to think about specific muscles while you are dancing, by understanding what muscles are responsible for dance movements, you can give yourself clear images of how you want to achieve dance movements. In this way you can empower yourself as a dancer to be an active participant in your training and artistry.

Alignment

One of your first goals in dancer wellness should be to address the issue of proper **alignment** for dance practice; in other words, examine how the parts of your body organize in stance and movement. The well-aligned body is aesthetically pleasing, and according to research it causes less wear and tear on the joints and muscles, which can translate into fewer injuries and a longer career. The easiest way to begin to assess alignment is to look at yourself in profile and observe the plumb line (see figure 2.11).

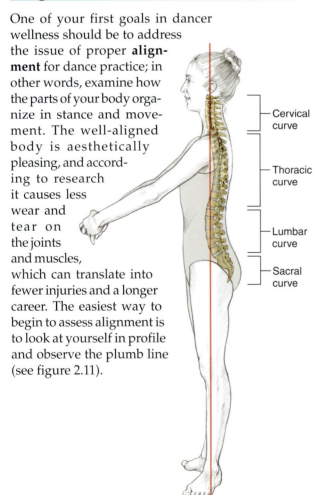

Cervical curve

Thoracic curve

Lumbar curve

Sacral curve

Figure 2.11   Plumb line.

Plumb Line and Spine Variations

The **plumb line** is an imaginary line drawn through the top of the head, center of the ears, bodies of the central cervical vertebrae, acromia of the shoulder girdle, bodies of the central lumbar vertebrae, heads of the femur, centers of the knee joints, and centers of the ankle joints. When the body is in good alignment, the plumb line is vertical in relation to gravity. Keep in mind that dancers in general actually stand in different alignment depending on the foot position. For example, dancers stand in better alignment in first position turned out than in fifth position turned out. Possible reasons for this difference are discussed later in this section.

Spine variations affect the body's alignment. Most of these variations can be corrected with an appropriate conditioning program, which you will be able to develop for yourself after reading chapter 3. The most common spine variations are as follows:

› Forward head (cervical hyperextension)
› Rounded shoulders (protracted scapulae)
› Elevated shoulders (elevated scapulae)
› Winged shoulder blades (scapula alata; inner borders protrude)
› Rounded chest or exaggerated thoracic curve (kyphosis)
› Protruding ribs (excessive tension in thoracic erector spinae)
› Swayback or lordosis (anterior pelvic tilt)
› Tucked pelvis (posterior pelvic tilt)
› Spine lateral curvature (scoliosis; also includes some spine rotation, and can be anywhere in the spine)

Alignment of the Upper Extremities

In the well-aligned body, the scapulae lie flat on the rib cage when viewed from the back. Looking from the side, the shoulders do not appear to be rounded forward. In fact, in nondancers the scapulae are 30 degrees anterior to the plumb line, but dancers work to open the front of the chest and align the shoulder blades in the plumb line. From the front view, the clavicles should make only a slight V or be in a parallel line to the floor; an exaggerated V indicates elevated shoulders.

In dynamic movement, most dance practices require the look of a long neck and an open chest. Therefore, in your dance training, you should work to inhibit shoulder girdle elevation and protraction, and maintain the scapulae in the neutral position, even when the arms are actively moving. At first this pattern can cause tension in the upper body, but eventually it becomes a habit that is easy to maintain.

Alignment of the Lower Extremities

Understanding the meaning of neutral pelvis can be challenging. In anatomical terms, the **neutral pelvis** is an organization of the pelvis and spine in which the anterior superior iliac spine (ASIS: the two bony projections on the front of the pelvis, often called "hip bones") is vertically aligned over the pubic bone. If the pubic bone is further forward, the pelvis is tucked; if the ASIS bones are further forward, the pelvis is in anterior tilt, or swayback.

Another alignment issue in the lower extremities involves the organization of the hip, knee, ankle, and foot. When the dancer is in parallel *demi-plié*, in general the centers of the hip joints should be directly over the centers of the knee joints, which should be directly over the centers of the ankle joints. In addition, the weight in the foot should be distributed evenly in a triangle created by the first metatarsal (opposite the big toe), fifth metatarsal (opposite the baby toe), and center of the heel. In any turned-out position (first, second, fourth, or fifth position) this arrangement of the knees over the feet and the even distribution of weight should still be the goal. Note that a certain percentage of dancers have a condition called **tibial torsion**, in which the tibia twists as it goes down the leg. For these dancers, the knee will not be over the foot in plié; for them the focus should be on the even distribution of weight in the foot. You can ask your dance teacher or a physical therapist to assess you for tibial torsion.

Finally, if your body is well aligned, the foot is neither supinated nor pronated in stance or relevé. These conditions can be caused by issues at the hip, such as forcing turnout, or weakness and lack of control in ankle and foot muscles. You can do a self-assessment to determine why one or both of these conditions exists, then create a corrective program or work on repatterning in turnout.

In addition to pronating the feet, you might do two other compensations to achieve the look of more turnout than you have anatomically. The first is allowing the pelvis to be in anterior pelvic tilt, which creates more turnout by taking the hips into slight flexion. Dancers tend to force turnout more in fifth position than other standing positions, which is why the pelvis will tilt more in fifth position. The second is torquing at the knee. When the knee is in, not bearing weight, and is flexed, the lower leg (tibia) can outwardly rotate in relation to the femur. Sometimes dancers use this process to get into turned-out positions and then attempt to straighten the legs. However, this action puts tremendous strain on the knee ligaments, and you should not encourage this practice in your dancing.

SELF-AWARENESS

Static Versus Dynamic Alignment

Sometimes you might be frustrated by the fact that you feel well aligned in stance (at the barre and center), but then feel that your alignment deteriorates to some extent as you move into dynamic traveling material. In fact, it is far more complex to align the body in traveling movement. If organizing alignment demands conscious attention in the early portions of class, it is likely that when attention is placed on complex combinations, alignment will suffer. Until good alignment is habitual and nonconscious, it will probably not carry over to complex movement. This process has more to do with the brain and the neural components of movement than whether or not the muscles are sufficiently strong and flexible to support proper alignment at each joint. Working with a partner from your dance class, take turns assessing each other from the side. Determine whether your bony landmarks line up with the plumb line. Also look at each other in demi-plié, and assess your hip–knee–foot alignment. Finally, watch each other doing a complex movement phrase, and notice whether proper alignment is maintained.

Specific Concepts in Dance Technique

Technique is a broad term that can cover any aspect of your training from functional body elements, such as core support and turnout, to specific dance skills, such as turning, elevation steps, and balancing. This section provides a general overview of some of these topics, but it is by no means a thorough and complete discussion of technical training. Some dance teachers approach technical training purely from aesthetic values, putting the emphasis on the look and beauty of the movement from a particular standard. This section describes these aspects of training from the health and well-being perspective and not from an aesthetic point of view.

Core Support and Use of the Spine

You might think that if you tighten the surface muscles at the front of the body, you are using your core. In fact, the muscles of the core lie deep in the body, and they are closer to the spine than these surface muscles. They are the transverse abdominis, the lumbar multifidi (part of the deep extensors), the pelvic floor, and the diaphragm. Good core support assists in balance and injury prevention without limiting range of motion or ease. The use of the core support muscles creates the sensations of narrowing at the waist, hollowing or drawing in the lower abdominal area, and freedom in breathing patterns. Many conditioning and training systems have developed methods to assist dancers in activating the core muscles, and no one method is the best. For more detailed information, see chapter 3 and the bibliography for this chapter.

Movements of the spine can explore full range of motion as long as good core support exists and you pay attention to elongation in all directions. For example, in arabesque, it is easy for you to arch the low back by crunching or collapsing the joint spaces. However, you can arch this area of the spine and still elongate or maintain joint space. This action not only protects the low back from injury, it is also far more aesthetically pleasing. The thoracic area of the spine is most limited in range of motion, and you should give some time in your conditioning program to work on increasing range of motion in this area. Every technique or style of dance uses the spine in different ways, not only in shape design but also in muscular effort. These can range from very bound and resisted movement to swinging and full release to gravity. You need to distinguish these various movements and their dynamic qualities, and train the body to do each in a safe and effective way.

Turnout

You create active turnout through external rotation at the hip joint. While anatomical contributions to turnout do exist down the lower leg and foot, you should not forcefully attempt to add to your turnout through these additional mechanisms, such as torquing at the knee and pronating the feet. Probably one of the most important ideas that you should embrace is that turnout is not a static position. It is an ongoing activity that is sustained throughout class and choreography. It is more important that turnout be maintained in a jump landing than held at a position at the barre. Until this dynamic patterning is habitual, you must attend to it consciously or risk injury to the lower legs. You must find indi-

vidual methods to ensure this patterning, whether through imagery, supplementary exercises, verbal cueing, or sensory feedback. You can empower personal training methods by being proactive and not relying on your teacher's cues and corrections to work on turnout.

It would be valuable for you to seek out a professional person with experience in functional assessment, and find out what your passive and active ranges of motion in turnout are. If a large discrepancy exists between the passive measurement and what you can achieve in active movement, you need to do exercises to increase active muscle use and control.

Use of Arms

Each dance technique and style approaches the use of arms differently. Even within modern and contemporary forms, a broad range of shapes and efforts exists with arm use. Perhaps the important issue for you in your training is be aware of these differences and find ways to shift from style to style as you go to different classes. In this way, you will be versatile and take responsibility for your training. Probably one of the more universal features in arm use is the aesthetic of the lengthened neck and open chest. As mentioned previously, it requires ongoing depression and retraction in the shoulder girdle to maintain neutral scapular alignment as the arms move through full range. However, the shoulder girdle must rotate upward and downward as the arms move, so thinking of locking or anchoring the scapulae is not useful and can create excess tension.

In recent years, a greater demand has been placed on the dancer for increased strength in the upper extremities. First, choreography is using more weight bearing on the arms, and many dancers do not have sufficient strength or control to do these movements safely. Second, partnering work is becoming increasingly complex, and female dancers are expected to lift other dancers as well as to be lifted. If you are currently in a dance company or school in which these tasks are expected of you, it would be advantageous to do strength training for the arms and upper body as part of your personal program.

Use of Lower Legs and Feet

The lower legs and feet probably have the highest potential for injury in elevation work (jumping). Jumping technique requires strength and power (strength applied at speed) in all of the extrinsic and intrinsic muscles of the feet and ankles. In addition, it requires excellent motor control, which refers to the messages from brain that organize the movement patterns. Further, being a strong jumper in one technique does not mean that you are necessarily prepared for jumping in a different technique. For example, the advanced ballet dancer may not be able to safely achieve jumps in parallel position given in a modern or hip-hop dance class.

Regardless of the style of jumps, landings should always be controlled and soft to absorb the force of the landing. When you push off for a jump, the muscles creating the movement shorten; this action is called a **concentric contraction**. When you land, the muscles need to elongate even though they continue working; this action is called the **eccentric contraction**. The eccentric contraction is the most difficult phase to train, and it is also what protects the lower legs from injury.

A dancer may have **hyperextended knees**, in which the back of the knee is bowed due to long ligaments, and also be able to pronate and evert ("wing") the foot. These movements are potentially problematic in weight bearing, because they put undue stress on the ligaments and structures of the joints. However, they can be safely used in gesture (nonweight bearing) if a choreographer requests it. If you are aligning your body this way, you must simply be aware that you return to neutral alignment of the joints when returning to weight bearing.

While these discussions cover only the most general areas of technical training and dancer wellness, the information can assist you in becoming aware of their issues and stimulate further thoughts and research. In this way, you can begin to develop personal strategies to enhance your technique. You can set progressive goals for future improvements, becoming your own trainer and teacher in the process.

A beautiful example of arabesque en pointe with elegant alignment of the knees and feet.

Karen Kain in *Romeo and Juliet* (ca. 1982). Photo by Andrew Oxenham. Courtesy of the National Ballet of Canada Archives.

GOAL SETTING

Create Short- and Long-Term Goals for Your Training

Understanding various aspects of dance technique can allow you to establish short-term and long-term goals. For example, if muscles are too weak or too tight for optimal function, you can set goals to correct any imbalances. Write in a journal stating what you would like to achieve in 1 month or 1 year, and then design a plan to accomplish each of these goals. Setting goals is an excellent way for you to motivate yourself and not become overwhelmed with what you hope to change.

Motor Learning in Dance

Motor learning refers to changes that occur with practice or experience that determine a person's capability for producing a motor skill. These changes are relatively permanent, and they are associated with repetition of motor skills. In dance, motor learning is the process that allows you to learn basic and sophisticated skills that are not acquired through typical human motor development. Specific examples include pirouettes, large jumps, and balances. In addition, the aim of motor learning is to gain these skills with the specific intent to improve the quality of performance by enhancing smoothness, coordination, and accuracy.

The Learning Process

The motor learning process includes these essential stages:

1. Attention and observation (perception) of a demonstrated skill
2. Replication (execution) of what has been observed
3. Feedback
4. Repetition (further practice)

In most formal dance classes, your teacher provides the initial information by demonstrating and explaining a dance combination. You then perform the movements, and those movements are encoded in your mind. With repetition, that movement becomes a part of your memory. When the same or similar movements are required, you must recall it mentally and transfer it to physical execution. By the time the motor skill is embedded in memory, it is an image or concept of the task that is recalled at this level of execution, as opposed to a complicated series of details, multiple body parts, or individual muscle activation. This step is the final goal of the motor learning process.

Perception

As the teacher demonstrates the combination or skill for the dance students, the process of motor learning starts with attention and perception. Perception has two components. First, you observe and organize your present experience; second, meaning is attached to that observation based on past experience. Perception is dependent on the senses (sight, touch, smell, hearing, taste). For example, you see the teacher demonstrate the shift from first position to retiré, and you might relate it to any number of childhood games in which you attempted to balance on one leg. You also hear the music for the exercise, giving the movement a temporal context. It is likely that the first attempts would include some wobbling and adjusting while the brain seeks strategies to accomplish this shift in a smooth, coordinated way as demonstrated by the teacher. Note that learning can be enhanced through use of attention (conscious focus on what is being learned or the environment), but perception does not necessarily demand attention.

In addition to the sensory information, perception relies on another way of sensing. The bones, muscles, tendons, ligaments, joints, and skin all have specialized tissues (nerve cells) that receive information during stance and movement, and they send this information to the brain; this type of sense is called **proprioception**. Considerable fluctuations exist in the ability of the brain to utilize proprioceptive information during some of the adolescent years, and deficits are noticeable during growth spurts. It is not uncommon to see dancers regress in ability to balance on one leg during these growth spurts. If you are already accomplishing multiple pirouettes, and a growth spurt occurs, you may suddenly find that you can no longer achieve this task; you might consider doing fewer turns during this phase and attend to other motor or artistic components of the skill.

Perceptual skills are those skills that are inherited rather than learned but can be enhanced by training. Perceptual skills include hand-eye coordination, rhythm, visual discrimination, spatial discrimination, body control, and balance. Thus, one of your goals is to take the innate skills that you bring to class and fine-tune these abilities. For example, some dance students have an innate ability to balance easily before any training has occurred, but they may do the given task by lifting the hip of the gesture leg and leaning the torso off to the side. You can learn ways to fine-tune your skills by listening to feedback (to be discussed later) that encourages a vertical alignment of the torso and a translation of the pelvis onto the standing leg.

From Perception to Movement

Motor learning is set in motion by perception and continues with **replication**; in this phase, you attempt to do the observed task. Learning a dance or movement skill depends partly on how the information is presented. Motor learning can take three general forms: visual, verbal, and **kinesthetic** (touch and sensation). You can become aware of what your preferred learning strategies are, to make the best use of class time. It is also of great benefit for you to observe your peers attempting the material, and working through problems and errors. By seeing others correct and improve the attempted skill, you can see what constitutes a successful strategy and try applying it to your own experiences. This process has the added benefit of encouraging the idea that making mistakes is a natural part of the process, a necessary component of learning to dance. When you develop an overwhelming fear of making mistakes, you can limit your progress.

DIVERSITY IN DANCE

Examine Your Preferred Learning Styles

Examine your learning strategies. How do you prefer to learn dance movement? Are you a visual learner? Are you a kinesthetic learner? Are you a verbal/analytic learner? Now think about how you might expand your learning strategies. What type of learning strategy would you like to be better at? How would you work on expanding your ability in this type of learning? If you can be diverse in your learning strategies, you can work easily with a larger group of teachers and choreographers.

Feedback and Repetition

Watching and doing should be the predominant strategy in motor learning, and verbal instruction should be secondary, especially when you are seeing and learning a task for the first time. After the initial attempts at the movement task, dance training involves considerable repetition. At this stage verbal input can be an important factor in the learning process. In the dance example, it might mean that your teacher will tell you that you did not shift your pelvis far enough onto the standing leg to achieve balance. You should listen to your teacher's feedback, and make sure that you understand what it is about. This feedback is an important component of the motor learning process. Repetition of material without feedback does not necessarily result in improved performance.

As you progress from recreational to pre-professional to professional, you can develop the capacity and knowledge to 'self-instruct.' As you become more and more advanced in your movement capacity, you should become less and less dependent on the teacher for actual teaching of skills, but make use of the teacher's artistic expertise for coaching the artistic qualities.

Setting Goals and Motivating Yourself

Establishing goals is an important part of the learning process. Even before you are attempting pirouettes, you may be more inclined to practice and refine your retiré balances if you see pirouettes and know that this is the goal. This forward-looking strategy creates excitement and anticipation, and motivation is key in skill acquisition. Thus, in addition to setting goals for your dance class, if you have a positive attitude, you will have more success at learning and achieving; in other words, you will have self-motivation. If you attempt your retiré balance after receiving corrections, you manage a cleaner weight shift to the one-legged balance, but the arms are still not correct, it is an opportunity to acknowledge your success in the improvement of the shift rather than criticize your arms. You can work on your arms in a later attempt; acknowledge and enjoy your successes.

Additional Factors Affecting Motor Learning

Two additional factors in motor learning are particularly noteworthy for dancers. One is the use of **transfer of training**, which is the effect or influence that skill or knowledge acquired in one circumstance has on learning skills and problem solving in another circumstance. The second is the use of mirrors, which are frequently seen in dance training settings, although they are not common in sporting activities.

Transfer of Training

Motor learning as it relates to dance involves the concept of transfer of information, called transfer of training. The ballet dancer practices skills at the barre that are repeated in the center. Similarly contemporary or jazz dancers sometimes practice skills on the floor that are repeated in center work. It has been suggested by more than a few researchers and dance teachers that this transfer of information does not occur as expected. For example, the barre work may not be preparing you for balancing that is needed in the center. Similarly, practicing skills on the floor can teach motor patterns in the spine and limbs, but they may not be preparing the balancing mechanisms that you will need to underlie these skills once you are standing.

It has also been long presumed that dance class promotes even development of the right and left sides of the body. However, recent research indicates that right and left sides of the body are not trained as symmetrically as one would presume. The right side is often the side that you probably use to mark combinations, and the number of repetitions of an exercise on the left side of the body can be less. Motor learning research also suggests that transfer of information from the preferred side (for most dancers, the right) to the nonpreferred side is more effective.

Use of Mirrors

It has long been assumed that using mirrors enhances learning, but evidence exists that visual information from the mirror is distorted (two-dimensional), which may diminish kinesthetic awareness and learning. In addition, evidence in the field of psychology suggests that constant use of the mirror may negatively affect your self-esteem. You can consider standing in an area of the studio where you cannot see yourself in the mirror for at least some of your classes.

The traditional dance class provides many excellent opportunities to train you and develop your artistry. As you develop self-awareness along with movement skills, you can arrive at personal goals and become empowered in your own training. The field of motor learning has much to offer you in approaching classes so that they are safe, productive, and exciting.

Applying Physics to Dance Movements

All of the movements that dancers do every day use the principles of physics. Some common ones are balance, turns, and jumps. Further, turns can involve a solo dancer or partner work. Often dancers are not consciously aware of the use of physics in dancing, nevertheless these principles are at play. Looking at some specific examples will help you understand how to use physics to your advantage.

Balance

One of the breathtaking moments in dance occurs when a spectacular arrest of motion is prolonged beyond the expected duration. It is that instant when the dancer captures a certain bodily architecture or shape in space and has the ability to suspend the position seemingly indefinitely. In finding that position, gripping the muscles or holding one's breath does not help but instead hinders the achievement of balance.

Balance occurs when the **center of gravity (COG)** of a body is in a vertical line with the support at the floor. For this purpose, the center of gravity is defined as that point where the downward force of gravity appears to act on the body as a whole. An example of center of gravity is the middle of a seesaw. Basically, equilibrium is the process of finding balance. All of the balances that you do in dance classes are either moving the center of gravity or changing the location of support. An example of moving the center of gravity would be going from a wide stance on two feet to being on balance on one foot in classical Indian dance. An example of moving the location of support would be jumping from the feet onto one hand in urban street dance.

Turns

Dancers spend considerable time practicing turns. You may want to be a natural turner, the kind of dancer that seems to have no trouble knocking out the perfect triple and quadruple turns in ballet class or turns with the body in a curve in modern dance class. Although some people do have that natural ability to produce turns, in fact you have the capability to control and master the level of turning technique based on certain knowledge of physics.

Turns Performed by a Single Dancer

In dance movements, **variables** are those characteristics or aspects of the movement that can be changed while still keeping the essence of the movement. Examples include speed, level, where you face in the space, and arm gestures. It takes several variables to produce a pirouette that can be examined using physics; examples include the force used by the feet on the floor, the distance between the two feet, the time it takes for the push-off and the turn, and the use of the arms.

Consider what seems to be the usual preparation stance for a pirouette: The usual stance is an open fourth position, turned out or parallel, which can create more momentum for the turn. Fourth position is useful as a wider preparatory stance. It has more stability than fifth position, and the width can actually help make a turn more successful because it produces more **torque**, the force that causes an object to rotate.

The arms store the momentum after the turn is initiated. When turning to the right, the right arm will start gaining momentum, which is transferred to the torso. Then the left arm starts moving toward the right arm, and this energy transfers to the torso. This sequence allows the momentum generated in the two arms to be shared by the body as a whole (see figure 2.12).

Considering each of these variables will help to tailor one's turns, eliminate repetitive practice, and still produce customized turns to suit the needs of the individual dancer.

Some turns, such as the body rolling turns in Limón technique or the spiral turns in Graham technique, use the torso rather than the arms as the primary producer of momentum.

Turns Performed Within Partner Work

Turning with a partner uses many of the same variables but adds other possibilities. The partner can provide momentum for the turn, and momentum can even be transferred from one turning body to another. Consider being lifted by a partner, as might happen in ballroom dance. As the partner begins to spin, you will also spin, even though you are off the ground. As the partner places you on the ground, you can easily continue spinning or rolling along the floor, using that partner's momentum.

Using the classical partnership, the pas de deux (dance of two), is an example of the previously mentioned principles that uses two people instead of one. Supported pirouettes are common in ballet partnering, and they usually consist of the woman

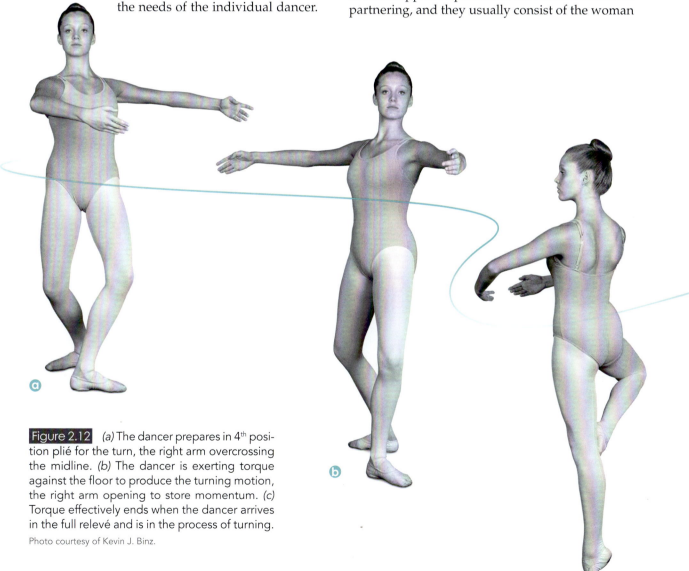

Figure 2.12 (a) The dancer prepares in 4th position plié for the turn, the right arm overcrossing the midline. (b) The dancer is exerting torque against the floor to produce the turning motion, the right arm opening to store momentum. (c) Torque effectively ends when the dancer arrives in the full relevé and is in the process of turning.

Photo courtesy of Kevin J. Binz.

initiating the turn in the way she usually would when dancing solo. She exerts forces with her two feet against the floor, which produce a torque that provides for her rotational motion around a vertical axis. The axis is in contact with the floor at the toe of her supporting foot. Suppose the choreography calls for a faster, more vigorous rotation than the woman can create on her own. She will need the man to exert the forces on her body that produce a turning movement of greater speed. The forces he exerts on her come from his two hands on her waist—one hand pulling back and the other pushing forward.

It is challenging for the male partner to exert those forces while simultaneously keeping his partner balanced upright as she completes a series of turns. Also, he must carefully arrange for her to complete the turns when facing the audience, in synchronism with the musical cue. When all of that movement is accomplished through body mechanics, body movements, and the use of applicable physics analyses, then the effects can be magnificent!

Jumps

While gravity is always a factor in dancing, its effect on the body is even more apparent when you begin doing jumps. Suppose you are in a class of dancers who are asked to do a series of vertical jumps without getting ahead of the music. During the first two jumps, the arms are held in a low position. On the third jump, dancers are told to carry their arms over their heads during the time their feet are pushing down against the floor. The first two jumps seem to make it nearly impossible to stay in the air with the music. However, on the third jump, it seems that the hang time (time in the air) is longer.

Physics can explain why this extra hang time occurs. If the arms are lifted during the time the feet are pushing against the floor, a fraction of the vertical momentum acquired by the body as a whole is absorbed by the arms. If that momentum is transferred to the body as a whole when the body is near the peak of its motion, then the body as a whole will have acquired more vertical momentum when it reaches its peak, and it will coast to a higher ultimate height before starting to descend.

When you apply the principles of physics, you can grow in execution and artistry. Understanding movement and the direct application of physics to dance can help you determine how to use your body effectively while preventing unnecessary wear and tear. Once you have a deeper understanding that encourages more efficient use of the body in space, you are on the path to ensuring a longer and more satisfying dance career.

Summary

Many areas of science can help you become a better dancer, as well as ensure your health and well-being. Anatomy gives you insight into how the bones and muscles create movement, and how the ligaments can protect your joints. Proper alignment is essential in your dance practice; it can prevent injury-producing wear and tear. Knowing how to develop core support, turnout, and the use of your spine, arms, and legs will serve you over a lifetime of dancing while protecting your body. While motor learning and physics are newer fields of study in terms of relating them to dance, they can provide invaluable lessons to make your training less repetitive and more effective.

This chapter discusses several areas of the scientific foundations of dance training, including anatomy, alignment, technique, motor learning, and physics. With this knowledge, you can begin to undertake a personal assessment and develop a plan to implement for improved performance.

First, evaluate your anatomical attributes. Examine your alignment in profile. Do you observe any misalignments such as round shoulders or anterior pelvic tilt? Do you see any asymmetries, such as scoliosis or one hip higher than the other? Can you evaluate your muscle imbalances? What might be too tight or too weak for good dance function?

Now examine how you work in technique class. Are you effective in using your core, or do you use tension and bracing for balance? Do you have a clear understanding of turnout, and do you control turnout well during dynamic movement?

Finally, assess how you accomplish particular skills in relation to principles of physics. Do you think you have good balance in your dance skills? Do you understand how to use momentum to create turns? Are you satisfied with your jumping skills? How might you improve them?

After you have answered all of these questions, you should have a clear idea of your current strengths and challenges and ways to improve your alignment, technique, learning strategies, and use of physics in your dancing. It can be empowering to act as your own teacher in how you work in class and how you develop your attributes in your own time. Make sure that you are setting realistic and timely goals, and track your work and your accomplishments. This process is rewarding and enjoyable.

Review Questions

1. Define bones, joints, ligaments, muscles, and tendons, and describe the function of each one.

2. What are the main muscles that you as a dancer need to know, and what are the various movements at all of the joints that you use in your practice?

3. Why is proper alignment important, and how can you recognize your alignment problems?

4. Discuss the main concepts for you as a dancer involving core support, the spine, turnout, and use of the arms and legs.

5. What are the motor learning issues for your age and level, and how can you improve your learning strategies?

6. In what ways does physics play a role in balances, turns, and jumps?

www For chapter-specific supplemental learning activities, study aids, suggested readings, web links, and more, visit the web resource at www.HumanKinetics.com/DancerWellness.

Cross-Training and Conditioning

Emma Redding, PhD, MSc, and Pamela Geber Handman, MFA

© Chris Nash, www.chrisnashphoto.com

Key Terms

adaptation

anaerobic capacity

cardiorespiratory endurance

compensation

cross-training

duration

flexibility

frequency

HRmax

individuality

intensity

isometric contraction

joint hypermobility

joint mobility

joint range of motion

muscular endurance

muscular power

muscular strength

neurological system

plyometrics

progressive overload

proprioceptive neuromuscular
   facilitation (PNF)

reversibility

somatic practices or somatic
   education

specificity

volume

LEARNING OBJECTIVES

After reading this chapter, you will be able to do the following:

❯ State the benefits of cross-training.

❯ Understand how to do a correct warm-up and cool-down.

❯ Describe these principles of training: adaptation, specificity, individuality, reversibility, compensation, and progressive overload.

❯ Consider the differences between muscular strength and power, flexibility, cardiorespiratory endurance, and anaerobic capacity, and determine which areas you need to develop.

❯ Understand the benefits of somatic practices and dance-specific programs.

At present, versatility is central to contemporary choreography; the skills required of dancers are extremely broad. Technique classes are still important as a part of a dancer's education, physical preparation, exposure to styles, and ways of working. However, for the most part, individually tailored conditioning programs provide dancers with a certain baseline of needed physical capacities. Supplemental dance conditioning has become not only increasingly popular with dancers, it has become essential for health and longevity. In the past, dance technique classes served as the main physical preparation for the performance of choreography. Currently dancers are expected to train in a wide variety of dance styles. To avoid risk of injury, dancers must find a conditioning practice that re-centers and grounds them with a basic level of balanced strength, flexibility, and endurance.

Musculoskeletal imbalances or inadequacies of strength and control, flexibility, and muscular endurance can be addressed in your supplemental conditioning program in a systematic, repetitive, and progressive manner. Through this process, you also deepen your understanding of your body, which places you in the driver's seat of your own practice. Your conditioning program must place attention on correct alignment, form, and coordination. The number of repetitions for each exercise can be set individually, building over time until your optimal performance of a given movement sequence is physically seamless, efficient, and does not sacrifice clarity of alignment and form.

This chapter addresses the advantages of cross-training and focuses on many of the principles and components of conditioning for dancers. It explores the importance of preparing for and recovering from dance training and performance so that you can get the most out of class, rehearsal, and performance and avoid injuries as much as possible. The chapter familiarizes you with principles of conditioning such as individuality, specificity, and recovery; if they are followed correctly, they lead to better performance and longevity in dance. In addition, the chapter explains the essential principle of progressive overload, which helps ensure noticeable improvements in performance. It is vital that you understand the differences between muscular strength, power, and endurance so that you can properly train these components of physical fitness and therefore be better prepared for the various demands inherent in various types of choreography. Dancers should improve both their cardiorespiratory endurance and anaerobic capacity, elements that are not often addressed fully in dance classes. Also included in this chapter are descriptions of conditioning systems that are specially designed for dancers or used as supplemental training by many dancers. This topic connects to a discussion on the value of somatic practices for dancers. Conditioning myths are detailed, exploring those that should be discarded as anecdotal versus those based on evidence. This discussion is put forth so that you can be clear about supplemental conditioning recommendations. The end-of-chapter application activity is an easy-to-use guide for putting all these recommendations into practice.

Benefits of Cross-Training

Cross-training for dance is any form of training other than dancing that has the goal of improving overall dance performance by making sure every part of the body and aspect of fitness is covered. If you cross-train wisely, you are less likely to incur injuries, especially those that stem from factors that you could control, such as alignment or form, coordination, strength, control, flexibility, or endurance. Ideal cross-training for dancers includes swimming, yoga, jogging, and cycling.

If you are already injured or ailing, a well-conceived, dance-specific conditioning program could help you heal faster and send you back into the dance arena more quickly. For example, if you have an ankle injury, you may not initially be advised to do high-impact exercise such as running or jumping; however, swimming may be recommended as a useful alternative because it is nonweight bearing yet beneficial for you. In addition to a conditioning program's effect on injury prevention and care, your performance will be enhanced. Conditioning can create these noticeable changes:

> An increase in a joint's range of motion, such as higher kicks

> Better central control, support, and balance

> Clearer articulation in fine motor movements, such as nuanced expression through the hands and feet

> More power or endurance in gross motor movements that travel through the space, change levels quickly, or propel off the floor

> Enlivened confidence and presence

As you can see, involving yourself in cross-training as a regular part of your dance training has many benefits.

DIVERSITY IN DANCE

Various Dance Forms Need Diverse Conditioning

Consider all of the dance forms that you currently study. Do they have different conditioning needs? For example, is the flexibility needed for ballet the same in tap dance? Probably not. Think about each of your classes (ballet, modern, tap, jazz, African, hip-hop, etc.), and determine what conditioning may help you become a better dancer in that form.

Preparing for and Recovering From Training

In order to be able to dance optimally and get the most out of class, rehearsal, and performance, you need to be fully prepared before you begin your full-out dancing. Essential for all dancers, this preparatory undertaking involves an effective warm-up. Further, in order to recover safely and effectively from dancing, you should perform a proper cool-down.

Warming Up

The aims of a warm-up are to raise the pulse, mobilize the joints, and gently stretch the muscles, as well as prepare the muscles for muscular work. In addition, the **neurological system** (the brain and its pathways to the body) needs to be considered in the warm-up; this involves mental focus, clarity, and centering, and it promotes both efficient alignment and effective coordination or physical patterning. The benefits of a warm-up include the following:

> Increase in body temperature

> Increase in metabolic rate within the muscles

> Increase in blood flow and oxygen to the muscles

> Gradual increase in the full range of motion of the joints

> Increase in the speed of nervous system transmission

> More efficient production of energy for fueling muscle contractions

> Arriving at a state of physical and mental preparedness for class or rehearsal

The first phase of the warm-up is the gradual pulse raiser, whereby the heart rate and breathing are increased to an intensity similar to that of light jogging. **Intensity** refers to the level of exercise and how difficult it is. Intensity is best raised through dynamic movements that use the large muscles of the body, such as jogging, skipping, knee lifts, and movements that change levels such as lunges, squats, or rolls down onto the floor and up out of the floor. It is important to work the muscles in greater range of motion; think in terms of large openings and closings, highs and lows, as well as big, full reaches in one direction followed by reaching to the opposite direction.

The second phase of the warm-up is the joint mobilizer, whereby the major joints such as the hips, knees, ankles, spine, and shoulders are moved repetitively within their range. This movement increases the temperature and fluid around these joints, preparing them for loading and action. Examples of joint mobilizer movements include pelvic circles and knee lifts (for the hip joints), folding and unfolding as well as rotating in and out at the hip joints, circling the ankles in both directions as well as raising and lowering in the ankle joints, swinging or circling the arms, flexing and extending the torso, bending sideways each way, and twisting.

The third phase of the warm-up involves short stretches, whereby exercises that lengthen the major muscles are carried out. Note that stretches should be brief (no more than 10 seconds) and target the main muscles in the calves (by dorsiflexing the ankle, which stretches the calves), low and mid back (by curving/flexing the torso, adding a twist each direction, and then side bending the torso each direction), as well as the hamstrings (flexing at the hip joints and doing so with a slightly bent knee at this early point), gluteal muscles (flexing and adducting at the hip joints, drawing the torso into a curved/flexed position as well) and quadriceps (extending through the hip joints and bending the knee). Ideally stretches should be dynamic and active (in motion) when they are done at the beginning of a dance session. It is important not to take joints to their extreme range at first. Avoid prolonged passive (using gravity or body part as weight) or ballistic (bouncing) stretching at this stage.

The fourth phase of the warm-up is the second pulse raiser, whereby movements are carried out to raise the pulse once again. These movements can consist of dance phrases you would do in class that are repetitive in nature, particularly ones that change direction and level, thereby also facilitating coordination. Weight-shifting through space, perhaps building from walking to jogging, as well as moving down onto the floor and up out of the floor again are beneficial at this stage.

These phases may well overlap, and they are not necessarily done in segmental or separate movement phrases. For example, leg swings can act as both a pulse raiser and a joint mobilizer, as well as contribute to stretching some of the large muscles around the hips. Deep pliés or squats that develop into a roll on the floor across your back (opening wide into an X shape and curling back into a ball) and back up to standing again can serve as a joint mobilizer for hips, knees, and ankles; a short, dynamic stretch for the hips and low back; and a pulse raiser as well. Locomotor movements through space, changing directions, and altering levels can similarly serve as both pulse raisers and dynamic stretches for many joints. All of these movements raise the body temperature, which is an important part of warming up.

Mental focus is essential during the warm-up. It promotes greater awareness and attention to the body. A brief moment of standing quietly and focusing your attention on your body, breathing, and your body's sensations can translate into greater physical clarity as well as performance presence later on. This experience, called mindfulness, is addressed in chapter 4. You may wish to close your eyes at first in order to eliminate visual input from your surroundings and to more easily concentrate on the proprioceptive sensations of your body. Tuning in mentally is essential to all phases of dancing and conditioning; it includes the warm-up and continues into the later aspects of class or rehearsal.

SAFETY TIP

Warm Up Properly

Remember that a warm-up should begin gradually. It should build in intensity and complexity, progressing from general to more complex movements, later involving more intricate coordination and finally more dance-specific movement. The warm-up should not involve deep stretching or begin with full-out sprinting. If the body is not already adequately warm, these movement activities can cause injury.

Cooling Down

At the end of a class, rehearsal, or performance, it is important to cool down. Performing a cool-down decreases the risk of feeling sore the next day and helps prevent injury. It is also a great time to stretch more deeply and relax both body and mind.

The aims of a cool-down are to gradually lower the pulse, and release and stretch the muscles. The benefits of a cool-down include the following:

> - Effective recovery from a training session or performance
> - Decrease in the likelihood of injury
> - Increase in flexibility of muscles
> - Opportunity to relax
> - Slowing the heart and breath rate, and lowering the body's temperature

The structure of the cool-down should be the reverse of the warm-up. It should include a gradual slowing down of dynamic movement in order to return the heart rate and breathing to normal. The gradual decrease in activity also allows more oxygen to be delivered to the muscles to assist with their recovery. Longer and deeper stretches can be carried out during the cool-down, and all major muscles should be stretched for approximately 20 to 30 seconds each. If certain muscle groups are especially in need of stretching, try stretching them a couple of times.

Dancers need to be fully prepared before they begin their full-out dancing by undertaking an effective warm-up, which includes several phases (pulse raisers, joint mobilization, and short stretches). In order to recover safely and effectively from dancing, dancers should also do a cool-down, which includes a gradual decrease in pacing as well as longer, deeper stretches and quieter moments for both body and mind to relax.

Principles of Training

Certain principles of training can help you get the most out of your dancing. This section explains the principles of adaptation, specificity, individuality, reversibility, and compensation. In addition, a well-designed conditioning program should follow the principle of progressive overload in order to help ensure improvements.

Adaptation

Adaptation is when changes occur as a result of training. This process may take some time. The key point is to not push the body too far, too fast. The body's skeletal structure is set after adulthood, but you can do a lot to train the muscles. In order for change to occur, you must set and stick to a regular conditioning schedule, expecting that it takes a few weeks of regular practice to experience any changes.

While some people by nature are more flexible, in terms of muscles and joint range of motion, and others are tighter, everyone can enhance all components of physical fitness. Change occurs more readily when you pay attention to bodily sensations while performing dance or other types of exercise. Don't tune out. This mental attention will help you make the transition from supplemental conditioning to technique class to performance.

Specificity

To have **specificity**, exercises in a dance conditioning program must mimic dance movement wherever possible. For the conditioning to adequately transfer into the dance studio and performance environment, the program must account for similar joint movement, muscle usage, range of motion, speed, resistance, and number of repetitions that would be done in dance. Too often, dancers reinjure

themselves soon after they step into the dance studio simply because the conditioning program in which they participated prior to returning to dance was not relevant or applicable to the demands of the dancing. For example, ankle sprain is a common injury that necessitates rest, ice, and once inflammation is gone, careful rehabilitative strengthening. If you do not add strengthening sequences that share the same range of motion, timing, and specific muscle usage as your dancing, you are more prone to reinjury. More specifically, slow work with exercise bands for strengthening the foot is important, but before you return to jumping, you should gradually build speed and resistance into your exercise regimen. Chapter 9 includes more in-depth information about dance injuries, prevention, and recovery.

Individuality

Individuality refers to training that addresses the particular needs of each person. Every body is different and has unique needs. Conditioning exercises can be modified so that they are tailored to each dancer's needs. An exercise that might be considered appropriately challenging for one dancer may be too difficult for another, so the conditioning program must address individual needs. For example, exercises designed for strengthening muscles of the

---

GOAL SETTING

Broaden Your Individual Strengths

Consider what type of dancer you are. You may notice that you often receive praise for a certain type of movement. Are you best at adagio (slow) phrases with lots of balances? Do you excel at high jumps and fast falls? Now consider how you might broaden your best features. What areas of conditioning could make you a stronger dancer in ways that are not typically your favorite dance movements? Set some reasonable goals for improvement in those areas. Also, consider participating in a dancer screening or assessment, which is usually performed by a knowledgeable dance teacher who has a background in anatomy or kinesiology along with a licensed physical therapist. A full one-on-one dancer screening or assessment can be invaluable, if this is available to you, in terms of clarifying specific goals while considering your individual assets, current level and type of training, and performance needs. Information about screenings is provided in chapter 10.

arms or legs often need to be performed with control through the torso. If you are not able to perform the full range of motion of the arms or legs without losing core control, then you should work the limbs in a smaller range while working on core support. By comparison, you might be a dancer who is more flexible and needs to focus more on muscular control rather than the full range of motion. On the other hand, if you are less flexible, you may need to focus on finding more easeful, full range of motion in the same sequence. You may also need to remain longer in a stretch in order to gain the same benefit as the more flexible dancer.

Reversibility

Reversibility means that if you are not consistent in your conditioning program, a de-training in performance can occur. A loss of strength rapidly occurs only 2 weeks after training ends. After only 1 month, a significant decrease in strength can occur—up to as much as 35 percent. Of all conditioning components, cardiorespiratory endurance appears to decline the fastest. You should understand the importance of adhering to a gradually progressive conditioning program so as to avoid reversibility and a decline in performance.

Compensation

Compensation occurs when you use muscles and alignment other than what is efficient or optimal because of fatigue or injury. For example, you may do a conditioning sequence in which you are trying to stabilize the body's core while dynamically strengthening muscles of the legs, going through pliés. A common misalignment that you might have is working with an anterior pelvic tilt rather than neutral pelvic alignment. You may begin the series with a neutral pelvis, but when some of the deeper abdominal muscles as well as the hamstrings get tired, the pelvis slips into an anterior tilt. Many muscles begin to work differently at that point even although you are still doing pliés through the legs. It is best to stop and rest when tired rather than compromise technique and form. Furthermore, trying to progress too quickly invites bad habits and injuries. Again, a gradual progressive conditioning program is ideal.

Progressive Overload

When designing a progressive conditioning program, you must consider several aspects of training, such as frequency, intensity, duration, volume, and rest or recovery. Each of these aspects determines the patterns of how often, how many, how much effort, and how much rest. Without considering these elements, you may not get the results you seek from your training. Therefore, you must understand the value of progressive overload. **Progressive overload** means that your skills and fitness develop optimally when the challenge of the conditioning exercises is increased gradually, and the demands are slightly beyond your limits. This progression allows the body to gradually adapt, improve, and become stronger. You should begin exercising right at your limit in terms of resistance and number of repetitions. In order for you to gain strength, you should gradually add more weight or resistance; to gain endurance, you should incrementally increase the number of repetitions. As discussed previously, maintaining proper alignment and form is essential as you add weight, resistance, or number of repetitions. Always perform exercises with good form; don't cheat!

Frequency

The term **frequency** refers to how often or how many times an exercise is carried out. For example, a flexibility exercise might be carried out for 30 seconds, twice per day and five times per week. If the principle of overload is applied in order to continue seeing improvements, you may increase the number of stretching bouts to three times per day. The frequency of a strengthening sequence could be 8 to 12 repetitions at a certain weight, repeated twice and done three times per week. If the principle of overload were applied here for strength exercises, you would gradually increase the number of times the exercises were performed each day, the amount resistance, or the number of days per week. In this case, however, it would be more effective to increase the intensity rather than the number of repetitions.

Intensity

Intensity refers to the level of challenge within an exercise and is usually measured in relation to your maximal capacity. Exercises are of varying intensity. For example, running is an exercise that is considered higher in intensity than light jogging. A balance on relevé would be considered higher in intensity than a balance on flat foot, and a jump from one leg is higher in intensity than a jump that takes off from two legs. If the principle of overload were applied to an exercise, the intensity would increase over a period of time in order to avoid a situation whereby the body becomes too accustomed to doing the same exercise and improvements no longer occur.

Duration

Duration refers to how long an exercise or set of exercises lasts. It is usually recommended that the duration of a warm-up be approximately 15 minutes, although it may be more or less depending on the activity to follow, the current temperature of the studio, your individual needs, or other factors.

If the principle of overload were applied to duration, the exercise would become longer over time. For example, you might do a balance exercise, such as standing on one leg with your eyes closed for 30 seconds, and repeat this exercise four times per week. At one point, this exercise would start to feel easier for you to complete; consequently, an appropriate overload would be applied. You might then do the balance exercise for 45 seconds increased duration while maintaining the number of times per week; that is, the frequency remains the same.

Volume

In this context, the term **volume** refers to how much exercise is carried out. You may take two technique classes one day followed by three classes the next day. This means the overall volume of exercise has increased from the first day to the second.

There is no ideal volume of conditioning or training for dancers, because what is ideal for one dancer may not be ideal for another. It is important to consider the frequency, intensity, and duration of an exercise when determining the ideal volume at any period of time. A reliable measure of a program's success is to take note of improvements across time.

Rest and Recovery

In order for the muscles to repair and grow stronger after an intense bout of exercise, they must be given adequate time to rest and recover. After a day of heavy class and rehearsal, a substantial meal and a good night's sleep is usually sufficient. After several days of intensive training, a full day of rest is often needed. The amount of rest and recovery needed varies from person to person. However, a good indicator that you are not getting enough rest is when overall performance is not improving over a period of time, even with progressive overload. For an in-depth discussion of rest and recovery, refer to chapter 6.

Within a particular conditioning session, it is important to include short rest periods for the muscle groups that have been targeted and intermittently work on another muscle group. For example, the hamstrings may need to rest while you focus on the upper body. Then you would swap back to the hamstrings or an entirely different muscle group.

This change in focus is particularly helpful during strength and power exercises in which the muscles replenish their energy stores for the next bout of exertion.

In summary, a dancer's conditioning program should use certain principles of training. The principles of adaptation, specificity, individuality, reversibility, and compensation are important when designing an effective program. For improvements to occur across time, progressive overload should be applied so that the body encounters a greater challenge than what it has been used to. The principles of training are discussed in more detail later in this chapter.

Muscular Strength, Power, and Endurance Training

Muscular strength is the ability to exert maximal force in one single contraction, such as lifting a weight that you could lift only once before needing a short break. **Muscular power** refers to a great force production over a short period of time, such as in fast leg kicks and explosive jumping. **Muscular**

This dancer displays muscular strength as well as flexibility in this difficult balance.

CPRowe Photography 2012, University of Utah, Modern Dance.

endurance is when less force is sustained over a longer period of time such as in gallops, skips, pliés, and swings. Dancers often confuse endurance with strength, so it is sometimes useful to think of endurance as continuous and strength as maximal.

In dance you are required to jump, catch partners, move down onto the floor and up out of the floor at fast speeds, and perform other explosive movements. These movements require a level of muscular strength and power. While technique classes can improve muscular strength and power, it is not necessarily the main goal. Some current dance technique classes are increasingly asymmetrical (practicing coordination on one side only) and are more focused on stylistic and artistic aspects of dancing rather than adequate repetitions to develop strength, power, and endurance. Therefore, you should do supplementary exercises for muscular strength, power, and endurance outside of your dance technique classes. Without a certain baseline of these important abilities, you are more likely to incur musculoskeletal imbalances and injuries. Injuries developed from muscular imbalances or from lack of core strength in large, explosive movements are common.

You need a good level of muscular strength, power, and endurance in order to effectively perform a variety of dance movements such as lifts, jumps, and explosive movements. An adequate level of muscular strength, power, and endurance not only assists the technical and aesthetic aspects of performance, it can also minimize the risk of injury by increasing joint stabilization and improving bone health.

A common method of strength training is with resistance machines or free weights, such as dumbbells. Even more common for dancers is using exercise bands or stretchy surgical tubing as resistance. You can also do strength training using your own body weight, such as in push-ups and leg lunges. You should exercise larger muscle groups before smaller ones, because smaller ones fatigue more quickly. It is important to alternate muscle groups to allow for recovery before performing another exercise on the same muscle group. For muscular strength gains, you should exercise a muscle through its full range of motion for 8 to 12 repetitions. The amount of weight or resistance should be challenging; after the set, you should feel muscular fatigue. Young teens or dancers rehabilitating from an injury should use lower weight or resistance and higher numbers of repetitions. For exercises targeting muscular power, remember to perform fast repetitions. You can repeat exercises

two or three times in a given conditioning sequence.

When exercising for muscle strength, you should isolate the muscles to be strengthened; carry out the correct motion fully in a smooth and controlled manner without other muscles compensating. People tend to compensate when they are tired, which is when other muscles take over for the fatigued muscles. When you are exercising, be mindful of this tendency and make adjustments in resistance in order to isolate the appropriate muscles. Whenever possible, exercise a joint through its full range of motion so as to work the entire muscle and not to use too much weight or resistance during the end of a motion.

Apply the principle of specificity by replicating movement patterns of dance as closely as possible and stressing muscle groups that are most needed in current dance activities. For example, when you are returning to technique class or rehearsals after an ankle sprain, you will need to condition the ankle to be able to jump. It is best for you to incorporate foot exercises that best match the jumping speed and range of motion similar to what occurs in dance jumps. While slow and sustained strengthening exercises, such as work with an exercise band, are recommended, you will benefit from restrengthening the feet with an increase in tempo, coming as close as possible to actual jumping speed and with a similar range of motion.

To realize gains in strength and power, apply the principle of progressive overload. Overload should happen in a gradual and progressive manner whereby intensity, duration, and frequency of the exercises are steadily increased. It is a good idea to begin with an initial 2-week period of high-repetition (15-25 reps) training with low resistance. Following this period, increase load with fewer (8-12) repetitions, allowing the focus of the exercise to shift from endurance to strength. A rest period of 60 to 90 seconds between each set is important, and exercises for the same body area should not be done on successive days. You may not notice results for 5 to 10 weeks, but do not become discouraged; results will occur.

You can train muscular power by incorporating explosive exercises after seeing initial strength gains. **Plyometrics** training is a form of jump training in which you exert maximal force in short intervals, which has been shown to effectively increase leg power. Usually exercises are quite short but fairly explosive. An example of a plyometrics exercise is 6 to 8 high tuck jumps followed by a rest and then repeated twice more. If progressive overload is applied here, the frequency of the jumps may increase from 3 to 4 bouts and the number of repetitions may increase from 6 to 8 jumps, to 8 to 10 jumps, and so on.

Dance technique classes cannot be solely relied on to provide the conditioning exercises needed to target various components of physical fitness such as muscular strength, power, and endurance. These aspects of conditioning allow you to perform dance movements such as jumping, catching a partner, moving down onto the floor and up from the floor at fast speeds, and other explosive movements. It is therefore recommended that you do supplementary exercises for these aspects of conditioning outside of dance technique classes.

Flexibility Training

Flexibility is range of motion in a joint and the length in the muscles that cross the joint. As a dancer, you are often required to take your joints to extreme ranges of motion, and it is important that you understand how to increase your flexibility safely and effectively. In order for you to extend your legs higher in space, flexibility in the muscles around the hip and knee joints is important. You need to stretch your hamstrings in order to do an extension (battement) of the gesture leg higher to the front. In order to lift the leg higher to the back (arabesque), the muscles in the front of the gesture leg's hip need to be stretched. It is a common misconception that flexibility in the hip muscles is the sole factor in getting one's gesture leg high in the air. A combination of flexibility and strength is in fact needed.

The benefits of flexibility training include discovery of a greater range of joint motions. For the hip joints, it may lead to higher leg extensions. There are many other reasons to work on flexibility, including enhancement of dynamic alignment (efficient upright posture during movement) as well as necessary balancing of opposing muscle groups around a joint. For example, you may be tight in your low-back muscles and your hip flexors and may habitually stand with a swayback, pelvis tilted anteriorly. By lengthening the low-back muscles and the muscles at the front of the hip joint, in combination with strengthening the deep abdominal and hamstring muscles, you can more easily stand in a more centered, efficient alignment through the lower torso, pelvis, and hips. In general, many dancers are muscularly tighter on one side of a joint and less tight (longer) on the opposite side. For example, it is common for many dancers to have tight quadriceps and hip flexor muscles, but they have

Dancers need flexibility in movement, as demonstrated by this leg split.
CPRowe Photography 2012, University of Utah, Modern Dance.

flexible hamstrings and other hip extensor muscles. In many dancers, outward hip rotator muscles are often tighter than the inward hip rotator muscles. In the shoulder joints, the muscles in the front of the shoulder, including the pectoralis major and minor, are typically tighter than the muscles in the back of the shoulder joint, such as the posterior deltoid or posterior rotator cuff muscles. For better stability and overall health for one's joints, the tighter side needs to be lengthened and the flexible side needs to be strengthened. Incorporating exercise sequences to specifically address the imbalance between the two opposite sides (called the agonist and antagonist muscles) can prevent potential injuries from occurring.

The process of acquiring flexibility involves the elongation of the muscles, including tendons and connective tissue through the joint range of motion. **Joint range of motion** refers to the degree of movement at a given joint based on its bones and ligaments. Joint range of motion is influenced by anatomical, biomechanical, and physiological factors.

Many types of flexibility training exist. As a dancer, you should learn what they are and which ones are appropriate to do at particular times. *Dynamic flexibility training* refers to controlled movements, which move through a range of motion at a joint. Some examples include yoga sun salutations (in which you fully extend and open the torso and hips followed by a full flexion, or folding, of the torso and hips), grand battement (in which the leg swings into the air in front and progressively moves into a leg swing to the back), and also a full extension of the legs followed by a deep plié. *Static flexibility training* is when the muscles being stretched are elongated to their tolerance and the position of stretch is held for a period of time. For example, gentle leg swings provide a dynamic stretch for the front and back of the hip, while hanging forward is a static stretch for the muscles along the back of the leg. *Passive flexibility training* is when stretching is assisted by gravity, one's own body weight, or external force such as a wall, floor, barre, or friend.

SAFETY TIP

Stretch Safely

The external force placed on the body during static flexibility training should never be excessive. A stretch should never include sharp pain or involve shaking. If either occurs during a stretch, release some of the force or lessen the range of motion such that breathing is full and deep. You should not experience excessive pain.

Another well-known form of flexibility training is called **proprioceptive neuromuscular facilitation (PNF)**, a form of stretching using muscle reflexes and responses to aid in flexibility gains. Because of the potential for injury to the muscles, it is not recommended that you do this form of stretching on your own or with a friend. It is best to have a qualified medical practitioner, such as a physical therapist, or a dance teacher trained in this method to use PNF. The two main forms of PNF stretching are called contract–relax (CR) stretch and contract–relax with antagonist contraction (CRAC) stretch. Using the example of hamstring stretches, in the CR stretch, the hamstrings are taken to an easeful, elongated position (known as *end range of motion* or *end range*) and then contracted. After this brief but intense contraction, the hamstrings are voluntarily relaxed while being stretched a bit farther. In phase 1 of the CRAC stretch, the hamstrings are first contracted near their end range of motion, just as in the CR stretch. In the next phase, the hamstrings are voluntarily relaxed while being stretched a bit further, and at the same time the quadriceps are contracted. It is during phase 2 that the quadriceps contraction encourages further hamstring relaxation.

Proper Stretching

Specific rules make stretching more effective. These rules relate to how long to hold a stretch, how often to perform stretches during the week, and what time of day to perform stretches in relation to other dance activities. Extensive stretching before class or performance could reduce strength and power, so it is best to leave the deeper stretches until later. Major muscle groups should be the focus of flexibility training before class; whereas those muscles, which have been worked specifically in class, should be stretched out after class. It is important to isolate the muscles to be stretched by moving the origin and insertion away from one another. Stretching should feel good and free of pain. Pay particular attention to stretching the major muscles that are used a lot in dance. Typically, but not always this includes stretching the quadriceps, hip flexors, hamstrings, and calves in the legs as well as the gluteal muscles and deep outward hip rotators in the hips. In the torso, stretching all sides of the major muscles by flexing, twisting, and extending through the body is recommended as well as stretching the shoulder and scapular muscles, especially the pectoralis muscles, by opening through the front of the shoulders. You can also stretch the rhomboids, trapezius, and latissimus dorsi muscles by curving the spine forward and taking the arms forward, perhaps crossing them in front of the body to deepen the stretch of these muscles in the back. The muscles that need the most stretching are the ones that have most readily been used and are likely feeling tight or sore.

You should avoid stretching ligaments or joint capsules, because they provide stability and do not need stretching. Such stretches could compromise the stability of the joint and perhaps lead to injuries. Stretch so that you feel the sensation of the stretch in the middle portion of the muscle (the muscle belly) and not at the joints. If you feel sensations of either stretch or pain at the points where the muscles attach near the joints, it may indicate that ligaments or joint capsules are being stretched.

As mentioned earlier, dancers' bodies should be fully warmed up before deep stretches can take place. The stretch will be much more effective if your muscles are warm, because warm muscles are more extensible and responsive. As a guide, include 2 to

Elastic bands aid in stretching the hamstrings.

Photography by James Keates, Trinity Laban Conservatoire of Music and Dance.

4 repetitions of each stretch, for a total duration of 60 seconds for each muscle group targeted. Dancers should perform a stretching program a minimum of 2 days per week, and preferably daily.

Muscles work in opposing (agonist/antagonist) pairs, so you must ensure a balance of stretching and strength training in opposing muscle pairs. For example, the biceps and triceps work as a pair; as the elbow bends, the biceps contracts, acting as an agonist, while the triceps lengthens, acting as the antagonist. A muscle that is not flexible can be torn when it acts as antagonist to its concentrically contracting, opposing (agonist) muscle group. The antagonist's lack of flexibility can also prevent the agonist from fully contracting, limiting range of motion. Finally, studies have shown that a strength program combined with proper stretching leads to greater gains in flexibility than stretching alone.

Hypermobility

While dancers with extreme flexibility are sometimes admired, too much flexibility can lead to problems. **Joint hypermobility** refers to a joint that can be extended beyond normal range of motion. For example, some dancers have hyperextended knees, sometimes called swayback legs. Although certain hypermobile joints may be aesthetically pleasing in certain genres such as classical ballet, they are less stable and require specific attention in terms of conditioning.

If you are a dancer who is hypermobile, you will tend to need a slower paced training in order to learn proper and safe alignment, and you may have to work harder to develop good proprioception and stability around the hypermobile joints. It is advised that if you have hypermobile joints, you should be especially cautious when bearing weight on those joints. For example, standing on a leg with a hyperextended knee will have a domino effect through other parts of the body, such as the standing leg's foot, ankle, and hip as well as torso, neck, and upper limb. If you bear weight on a hyperextended limb, even working on the hands but hyperextending your elbows, you are supporting your bodyweight without using adequate strength and control. Instead, you are pushing into your joint's end range, stressing the joint's ligaments.

As a dancer, you are often required to take your joints to extreme ranges of motion, so it is important that you understand how to increase your flexibility safely and effectively without sacrificing muscular control. As described already, you can stretch in several different ways; the type and duration of each depend on your body type and whether or not your body is generally more tight or loose. A successful stretching regimen is best undertaken when you are fully warm, which is usually toward the end of your dance technique class, conditioning program, or after a physically demanding performance.

Cardiorespiratory Endurance and Anaerobic Capacity

You may sometimes be concerned about your endurance and whether you have enough energy to get through the choreography without feeling too tired. Fatigue is one of the biggest causes of dance injuries, yet a good level of fitness can delay the onset of fatigue during dancing and potentially prevent injury.

Dance is most often an intermittent form of exercise, meaning that it requires dancers to move between fluctuating periods of activity at varying levels of intensity. The physical demands of jumping are quite different to the demands of balancing, lunging, or walking and require different means of generating energy. The physical demands when learning new choreography seem more challenging than ever before. Therefore, dancers need to improve their cardiorespiratory endurance and anaerobic capacity in order to be able to meet such demands and perform optimally. The typical technique class is not usually designed to improve dancers' endurance, because the overarching purpose of the technique class is to develop skill and artistry. There appears to be a discrepancy between the intensity levels of technique training and performance. Therefore, you should look for other ways of improving your cardiorespiratory endurance and anaerobic capacity, such as through supplemental training.

Cardiorespiratory Endurance

Cardiorespiratory endurance (sometimes called aerobic fitness) is the body's ability to supply oxygen to the working muscles during physical activity. Regular aerobic exercise enhances the body's ability to continue moving for a sustained period of time, because the heart muscle becomes larger and stronger and is therefore able to pump more blood and oxygen more effectively throughout the body. Regular aerobic exercise also improves the body's ability to inhale more oxygen at a given exercise intensity. Examples of aerobic exercise are jogging, cycling, skipping rope, swimming, and using machines such as elliptical trainers. All these exercises use large muscle groups in a repetitive manner over a sustained period of time.

Regular cardiorespiratory endurance training can help you recover more quickly between exercises as well as develop the endurance needed to sustain long periods of dancing. If you have a higher level of endurance, you are less likely to experience fatigue while dancing; this means you will be able to perform optimally for longer. Good cardiorespiratory endurance is therefore key to reducing injury and enhancing performance.

Anaerobic Capacity

Anaerobic capacity is the body's ability to generate energy during very high, intense bouts of physical activity without the use of oxygen. Many dance movements utilize the anaerobic energy system. Regular anaerobic exercise helps the body perform better during short-duration, high-intensity activities, which last up to about 2 minutes. It is nearly impossible to maintain such high-intensity bursts longer than that. Examples of anaerobic exercise are sprinting, burpees, continuous jumps, petit and grand allegro, or other extended fast combinations. These forms of exercise use large muscle groups in an explosive manner for a short period of time.

Anaerobic training can help dancers perform short, maximal, and explosive elements of dancing. If you have a higher level of anaerobic capacity, you can more effectively execute powerful movements such as jumping, catching partners, and moving down onto the floor and up out of the floor very quickly.

Improving Cardiorespiratory Endurance and Anaerobic Capacity

In order to improve cardiorespiratory endurance, you need to work hard enough and regularly enough for positive changes to occur. Trying to do 20 minutes of continuous big jumps would be impossible without high levels of cardiorespiratory endurance. Appropriate activities are swimming, cycling, jogging, or exercising on gym equipment such as stationary bikes, elliptical trainers, and treadmills. You may also enjoy dance-based training such as aerobics classes. If you choose to jog, it is best to do so on soft ground (such as a track in a park) rather than concrete to lessen impact on the joints of the legs. In addition, jogging should be followed by stretches for the calves, quadriceps, and low back, which can become tight with regular jogging.

For cardiorespiratory endurance, you should maintain a heart rate at a pace between 55 and 80 percent of its maximum (**HRmax**) for a sustained period of time; in other words, exercise at an intensity that creates exertion but does not exhaust the body after a few minutes. The simplest way to determine your maximum heart rate is to take the number 220 and subtract your age. For dancers under 20 years old, consider the maximum to be 200 beats per minute. This intensity should be maintained for approximately 20 to 40 minutes, at least three times a week.

In order to improve anaerobic capacity, you must exercise using short bouts of near-maximal effort with rest periods in between. Exercise time can vary from a few seconds to 60 seconds in order to mimic the kinds of work-to-rest ratios seen in different forms of dance. The intensity for the whole period of exercise should be near maximal heart rate (e.g., 90-100% HRmax), but this level of work should be gradually achieved across several weeks. Good exercises for anaerobic training are sprints, quick steps, burpees, jumps, and fast skipping as well as circuit and interval training.

General cardiorespiratory endurance training should take place before anaerobic fitness training, and ideally, such training should be undertaken as either a preparation for or done alongside technical training. Cardiorespiratory endurance can also be incorporated within dance technique classes. All endurance training should start more generally and become more dance-based across time. You should assess your current technique classes to see if they are providing adequate cardiorespiratory endurance and anaerobic capacity training. From there, you should build your conditioning regimen accordingly, adding what you are not getting from technique classes alone. More commonly, dance technique classes tend to address anaerobic capacity rather than cardiorespiratory endurance.

You should enhance both your cardiorespiratory endurance and anaerobic capacity in order to be better able to meet the physiological demands of dance. If you have a good level of cardiorespiratory endurance, you will have better endurance and better recovery delaying the onset of fatigue, thereby preventing injury. Further, if you have a good level of anaerobic capacity, you will have enhanced abilities to perform explosive, powerful movements and the stop–start nature inherent to some dance forms.

EMPOWERMENT

Take Charge of Your Endurance in Dancing

Perhaps you find that by the end of class or rehearsal you are very tired, or maybe you feel that you don't have enough energy to get through performances. Begin a simple cardiorespiratory endurance program. Maybe you decide to swim for 30 minutes, three times a week. Keep a journal of your program, noting how you feel in class and rehearsal daily. You may well begin to feel more energetic and less fatigued as time goes on. This increased endurance will be very empowering, and it can increase your confidence as you approach performances.

Dance-Specific Systems and Somatic Practice

Dancers use a multitude of training systems to supplement their dance technique classes and provide them with specific exercises and approaches for individualized, supplemental work. Some of these systems can provide you with not only specific movement sequences for the development of strength or flexibility, they provide ways of practic-

ing that can be extremely helpful as you move from supplemental conditioning to dance performance and embodiment of artistry.

Several training modalities, such as Pilates, focus on central control and clarity of alignment through a dancer's range of motion. Forms such as Gyrotonic and Gyrokinesis take these ideas into more three-dimensional movement patterns. They include exercise sequences using specific machines with varying levels of tension through springs or weights for resistance training and immediate proprioceptive feedback. These conditioning systems also include mat work and movement exercises with smaller props. Similarly, many movement systems use exercise bands or surgical tubing, called upon to aid with strength, flexibility development, control, and smooth muscle contractions.

Pilates

Pilates is one of the better-known conditioning programs used by many dancers and nondancers as well. Developed by Joseph H. Pilates, an early fitness advocate, this system teaches participants a series of exercises on the Pilates Reformer, an apparatus with varying resistance via springs, or on a mat. Other equipment sometimes used in Pilates includes the trapeze, tower, chairs, barrels, and arcs. Overarching themes in Pilates include the following: development of core strength and control, overall body awareness, stability, good posture/alignment, breathing, economy of motion, and finding smooth movements through a full range of motion. Pilates can help you build strength without bulk. You can find many Pilates instructors who are certified in different approaches, which you can find on the Internet. Pilates websites contain information about Pilates, DVDs and video demonstrations, as well as locations of Pilates certified instructors and studios around the world. It is advisable that a first-time Pilates session be one-on-one or in a small group if possible. By working more closely with a trained instructor, you can get detailed feedback as to your alignment and form.

Gyrotonic Exercises

Under the umbrella term of Gyrotonic Expansion System emerge two forms, Gyrotonic and Gyrokinesis. These forms were created by Juliu Horvath, a former dancer and swimmer, originally from Hungary. After relocating to New York City, he developed these techniques as a means of taking care of his own injuries through regaining strength as well as full, three-dimensional mobility, and preventing other injuries from occurring. The exercises can be very helpful to you as a dancer. Gyrotonic exercises are performed on a custom-designed apparatus using weights as resistance. Rather than using springs to change the resistance through the range of motion, the weights provide seamless resistance in each exercise. Gyrotonic exercises are usually performed one-on-one or in small groups with an instructor, and the sequences involve repetitive circular or spiraling movements that flow together, corresponding with breathing and rhythm. There is no compression on the joints, as all movements are sequenced smoothly from one to the next. Gyrokinesis exercises are done on either a mat or chair and usually can be practiced in a group setting, led by an instructor. These exercises are similar to those on the apparatus, involving repetitive, circular movements. Central to all Gyrotonic and Gyrokinesis exercises are the following principles: core control through three-dimensional range of motion, balance of muscular effort, movement efficiency (economy of motion), dynamic strength, mobility, and flexibility. For more information on these systems, see the Gyrotonic website at www.gyrotonic.com.

Floor-Barre

Floor-Barre technique was created by Zena Rommett, a pioneer in injury prevention and rehabilitation. Originally from Italy, she moved to New York City and developed her technique during the time she was teaching ballet at the American Ballet Center under the direction of Robert Joffrey. The Floor-Barre technique was specifically designed for dancers, stemming directly out of ballet training and initially meeting the needs of ballet dancers. In the floor work, the technique addresses alignment, helps build strength and flexibility, and fine-tunes efficient coordination without the same gravitational stresses in standing. Further, it addresses the slow work and mental awareness found in somatic practices. For more information, you can go to the Floor-Barre technique website at www.floor-barre.org.

Conditioning With Imagery

Conditioning With Imagery (C-I Training) was developed by Donna Krasnow, dance educator and researcher in Canada and the United States. C-I Training is dance specific in its movement choices. It merges conditioning exercises for muscular strength, endurance, and flexibility with the visualization and imagery work done in somatic practices for movement reeducation, alignment work, and mind–body integration. In addition, it can assist you in transferring the training from the conditioning work to movement practices in classes, rehearsals, performances, and daily life. The applications of C-I Training can also assist you with injury prevention, improved training practices, and appropriate warm-up procedures. Available is her book titled *Conditioning With Imagery for Dancers*, co-authored with professional dancer Jordana Deveau, as well as DVDs and videos in which dancers can learn the exercises. For more information, go to the C-I Training website at www.citraining.com.

Neuromuscular Training

Irene Dowd, based in New York City and mentored early on by Ideokinesis creator, Dr. Lulu Sweigard, maintains a practice in neuromuscular training for many dancers as well as nondancers. Addressing musculoskeletal imbalances and coaching efficient and coordinated movement patterns, Dowd has choreographed a series of movement sequences detailed in several videos, including: *Spirals, Warming Up the Hip: Turnout Dance and Orbits*, and *Trunk Stabilization and Volutes*. The DVDs are available on Dowd's website or through Canada's National Ballet School in Toronto. Dowd also has a book titled *Taking Route to Fly: Articles on Functional Anatomy*.

Franklin Method

Developed by dancer and movement educator Eric Franklin, the Franklin Method uses dynamic imagery and anatomical embodiment of concepts as a means of facilitating greater ease of motion, economy of muscular effort, clarity of joint mechanics, centering, control, and more range of motion in a coordinated fashion. Franklin has published many textbooks and has information available on his website at http://franklinmethod.com.

Many other movement systems exist that can be beneficial for you, many of which fall under the umbrella of somatics. **Somatic practices** or **somatic education** refer to learning methods that focus on sensation and awareness to make changes in the body's habitual movements and alignment. Somatic movement forms have greatly impacted and influenced dancers' training in the last 25 years. Many dancers are drawn to somatics, a term first coined in 1928 by a philosopher named Thomas Hanna to describe the sensing from within one's own body. For many dancers supplemental conditioning tends to include somatic principles and practices. At the core of somatic practice is the belief that the body and mind are completely entwined with one another. Dancers studying somatic forms are asked to be aware not only of the movements but also their feelings and intentions in relation to those movements. As you move through a series of sequences, self-awareness is heightened. You practice being increasingly awake and attentive to what is happening, thereby developing the skills necessary for both clear physical coordination and nuanced expressiveness. You can otherwise go through the motions, practicing and repeating movements without much awareness of how you are moving at that moment.

Central to mature dancing and performing is the full involvement of the self. Like a child learning to crawl for the first time, you can practice moving in a state of play and thus with the right somatic cueing, figure out more efficient, coordinated, whole-body movement patterns. Through many somatic areas of study, you can find greater core support and control. It may seem like more of a back door approach than typical abdominal or back strengthening exercises, yet you can reap similar rewards. Central themes within somatic forms include a quest for movement efficiency (less frozen, less habitual tension), better stability, greater easeful mobility and range of motion, clarity of movement initiation and follow-through, whole-body and whole-self integra-

tion, and tuning into sensation. Discreet somatic forms include Alexander Technique, Feldenkrais Method (Awareness Through Movement), Body–Mind Centering, Bartenieff Fundamentals, Rolfing, Structural Integration, and Ideokinesis, and some would include much older forms such as yoga and tai chi. For more information about somatic practices, see chapters 4 and 6.

Many specially designed training systems have been developed for dancers to improve strength and flexibility as well as prevent injury and help with recovery from injury. While several examples have been provided in this section, others exist, too. Find a dance training system that suits you and your needs.

Conditioning Myths

As a dancer today, you may have inherited certain myths about supplemental conditioning that are not necessarily true nor helpful. Two main myths in dance are as follows:

The first myth states that you must have extreme hypermobility in order to have a successful career in dance. In fact, you can do more harm than good if stretching goes on too long or too early, before a thorough warm-up. It is important to recognize

Yoga is an effective form of flexibility training, and the practice also enhances awareness.
Photography by James Keates, Trinity Laban Conservatoire of Music and Dance.

that hypermobility is often coupled with lack of strength and control, leading to injuries down the road. Passive flexibility is different than dynamic flexibility, and in the moment of performing a leg extension, you need strength to get the leg higher in the air along with flexibility and coordination of the body as a whole. The desire to get your leg higher in the air will not come by doing a series of floor stretches alone, because they are invariably passive stretches rather than active stretches.

The second myth is that strength training will increase the size of the muscles to a large extent. In reality, the only way in which you will develop massive bulkiness is if you take supplements alongside your training and have a certain genetic predisposition. For women, it is nearly impossible to attain excessively large muscles because of the lack of testosterone in their bodies. In fact, dancers who do strength training can reduce body fat and increase fat-free mass. This clearly discredits the notion that strength training is correlated with an increase in size or bulk. If you fear losing your leaner, smaller frame, this is actually more of a reason to strength train rather than not. Smaller typically means weaker, and without adequate muscular strength, the body will not be able to keep up with the physical demands expected of it. Another common misconception about strength training is that strength training with lighter weights or no weights, done with high repetitions, is better. Activities such as dozens of abdominal curls will increase muscle endurance, but they will not assist in strength gains. In contemporary choreography,

women are often asked to lift other dancers just as often as men. Therefore, strength training for women is essential.

As you can see, sometimes ideas in dance that have no scientific basis are taught or passed on. Working to be hypermobile and avoiding strength training for fear of muscle bulk can predispose you to injuries, and it will not improve your dancing. If you need additional flexibility or strength, you have many excellent and safe ways of achieving these goals.

Summary

Technique training today is often a mix of approaches from traditional dance forms to cultural dances, martial arts, contact improvisation, and inclusion of somatic approaches. Dancers are asked to be increasingly versatile. The physical demands that are placed on dancers are vast, and at times they can lead to musculoskeletal imbalances. It is recognized that you cannot rely solely on technique classes to provide you with everything you need to enter today's professional world of dance. Supplemental dance conditioning has become an acknowledged necessity for optimal performance, health, and longevity. While several dance conditioning systems are available, it is important that you understand the principles of supplemental conditioning so that you can foster a greater sense of responsibility for your own development and create an informed idea of what would work for you as an individual artist.

Often gaps exist from technical training to rehearsals and performance, which can be addressed in your supplemental conditioning program. In this way, injuries are more likely avoided and musculoskeletal imbalances leading to injuries are lessened. It is incredibly empowering to place yourself in the driver's seat of your own dance training, better understanding your own body and respecting your specific needs in order to be a healthy, versatile dancer. Make sure that you are setting realistic and timely goals, tracking your work and your accomplishments. You will find this process rewarding and enjoyable. It is also recommended that you seek advice from a dance professional, physical therapist, dance-specific conditioning system expert, or certified somatic practitioner. These professionals can provide you with specific feedback and guidance along the way.

SELF-AWARENESS

Learn About Your Body's Conditioning Needs

The next time you are in dance class, think about what your greatest challenges are. Do you find it difficult to do higher leg extensions? Do you struggle more with powerful jumps, lunges, and falls? Do you find partnering work in rehearsal difficult to achieve? Now consider what areas of conditioning work you probably need to give the most focus. This exercise in self-awareness can broaden your ability to make choices about supplementary training and positive changes in your dancing.

Application Activity: **Assess Your Training and Conditioning**

Begin by thinking about your warm-up. Do you cover all of the components of a good warm-up? If not, think about how you would alter your warm-up to make it more effective. Now consider what supplemental training you need to do. What areas of your body would benefit from strength and power conditioning? Are there stretches you might add at the end of your class or your day to enhance your flexibility? Consider the various cardiorespiratory endurance activities, and decide which one you might enjoy. It might be beneficial for you to go to a fitness center and try out some of the equipment. Finally, can you identify a somatic practice that you would like to add to your weekly training? All of these areas of conditioning can improve your dancing.

Review Questions

1. What is cross-training, and what are the benefits of cross-training?

2. What are the components of a correct warm-up and cool-down?

3. What are the various principles of training, and how do they apply to dance?

4. What are the differences between muscular strength and power, flexibility, cardiorespiratory endurance, and anaerobic capacity?

5. What are the benefits of somatic practices and dance-specific programs?

 For chapter-specific supplemental learning activities, study aids, suggested readings, web links, and more, visit the web resource at www.HumanKinetics.com/DancerWellness.

Part II

Mental Components of Dancer Wellness

Many mental factors come into play in training dancers. To learn about the human brain and how it controls and directs movement and to develop mental strategies that enhance technique, you can use imagery and somatic practices (chapter 4). Dancers can also learn about the psychological side of dance (chapter 5). Dance psychology is the study of aspects of psychology that are specific to dancers, including self-esteem, perfectionism, body image, stress, anxiety, competition, and social pressures. A third area dealing with mental components examines how rest and recovery affect learning, technique, and injury (chapter 6). Each of these mental aspects of dance can dramatically affect health and wellness. Understanding how to create the best mental training and psychological environment is key to dancer wellness.

Chapter 4 deals with mental training. Mental training consists of any methods or practices that help you create a mindset or way of working that allows you to consistently perform up to your abilities and talents. Two important techniques that you can use as part of mental training are imagery and somatic practice. Imagery is a psychological activity that suggests the physical characteristics of an object, picture, sensation, or event; for dancers it is usually used before or during movement. Somatic practices are a group of systems that allow you to explore individual anatomy and teach you to use mind–body focus to enhance your dancing. These two tools heighten awareness and allow you to best accomplish a dance skill.

Chapter 5 explores psychological wellness. You can benefit from understanding the psychological components of mental training as well as developing strategies to help you cope with the negative aspects. Although the class atmosphere and the teacher's style can have a major impact, you can empower yourself to have control over your mental attitude. Aspects of psychology such as self-perception, self-esteem, self-efficacy, perfectionism, and body image can all improve when you better understand these facets. Similarly, when you know the psychological barriers to performance, such as stress and anxiety, you can develop coping strategies to overcome them. Finally, a strong social network is beneficial for mental health.

Chapter 6 deals with rest and recovery. Dancers are only now beginning to understand how important rest and recovery are to both memory and successful accomplishment of skills. All dancers have experienced class or rehearsal on too little sleep or with an overworked body. Concentration suffers, skills diminish, and injuries are more likely. One of the more inhibiting psychological states is burnout, which manifests as poor dancing, tiredness, or lack of interest due to prolonged overwork. Ignoring the warning signs of burnout results in illnesses or injuries that become more difficult to treat and take longer for recovery. You can actively set goals and build a personal tool kit of resting practices.

In summary, mental components of wellness are far reaching, and they cover a range of aspects such as the training tools of imagery and somatic practices, and understanding and dealing with stress and anxiety. You can benefit from adding rest to your schedule and developing personal coping strategies for all of these issues. The first step is becoming aware of these barriers to superior performance and health. The next step is setting personal goals for achieving greater self-esteem and better enjoyment of dancing.

Mental Training

Janet Karin, OAM, Patrick Haggard, PhD, and
Julia Christensen, PhD

Photo by Sergey Konstantinov. Dancer: Mason Lovegrove, The Australian Ballet School and The Australian Ballet.

Key Terms

feedback
flow
imagery
kinesthetic
kinesthetic imagery
mental practice
mental rehearsal
metaphorical imagery
mindfulness
mirror system
motor plan
motor system
movement planner
postural reflex
primary motor cortex
proprioception
reflex arc
sensorimotor system
sensory awareness
sensory feedback
subjective imagery
visual imagery

LEARNING OBJECTIVES

After reading this chapter, you will be able to do the following:

❯ Explain how the various parts of the brain contribute to planning and coordinating movements in dance.

❯ Understand the various forms of feedback and how you can use them to improve your dancing.

❯ Develop sensory awareness of your body while dancing.

❯ Describe the various types of imagery and how you can use imagery to your benefit.

❯ Realize the power of mental rehearsal, and know how to incorporate it into your daily training.

How many times have you used wonderful, vibrant images to inspire expressive movement in your dancing? You may have also used images to work on your alignment, such as the image of the head floating like a balloon above your spine. You may even have spent time quietly resting while you visualize a section of choreography that you are rehearsing. Training the mind in conjunction with training the body improves your performance and well-being through the use of various forms of imagery. Imagery has a wide range of purposes that can all affect your dancing in powerful ways. This chapter describes the role of the brain in movement, sensory feedback, mental imagery, mindfulness, and flow, and it explains how you can incorporate these concepts into your dance training.

The Role of the Brain in Moving the Body

The brain and other parts of the nervous system work together to control your movements. While muscles move the skeleton, without messages from the brain and spinal cord, no movement could occur. The brain plans movement and determines which muscles can best achieve each movement task. This section discusses how the brain works to improve movements and how you can best achieve improvements. This section also describes the different types of feedback available to dancers, how they are processed in the brain, and whether they help to improve your dancing.

SELF-AWARENESS

How You Use the Mirror

The next time you are in dance class, think about how much you use the mirror to correct your movements. Become aware of the mirror's place in your daily training. Select a day that you take class without using the mirror at all. Are you aware of the sensations in your body? Can you correct yourself from the sensations alone? Also think about what it is like to use the teacher's comments and corrections without using the mirror. This exercise in self-awareness can broaden your ability to make positive changes in your dancing.

The Motor System

When you move, specific parts of your brain's **motor system** are activated. (The word "motor" means movement.) The key elements of the motor system are the brain, which issues the instructions to move; the muscles, which perform the actual movement; and the nerves that carry signals from brain to muscle, and also from the muscles back to the brain, to close the loop (see figure 4.1).

How the brain's motor system reacts is very receptive to training, so when you train your motor system with a dance focus, your motor system is more responsive to dance than a nondancer's motor system would be. For example, when ballet dancers watch ballet movements, their motor areas react much more strongly than when they watch an unfamiliar dance style. Also, the same motor

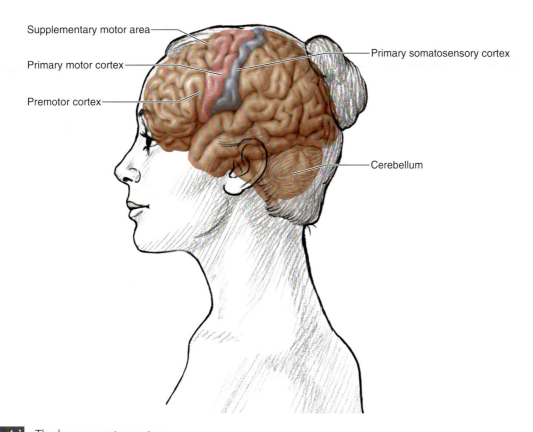

Supplementary motor area

Primary motor cortex

Premotor cortex

Primary somatosensory cortex

Cerebellum

Figure 4.1   The human motor system.

Recreated by Human Kinetics from original by Janet Karin and Gregory Cromie.

areas in the brain react when you do a movement and when you merely imagine it. The interaction of your body senses and your motor system is crucial to all movement; together they are known as the sensorimotor system.

Sensorimotor System

Different parts of your brain perform different functions. In all movement the **sensorimotor system** is essential for planning an action, controlling the muscle contractions that actually move your body, then processing the sensory information that your body sends back to your brain. The word "sensory" refers to messages from those senses that begin in the body itself; as mentioned earlier, "motor" means movement. Therefore, "sensorimotor" refers to the collection of brain systems that tell you about the state of the body. The brain uses that information to control how the body moves. This section explains the brain mechanisms that underlie skilled movements in dance.

Dancers sometimes think of their muscles as the key to performance, but a muscle does nothing by itself. When you want to make a specific movement, such as a leap, your **movement planner** (the area of your brain that works out what you will do) retrieves from memory exactly which muscles need to contract, when, and by how much, and translates all this information into a **motor command**, which is a series of electrical signals. The signals are sent through the **motor neurons** (nerves) in your spinal cord to the relevant muscles. All these processes can occur without your conscious thought. With proper training, you will learn to perform the leap almost automatically.

Reflexes

Your brain and spinal cord control most movement automatically without you needing to think about the details of what you are doing. Walking is a great example. When a person walks the action is automatic, but when scientists try to build robots that walk as well as humans do, they find it very hard to program all the coordinated movements that people make without any thought. This automatic quality of movement is partly due to the circuits of neurons called **reflex arcs** that automatically maintain body posture. These neural circuits run through the spinal cord, and they can coordinate a lot of your movement without much help from your brain. The **postural reflexes** are a particular series of muscle reflexes that maintain balance and dynamic alignment throughout all movement. The stretch reflexes react to maintain stability and to avoid muscle damage through overstretching. This reflex is apparent when a doctor taps your knee; the tap stretches the patellar tendon, which activates the reflex in the quadriceps, making your lower leg kick forward (see figure 4.2).

To understand how useful these reflexes are, take an empty cup and fill it up from a tap. As the water falls into the cup, the weight stretches your biceps muscle in the front of your upper arm. This weight would make your hand and the cup move downward if the muscles did not respond. However, your biceps muscle increases its level of contraction to maintain the placement of your hand in space. Even though the load changes as the cup fills up, your hand stays still. If you now close your eyes and get a friend to switch the tap on and off at random, your hand will move downward whenever water lands in the cup, then bounce back up again. The hand bouncing back is a reflex response to keep the hand in the same place as the weight changes.

Reflexes help with dancing in countless ways. For example, you stay standing up because any tendency to fall causes a stretch in some muscle, which is immediately resisted by reflex arcs or postural reflexes. The spinal reflex circuitry allows you to hold your body in a given position. Even more important, it allows some parts of your body to stay still while others move. For example, if you lift one arm to the side of the body, the change in your body's center of mass stretches the muscles on the opposite side and your reflexes act to stop you tipping over.

The Brain's Motor Systems

One key brain structure in producing movement is the **primary motor cortex**. This structure is another part of the motor system, which stretches from the top of your head to roughly just under your ears, as shown in figure 4.1. From the dancer's point of view, one of the most relevant features of the primary motor cortex is its plasticity, or ability to change. The relationship between neurons and muscles in the body can change with experience. This change can occur within just a few minutes. In other words, practicing a dance movement correctly for a few minutes may actually change your brain!

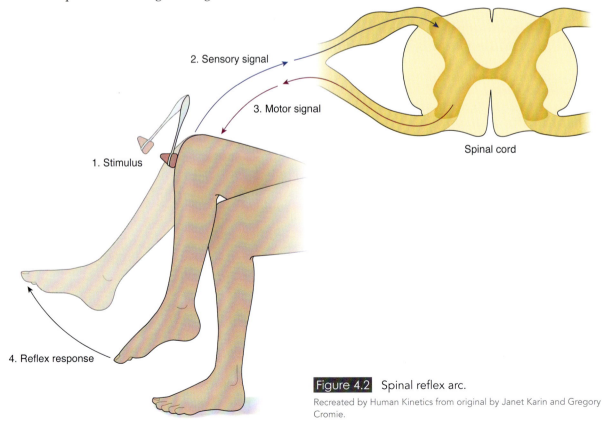

Figure 4.2   Spinal reflex arc.

Recreated by Human Kinetics from original by Janet Karin and Gregory Cromie.

Your motor cortex sends the final instruction to your muscles, but no single brain region exists that tells your motor cortex what instruction it should send. In fact, motor systems of your brain consist of loops rather than a simple chain. Two loops funnel information from many parts of the brain into the frontal motor areas that lie at the front of the brain and drive the primary motor cortex. The first of these loops is concerned with why you move; it motivates and drives the actions you are about to make. This loop sends feedback when an action has been successful so you can repeat the action. The second loop is concerned with how you move. Billions of neurons control the timing and amount of movement across many different muscles to coordinate your movements. The cerebellum, which is part of the second loop, is involved in learning and also in making complex, multijoint movements. It is believed to be one of the key areas for the complex movements in dance.

The Motor Plan

When you move, you are only aware of a tiny portion of what is going on in your body and brain to generate that movement. If you want an apple, you simply reach out and grab it. Your brain has already stored a complex reach-and-grab **motor plan**, which is made up of a series of motor commands (electrical signals) that will occur in a particular order. When your brain receives the order *Grab the apple,* your movement planner converts the order into a set of motor commands and the motor plan is executed automatically. Fortunately you don't have to think about all the details (reach out, adjust hand position, arm position, finger position, etc.). Generally this automatic execution is an advantage. However, it can also be inconvenient, because you cannot consciously access the motor plan to improve the movement.

As you can see in figure 4.3, the intended movement (the movement you want to make) is activated by fast internal signals from images within your brain, shaded in gray, and slow external signals from your teacher and the mirror. The fast circuit sends the images straight to your movement planner, which selects the motor commands and sends them from your motor cortex to your muscles. The motor commands also predict whether the commands will achieve the intended movement.

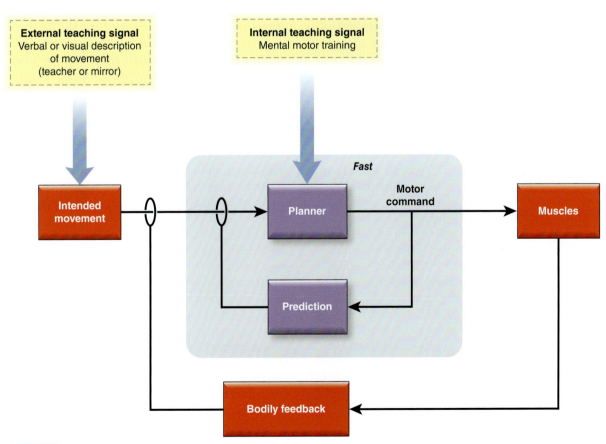

Figure 4.3   Movement control system of the brain.

Figure design by Patrick Haggard.

The organization of the brain and how it sends messages to the muscles are complex and quite amazing. Even with complicated dance movements, your brain organizes all the details so you don't need to think of them. However, little of your dancing would be possible without ongoing feedback from the body and the environment.

Types of Feedback

Feedback consists of messages about the body's position and movement that are sent to the brain. The main types of feedback that you can use in your dancing are sensory, tactile, verbal, and visual. An example of sensory feedback is the feeling of a stretch in your muscles that lets you know you have reached the end range of your movement. Your teacher might suggest that you widen your shoulders by placing hands on this area of your body (tactile feedback), or the teacher might say "Open the front of your chest and feel wide" (verbal feedback). And by looking in the mirror, you can correct the line of your arms in a dance movement (visual feedback).

Sensory Feedback

Sensory feedback is perhaps the most important form of feedback. It is ongoing, and it can occur in every situation, whether class, rehearsal, or performance, unlike visual feedback from the mirror that cannot be used in performance. As you move, **sensory feedback** from your muscles, skin, tendons, and joints tells your brain about the success of the movement. At this stage, tactile and verbal feedback from your teacher and visual feedback from the mirror enter the process. However, this type of feedback is slow and only tells your motor system how you want the movement to look eventually.

You might think that you learn by looking in the mirror and adjusting your movement until it looks the way you want it to appear. However, sensory feedback (including feedback from vision) is simply too slow to help in controlling rapid movements such as dance. It takes at least one fifth of a second to react to a touch on your hand and much longer for similar messages to travel the extra distance from your foot and back again. Visual signals take even longer. It would take around a quarter of a second to look in the mirror and then correct a movement. Visual feedback can help with pinpointing problems when you are practicing, but it is much too slow to control most movements while you are dancing. In addition, responding to slow visual signals can lead to jerky stop–start movement.

Instead, neuroscientists think that sensory information helps control movement in three ways. The first is through sensorimotor reflexes, described previously. Second, your brain compares the original motor command with sensory information about what is actually happening in your body through proprioception (discussed later). For example, when doing a slow leg extension the sensations in your body will give information to the brain, letting it know if the movement is happening as you intended.

Third, the final visual effect of a movement can serve as a goal. If the movement goes well and looks correct, a signal meaning "*Learn this*" is generated in your brain so you will be able to repeat it. It is like a reward that encourages you to do it the same way next time. If the movement is not happening as you planned, visual feedback is not fast enough to rescue it while you are moving, but you can use this information to improve the next attempt.

Using Feedback to Improve Your Practice

You may wonder about the importance of feedback, particularly visual feedback, in dance. You cannot see your own body during performance, so you cannot always rely on visual feedback. Sometimes you need to try a movement many times before you perform it successfully, simply because you need to refine the movement's motor plan. Your teacher can help with tactile, visual, or verbal feedback. Feedback from the mirror can help you to become aware of your movement quality and the end result. However, research suggests that relying too frequently and consistently on the visual feedback from the mirror can diminish the sensory or **kinesthetic** awareness so necessary in dance.

When using visual feedback, you may be better off relying on your dance teacher's visual system than on your own image in the mirror. First, you should be busy concentrating on the feeling of the movement, so you cannot attend to all the visual details in the mirror anyway. Second, your teacher has a viewpoint closer to what the audience sees. Third, the dance teacher has ideas about what looks correct or incorrect and also knows which features of your movement you need to adjust. Your own brain is responsible for all the motor learning needed for successful dance movements, but the critical knowledge of results and knowledge of performance often come from your teacher. *Knowledge of results* refers to feedback that gives you information about the outcome (result) of your movement and whether or not you achieved your goal. *Knowledge of perfor-

mance refers to feedback that gives you information about the aspects or features of what you did that caused the resulting movement. The mirror can help you to understand what the intended movement should look like and whether you have reached it. However, the mirror may not help you to get better at performing the whole movement, because it will not give you enough information to help you correct errors.

Different dancers need different amounts of feedback. How much feedback you need depends on your individual body awareness and on your own body. Some dancers may need more verbal feedback about what is correct to form specific motor memories in the brain. Others may not need as much verbal feedback because they can use other forms of feedback to find the best movement pattern for the movement. In any case, you can improve your own skills and enjoyment by practicing mental and physical training.

DIVERSITY IN DANCE

Explore Diverse Types of Feedback

Think about what kinds of feedback work best for you. Do you rely on the visual feedback of watching the teacher and other dancers demonstrate the movement? Do verbal corrections work best, or do you prefer hands-on, tactile corrections? Once you have come to understand your preferred feedback, try to diversify your strategies in class and rehearsal. Instead of asking to see a phrase again, ask for a verbal explanation. Perhaps ask a friend to give you some tactile information to help you learn a new movement. The more you can rely on diverse forms of feedback, the faster you will progress.

The Mirror System

The **mirror system** is an essential part of human communication, and it is also the basis of learning to dance. When you watch someone performing an action, some brain cells in your motor system that are responsible for your own movements fire in the same way as when you perform that action yourself. Scientists suggest that you understand people's feelings because your mirror systems reflect their posture, their movement, and their facial expressions. When you say that you feel for a friend who is crying, you are describing an actual fact. Your mirror system shares the physical sensations of your friend's sadness, reminding you of your own emotion that made your body respond

in the same way. Thanks to the mirror system, the audience shares the grace, freedom, excitement, power, and emotions that you are experiencing. If you see another dancer performing well, your mirror system can send their movement experience to your own movement planner.

Somatics and Sensory Awareness

Dancers use their bodies to communicate thoughts, emotions, and sensations. Therefore, it makes sense for dancers to become knowledgeable and skilled in recognizing the sensations of their own bodies and in translating somatic cues into movement. The terms *somatic practices* and *somatic education* refer to learning methods that focus on sensation and awareness to make changes in the body's habitual movements and alignment.

All somatic methods focus on **sensory awareness**, which is the direct focus on sensory aspects of your body and requires that you are paying attention. When you experience somatic techniques early in your training, you benefit from increased awareness of your alignment, muscle activity, and coordination. Without this advantage, you may be limited to an external view of your body, as if you were looking from the outside. In an attempt to force your body into desired shapes, you may overwork your muscles and distort your alignment. Somatic practices offer you an inner sense of how your body is behaving at rest and in movement. By working with your body rather than against it, you can find well-coordinated, seemingly effortless movement. The most difficult techniques can look and feel completely natural.

GOAL SETTING

Tune In to Your Body's Messages

Take some time to think about how you approach your movement goals. Do you mainly think about how you look and what your image in the mirror looks like? Do you find yourself comparing your image with the dancers around you? Now spend some time thinking about and experiencing how the movement feels. Are you forcing movement in a way that causes discomfort or tension? See if you can find a way of doing the movement that is pleasurable and enjoyable. You may even discover that your movement looks better when you take this approach. Make it a goal in every class to spend at least some of the time focusing on sensation to accomplish the task.

Proprioception refers to your ability to sense the position and movement of your body and limbs in space. The word "proprioception" comes from *proprio*, which means your own, and per*ception*, which refers to awareness. Your brain uses information from all your senses, including the sensory neurons in your muscles, tendons, ligaments, joints, skin, and the balance system in your inner ear, to give you the experience of proprioception. It enables your brain to adjust your muscle actions so that you can achieve the shape or position you want.

Good proprioception enables you to balance and to perform movements as you intend. Practicing somatic awareness can help proprioception, while muscle tension and anxiety can interfere with the process. Somatic awareness helps your brain to listen to proprioceptive information so that it can make small adjustments to improve your performance without adding unnecessary muscular effort (see figure 4.4).

Somatic practices are pleasurable in themselves because they reduce tension and allow you to move harmoniously and efficiently. They also help your motor system to translate your intentions into movement, thus making your dancing more expressive. Finally, they are useful tools to increase awareness and mind–body connection.

Figure 4.4 The dancer is using foam mats with her eyes closed to enhance her proprioception.

Photo courtesy of Nicholas Forster.

Sensory awareness is crucial in your dance training. Without awareness, it is difficult to make changes and even more difficult to improve in the ways you desire. Somatic practices are excellent for improving sensory awareness. A common tool in many of the somatic practices is imagery. Understanding and exploring imagery and its many uses can help you accelerate your training.

Imagery

Imagery is the key to unlocking your brain's potential to optimize your movement. It can help you overcome the limitations of verbal, physical, and visual feedback. **Imagery** involves sounds, tastes, smells, and kinesthetic and tactile (touch) sensations. Most dancers use imagery without being aware of it. Examples include being pushed by the wind as you run, rebounding off an imaginary wall, or wearing a crown. Imagining that someone is whispering behind your back may improve your head alignment without strain. Your body may feel lighter and may look more interesting if you imagine you are enjoying a beautiful perfume all around you. Remembering the sensation of chocolate melting on your tongue can encourage your movements to flow and run together.

Imagery is simply a message to your brain so it can coordinate your muscles, regardless of whether you want to eat your breakfast, get dressed, or dance. Imagining a movement trains the brain networks that are responsible for that movement, making your brain more expert in that movement. Another benefit is that if you do the movement perfectly in your imagination, your brain will use the same perfect networks to guide your movements when you actually dance the movement. Experiencing and understanding the various forms of imagery can improve aspects of your dancing such as alignment, therefore enhancing your wellness.

Visual Imagery

Visual imagery can include seeing objects and abstract shapes in the mind. For example, *Picture your sitting bones moving up and over a hill while you glide or leap to the side. Imagine darkness is falling as you let your body droop. Run in a zigzag.* You are not aware of how all the parts of your body cooperate to make the image you want, because your movement planner sorts out the details for you. Similarly, when you want to move the cursor around your computer screen, you are not conscious of the way your hand moves on the track pad

Images for Your Dance Training

Below are some images that you can explore that can enhance your dance training. For many more wonderful examples of imagery for dance movements, you can go to the web resource for this chapter. You can also explore the books and articles provided in the bibliography.

Imagery for Alignment and Stability

Imagine your body has been divided into a front half and a back half, with the division running through your main weight-bearing joints. The two halves should be the same weight and should have equal importance in your body image (see figure 4.5). Unfortunately, our brains easily lose interest in the back halves of our bodies and our alignment suffers. To encourage a full picture of your body, stand up, close your eyes and focus on your back half. Imagine the back half of your head and neck are growing bigger and extending into the space behind you. Imagine your shoulders and backs of your arms are becoming more important and filling more of the space behind you than usual. Do the same with the whole back half of your body, so that you are aware of the weight of each part and the space it takes. You may notice that you feel lighter, taller, and more energetic when your body is well balanced.

Imagery for Ribs and Spine

In a healthy person, the ribcage expands and contracts in all directions to move air in and out of the lungs. To achieve easy breathing and good rib alignment, practice focusing your breathing in your back, around the lower part of your ribcage. Focus on slow, easy breaths. Imagine that the lowest ribs in your back are gently expanding backwards and then relaxing, and also rising upwards from the rim of your pelvis. Imagine that your second bottom rib is rising above the lowest rib, and then your third rib is rising above the second one, and so on. Feel that your ribs continue to gently float upwards while you breathe. Keeping your focus on the back of your body, continue the imagery up through the bones at the back of your neck.

Imagery for Pelvic Stability and Hip Joint Mobility

Stand on your right leg in a reasonably turned-out position. Your left sitting bone should be roughly in line with your heel and your right sitting bone with your toes, so your two sitting bones, your toes, and your heel form a rectangle. Imagine your two sitting bones are floating on a calm lake until they are level. Imagine a spider-web from your left sitting bone to right 5th toe. The spider-web is slightly stretchy. Gently move your left leg around with the spider-web maintaining the connection between your left sitting bone and your right toe. The diagonal connection tells your movement planner that you want level sitting bones and a free left hip joint.

Imagery for Ankles

Standing on one leg with eyes closed, imagine that your foot is the base of an open laptop computer and your shin is the lid. Imagine that your foot is as long as your shin. Slowly close the lid in a large, smooth arc, folding your shin towards the imaginary end of your foot. Feel as if the hinge (ankle) is held in place by magic, allowing the lid to move freely. Try different foot micro-movements so you can feel which alignment gives the most freedom. Enjoy the effortless sensation as the "lid" lowers and rises.

Imagery for Knees

Sit on the floor with your legs in a comfortable second position. Keeping your leg muscles relaxed, bend over and grasp the metatarsal joints of your first two toes with your hand. Use your hand to adjust your leg until your hip, knee, and ankle joints are in line parallel with the floor. Keeping this alignment, extend your heel as far away as possible. The muscles in the front and back of your leg will need to work together to maintain your alignment. Ask someone to push on your heel while you push back. This teaches your motor system to respond to pressure on your heel by balancing your leg muscles and bringing your leg joints into a straight line. When you stand up, the floor will provide the heel pressure cue, and your leg will return to hyperextension when the pressure disappears.

or the mouse. Instead, your brain has learned how to coordinate your hand muscles to achieve your image of the cursor moving on the screen.

Kinesthetic Imagery

Kinesthetic imagery refers to imagined physical sensations such as sinking or weightlessness. An example is imagining that you are floating. Kinesthetic imagery allows your brain to imagine what your body might feel like. It is different from a picture that you want to reproduce. For example, *Imagine your sitting bones gliding smoothly along train tracks as you transfer from one leg to the other. Imagine placing tiny cushions between each of your vertebrae.* Notice the differences in your jumps when you imagine a rocket, a table tennis ball, an arrow, a bungee rope, a trampoline, a floating balloon, or a soaring eagle.

Subjective Imagery

Subjective imagery covers personal sensations such as sleepiness, fear, and pain. Some teachers suggest imagining you have been punched in the stomach to give you the feeling of a modern dance contraction. The image of sliding down into a hot bath can help you to feel relaxed and heavy as you sink to the floor. Try a gliding movement while imagining heat is radiating out of you, then try the same movement while imagining an icy wind is chilling you to the bone. Some images fit into more than one category. For example, these subjective images can also be considered kinesthetic.

Metaphorical Imagery

Metaphorical imagery uses words or phrases to communicate an idea or sensation that is not actually occurring. For example, the teacher who tells you to *let your feet sink through the floor* is unlikely to expect your feet to disappear from sight, but the imagery provides important information for your movement planner. The best imagery for a movement depends on the reason you are doing the movement.

Similes are related to metaphors, but they describe ideas and sensations by using "as if" or "like." You might be told to *hold your head as if you were wearing a sparkling tiara and beautiful necklace,* because those images tell your movement planner to lift your head and lengthen your neck. Similes help to convey the most obvious or memorable aspect of an object or movement without unhelpful details. The image *Feel like a swan* helps you to feel

serene and elegant without suggesting you copy a swan's big flat feet.

Many types of images exist, including visual, kinesthetic, subjective, and metaphorical, as well as others that have not been described in this section. For example, the kinesthetic image *Imagine your sitting bones gliding smoothly along train tracks as you transfer from one leg to the other* is also considered anatomical imagery. Find personal images that work for you, and develop your own imagery toolbox.

Imagery is the ideal way to communicate with your movement planner. It is your key to producing movement that is efficient, and therefore graceful and beautiful. Imagery can help you to understand what the teacher is asking, why other dancers move so well, and how your own body can achieve what you want.

EMPOWERMENT

Take Charge of Your Training

Think about what you like best in your dancing. Do you have a preferred dance style? Now create three images that you can use to help you feel empowered while you are dancing. Can these images assist in movements that are not in your strongest style? Work on creating images that empower you in all of your dancing.

Mental Practice and Mental Rehearsal

Mental practice means performing movements in your mind instead of doing them physically. You can improve your technique and overcome faults by imagining you are performing perfectly. Mental practice is particularly helpful when you are unable to dance in class. Any injury has an impact on the way you move, because your brain makes subtle adjustments to prevent pain or further injury. Mental practice helps you to restore and improve normal movement patterns before you return to full dancing.

Before starting mental practice to overcome a technical problem, you may need to check that your imagery for your alignment is accurate. If you have been misaligned for some time, your brain may have an inaccurate picture of your placement. Check yourself visually, moving your bones in and out of alignment until you can recognize where they are with your eyes closed. You can also have your teacher or another dancer check your alignment periodically and help you make further corrections. You may need to return to visual checks at different stages to ensure accuracy. When you are ready, practice some of your dance class exercises and some of the choreography you are rehearsing in your mind without performing them physically. Ask your teacher or a friend to watch you practicing physically to see whether your new alignment patterns have been incorporated.

Mental rehearsal involves imagining every aspect of a dance class, examination, audition, rehearsal, or performance, as if it were really happening. You can use mental rehearsal in any of these phases to improve your dancing. You can even use it as a way to practice when you may be too fatigued for more physical activity. Further, mental rehearsal aims to identify and neutralize any triggers that could cause anxiety and physical tension. Anxiety can become embedded in your behavior, so it may take weeks of careful mental rehearsal and many pause-and-rewinds to remove unhelpful habits. It might take even longer to get rid of stage fright, but the pleasure of relaxed, enjoyable performance is well worth every minute of practice.

All of the methods that you can use in your dancing, including imagery and mental practice, require that you can clearly focus your mind on the task at hand. While those who do not practice dance or sports often participate in exercise as mental relaxation, as a dancer, you need to have an alert and active mind as you practice. This type of intense concentration is called mindfulness.

Mindfulness

Mindfulness is intentional and nonjudgmental focus of one's attention on the present moment. When you practice mindfulness, your brain functions differently. Although it originated in early Eastern philosophy, mindfulness has developed in many different directions, some focusing on general wellness and others on high achievement. From the dance point of view, mindfulness means the following:

› Focusing deeply on what you are doing at the present moment

› Being aware of your own body, your imagery, and the music

› Accepting your body and movement as they are at the moment, without negative thoughts

It would seem obvious that you use some aspects of mindfulness in your dancing. You need to focus on what you are doing, and you need to be aware of the way you are moving. However, physical discomfort, fatigue, anxiety, personal problems, the teacher's instructions, or the sight of another dancer with higher legs or better jumps can distract you from time to time. It takes patience to learn to focus mindfully, but it can make your dancing easier and more rewarding.

The constant challenges of some techniques may encourage you to look ahead, with your mind on the next movement rather than on the present. They may cause you to look back, thinking about problems that have already occurred. Mindfulness shifts the focus to an involvement in the here and now (see figure 4.5).

Mindfulness is a technique, so you get better at it when you practice it regularly. In dance, mindfulness brings all the elements of your dancing into bright focus and harmony. Nothing else interferes. Complete absorption in dancing silences the nagging voice that says you have to try harder, you

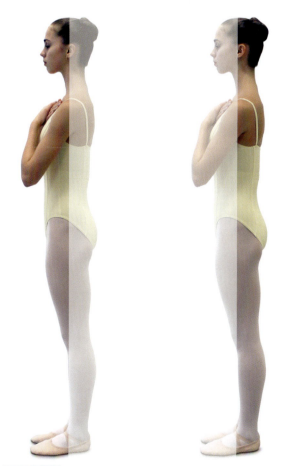

Figure 4.5 The dancer is focusing on the front and back halves of her body to increase her awareness.

Illustration: Marcus Bennett. Dancer: Isobelle Dashwood, The Australian Ballet School and The Australian Ballet.

have to force your body, and you will never be good enough. Mindfulness takes away your anxiety about doing well, about forgetting an exercise, and about criticism.

Flow

Flow is a psychological term for being what athletes call "in the zone." Mindfulness is something you actively work to achieve, but flow is a state of being that you enter through mindfulness. Although it is possible to achieve flow in everyday actions, flow in dance is a different level of harmony between your mind and body, your emotions, the music, and your movement. Flow produces extremely strong feelings of energy, creativity, and pleasure. In a flow state, you feel as if you can accomplish anything, as if your movement flows through you without any mental or physical effort. The sensation of flow is transmitted to the audience through their mirror systems. The experience is inspiring and satisfying for everyone.

The concept of flow is not new. Like mindfulness, flow has its roots in early Eastern philosophy. For centuries, Western artists have described a similar experience, but it was named "flow" during the 20th century. Mindfulness prepares you for flow. In the flow state you stop thinking, your dancing becomes completely natural, and you perform at a much higher level than usual. Musicians, actors, poets, dancers, painters, athletes, somatic practitioners, martial artists, and yoga practitioners have described experiences of flow, and all hope to return to that extraordinarily rewarding state as often as possible. However, trying to achieve flow is useless. To reach a flow state, you need to be completely involved in and accepting of what you are doing, with all your thoughts and senses directed to the here and now. Mindfulness and somatic awareness set the stage for the seemingly miraculous sensation of flow.

As a dancer, you are usually highly motivated. You can easily become caught up in your desire to be better, to have a stronger technique, to win the best role in a performance, and to progress to a higher level. Motivation is an excellent attribute, as long as it allows space for calmness and appreciation of the moment. Mindfulness gives value to the pleasure of movement and enhances the intrinsic rewards of dance.

Summary

While you probably think of muscles and joints as the source of movement, you now realize how important the brain is in planning and executing all movement, from everyday life to complex dancing. And feedback—whether sensory, tactile, verbal, or visual—is crucial to your ability to learn and finely tune your movements. As your training progresses you will add the use of imagery, somatic awareness, and mindfulness, often without being aware that you are using specific skills. Imagery, somatic awareness, and mindfulness ensure the brain's motor system performs at its best, so you can benefit by practicing them. If you are new to these tools, you may find it easier to develop them separately before integrating them into technique class and performance. By the time you can easily use these methods, you will experience the rewards of your efforts and notice how much they affect your dancing.

Application Activity: **Experiment with Mental Practice and Imagery**

Select a dance movement or phrase that you have been working on—perhaps struggling with—from your dance class or rehearsal. Begin by sitting quietly and doing a mental rehearsal of the phrase. Can you see in your mind the sections that are giving you problems? Next, think about images that you can create that might make the movement easier for you. Experiment with different types of images, perhaps trying out visual, kinesthetic, or metaphorical images, for example. Now try to do the phrase without thinking about how you are doing it technically; instead concentrate on the images and sensations. It may be helpful to you to add an awareness of your breathing and how it is timed with the music and your movement. Does the phrase seem any easier? Does it seem effortless and more enjoyable? Repeat this process, experimenting with various images, being mindful of the sensations arising from each image. You may need to try this activity many times over several weeks before it becomes part of your practice.

Review Questions

1. What are the parts of the brain that contribute to planning and coordinating movements in dance?

2. How can you use the various forms of feedback to improve your dancing?

3. What is meant by *sensory awareness* and *mindfulness* as they relate to dance practice?

4. What are the various types of imagery? Does the use of imagery benefit you?

5. What is mental rehearsal? How can you incorporate it into your daily training?

 For chapter-specific supplemental learning activities, study aids, suggested readings, web links, and more, visit the web resource at www.HumanKinetics.com/DancerWellness.

Psychological Wellness

Lynda Mainwaring, PhD, and Imogen Aujla, PhD

Lynda Mainwaring, PhD, and Imogen Aujla, PhD

Photo courtesy of Jake Pett.

Key Terms

approach-avoidance coping
autonomy
basic needs
body image
cognitive anxiety
competence
coping
emotion-focused coping
extrinsically motivated
intrinsically motivated
mastery oriented
performance anxiety
performance oriented
problem-focused coping
relatedness
self-awareness
self-compassion
self-concept
self-confidence
self-efficacy
self-esteem
somatic anxiety
stress
stressor

LEARNING OBJECTIVES

After reading this chapter, you will be able to do the following:

> Explain the difference between intrinsic and extrinsic motivation.

> Understand self-concept, self-awareness, self-esteem, self-confidence, self-efficacy, self-compassion, and body image, and how these psychological factors influence your dancing and your motivation.

> Describe the various stressors that affect you as a dancer, and identify the symptoms of and responses to stress.

> Recognize performance pressures and anxiety, and develop a plan to deal with these influences.

Every dancer knows how difficult it can be to dance when the physical body is injured or sick. However, your psychological well-being is just as important as your physical state is to your dancing. Psychological well-being is dynamic, multifaceted, and necessary for dancer wellness. It is the point at which a balance is achieved between your psychological, social, and physical resources and the challenges you face in life. Dance has a unique and distinct context and culture that creates challenges, expectations, specific ideals, and messages. The culture of dance influences the way you see the world and what you value as important. Social hierarchies, divisions, and inequalities are well established. The dance environment is full of messages about what is acceptable and what is not. These messages contribute to the enormous satisfaction gained from dancing, and they create pressure to perform in a certain way. Sometimes these pressures can have a negative effect on your well-being, because they may cause feelings of anxiety or reduce confidence. However, you can develop resources to manage—and bounce back from—these pressures and challenges.

The aim of this chapter is to help you understand psychological wellness, factors that affect it, and how to improve it with specific skills and techniques. The chapter discusses the importance of motivation, introduces factors such as self-confidence, body image, stress, and coping, and identifies specific psychological strategies for optimal performance. It concludes with some broad questions about how you feel as a dancer in relation to these topics. Dance can offer positive experiences to all, and dancers can play a critical role in developing their own psychological well-being.

Motivation to Dance

Dancers are involved in the practice of dance for a variety of reasons. Motivation can be intrinsic or extrinsic. Dancers are **intrinsically motivated** when they participate in dance for reasons inherent in the activity, such as for enjoyment, to master new skills, or out of curiosity. Dancers are **extrinsically motivated** when they participate in dance for reasons outside of the activity, such as to achieve desirable outcomes (e.g., winning prizes at competitions) or because of obligation or guilt. Your motivation for dancing can impact your psychological well-being.

SELF-AWARENESS

Why Do You Dance?

List all of the reasons you dance. Chances are that you have several reasons, and some are more important than others. It is also likely that your motives for dance have changed over time, and they may be different for different dance-related activities (e.g., class versus performance). However, try to think in general terms about your overarching reasons for dancing. What do you think most powerfully motivates you to dance? Are these most powerful motivators more intrinsic or extrinsic?

People usually have a combination of both intrinsic and extrinsic motives for any activity, but ideally the stronger or more dominant motives will be intrinsic. When you are intrinsically motivated, you dance because you love dance in and of itself, not for some external reason. This means that you are more likely to enjoy and be satisfied by your engagement in dance, will use more effort, and will persist longer. This type of enjoyable and satisfying engagement is crucial in achievement contexts like dance, because it takes a lot of hard work and dedication to succeed. Indeed, intrinsic motivation is a key determinant of long-term engagement and progress.

On the other hand, if you are more extrinsically motivated, your dance involvement depends on external reasons such as a desire for praise or because you do not want to let other people down. So, you may not find dance in and of itself enjoyable or interesting, and as a result will put less effort into dance and be less committed to it. Consequently, extrinsically motivated dancers will not progress at the rate they desire, which may lower their motivation to the point that they eventually drop out from dancing altogether.

Motivation can change over time. For example, you may have loved the joy of moving when you first started dance classes, but as you started to progress, your classes became more serious. Classes had less creative play, they placed more focus on repetitive technical exercises, and your teacher became stricter. These changes turned something you once loved and found intrinsically motivating into a chore. However, you can maintain your intrinsic motivation for dance even when the environment around you changes.

Becoming More Intrinsically Motivated

Intrinsic motivation develops when your psychological **basic needs** (autonomy, competence, and relatedness) are met. **Autonomy** means that you have a sense of choice and a say over what you do. **Competence** means you know you are capable of success. **Relatedness** refers to the psychological need to feel connected to others in the social environment. When you experience lower levels of these needs, you tend to be more extrinsically motivated. For example, if you do not feel autonomous, you might believe that you have no control over what you are doing or why you are doing it; if you do not feel competent, you will struggle to continue in the face of poor progress; and if you do not feel related to others, you will not enjoy what you are doing. However, motivation is not a set trait; you can become more intrinsically motivated by meeting your basic needs. The following sections outline two ways to enhance your intrinsic motivation.

Increase Autonomy

You can do a number of things to increase your sense of autonomy. For example, in dance class you can speak up, ask for clarification, and respond to teacher questions. If you do not yet feel confident in doing these things, you can choose to work on self-selected goals in class so that you are not entirely reliant on the teacher's direction and feedback. When working on your own, identify the purpose of each exercise, such as helping with developing strength, preparation for a more complex exercise later in the class, or relating to a performance piece. Perhaps the music gives you a particular idea for performing the phrase. Maybe you could work on certain dynamic qualities or think of ideas to express. The more you think about an exercise from your own point of view and are informed by your own ideas and goals, the more you will want to perform it well, and the more autonomous you will be.

Relate to Others

To increase your sense of relatedness, ask for a tutorial with your teacher to discuss your progress, which will also aid in your sense of autonomy. You might ask to talk with your teacher about other concerns, such as dance careers. Compliment peers on their performances, or ask them for advice. If your teacher prefers silence in the studio, try to arrive early for class or leave a little later than usual so that you can spend some time interacting with your peers.

Enhance Your Sense of Competence

You can set and monitor your own goals in order to acknowledge your progress and accomplishments and to help you increase competence. Tracking progress in this manner can also increase autonomy, so a good place to start is with the Application Activity at the end of the chapter and use it as a basis to start setting goals. However, the way in which you judge your own competence can make a difference to your motivation and well-being. Specifically, consider whether you make judgments about your abilities based on your own progress or based on comparisons with other dancers, which is important because it represents your goal orientation.

When you judge your competence according to your own personal progression, you are **mastery oriented**. To you, success and competence mean improving in relation to your previous performances.

If you are a mastery-oriented dancer, you tend to have more intrinsic motives for participating in dance; you are motivated by learning, improving, and lifelong progression.

When you judge your competence in relation to others, you are **performance oriented**. To you, success and competence mean outdoing others and demonstrating superior ability. Your reasons for participating in dance tend to be more extrinsic in nature, such as for social recognition and feelings of superiority.

As with intrinsic and extrinsic motivation, people have different levels of each type of goal orientation, and a dancer's goal orientation can have an impact on various well-being and performance outcomes. For example, a mastery orientation is associated with feeling in control of your progress; that is, you believe that if you work hard you will improve, your effort levels are higher, you possess greater confidence, and you are more persistent. The opposite is true of performance-oriented dancers, because their sense of ability depends on the people around them. If you are a performance-oriented dancer and you are the best in the class, then you feel confident and positive about your abilities. However, if you are not the best in the class, you lack confidence and feel anxious, and you are not likely to persist. Even being the best in the class can be problematic for performance-oriented dancers; you may eventually lose motivation because you do not have to work hard to succeed.

It is possible for you to change your goal orientation to become more mastery oriented. One of the best ways to do so is identifying personal goals that are relevant, meaningful, and achievable. You should strive to focus on yourself and the task at hand rather than focus on others. This task is difficult, but it will benefit you in the long run. For example, when you attend an audition, if you are mastery oriented you can focus on producing your best personal performance rather than worry about the ability of those around you. As well as setting personal goals, you can pay attention to feedback teachers give to other dancers, and use this feedback as information rather than assume that the other dancers are better or more skilled. When you become more mastery oriented, you will enhance your feelings of autonomy and competence, meeting your basic needs and increasing your intrinsic motivation.

Whether you dance at a recreational or professional level, motivation is a critical indicator of how and why you engage in dance. While teachers can have an effect on motivation, you must recognize that you can take an active part in the process of becoming more mastery oriented and intrinsically motivated. By identifying your dominant types of motivation and employing strategies to become more autonomous, competent, and related, you can pave the way for a more positive, challenging, and rewarding dance experience.

Contact improvisation is one way dancers learn to bond and trust each other, which enhances socialization and therefore helps to meet the basic need for relatedness.

Photo courtesy of Rachel Cherry, University of Bedfordshire.

The way you feel about yourself can also affect your motivation. Self-concept, self-awareness, self-esteem, self-confidence, self-efficacy, self-compassion, and body image can play a major role in psychological wellness. The following section discusses these ideas.

Dancing and the Self

The essential qualities that make each dancer unique are defined by the self. It drives motivation, perception, thinking, feelings, and personal and social identity. The self can be represented in many ways. Personal identity (also called self-identity) refers to personal qualities, whereas social identity refers to how you identify yourself in relation to others or by membership in certain groups. Your social (also called collective) identity represents who you think you are based on qualities you take on from membership in a particular group. Your identity is influenced by the dance culture, your peer groups, your family ties, and any social memberships you may have. This section describes the dimensions that make up the self.

Self-Concept

Self-concept is a set of stable beliefs about your personal qualities and characteristics. It is how you describe who you are and what characteristics define you. The descriptions form the basis of your self-concept—how you see yourself. Your self-concept influences how you behave, how you dance, and how you react with others. It is related to or is the foundation for many of the psychological constructs identified next.

Self-Awareness

The Greek philosophers said, "Know thyself." You should know what motivates you, what you like, what you dislike, what you fear, and what is comfortable to you. **Self-awareness** is a gradual process of knowing all about you and who you are. It is developed from a lifetime of growth and learning. If you know your strengths, weaknesses, limits, and boundaries, you can relate to others in a healthy way.

Self-Esteem

Self-esteem reflects how you feel about who you are and your abilities. It can be developed or whittled away. You learn what to feel about yourself. You might feel good about yourself in one situation and not so good in another. However, you should always value who you are and feel good about yourself even if your behaviors are not what you expected. For your psychological wellness, you need to accept yourself as a work in progress and strive to learn from mistakes, respecting yourself along the way.

Although it happens often in dance, it is not a good idea to compare yourself with others. Some would argue that dancers should work without mirrors to remove the constant comparison of mirror images of self and others. You are an original work of art and offer the world and others special qualities. Of course, you always have room for improvement, and it is good to grow and develop, but you must respect yourself along the way and accept that you have both strengths and weaknesses.

Dancers typically have high self-esteem, but they can develop low self-esteem if they are constantly criticized or if they put themselves down. Dancing can make you feel great, but it can also set the stage for feelings of low self-worth. Dancers who have high levels of perfectionism often have low levels of self-esteem; they think that they are never good enough. These dancers need to get some supportive counseling to help them get back on track.

Self-Confidence

Self-confidence is a set of beliefs about self-worth and competence. It is the extent to which you feel capable of achieving something and how you appraise yourself. It involves a positive attitude and is closely tied to self-esteem. Self-confident people perceive themselves (and are perceived by others) to be successful, satisfied, competent, self-assured, and assertive.

Self-Efficacy

Another aspect of self-concept is **self-efficacy**, which is the belief that you are able to accomplish a specific task successfully. Believing that you can do something has enormous implications for whether or not you can perform the task. If you believe that you cannot do it, you set yourself up for failure before you start. Self-efficacy is a powerful determinant of behavior. So, if you believe you can do something, you are also more likely to follow through with the behavior. For example, if you believe that you can stop smoking, you will persist through the difficult times more than if you do not believe you could do it. Similarly, if you believe that you can execute a complex new movement sequence, then you will have a positive frame of mind to keep practicing.

Taking time to build relationships and discuss common concerns can help dancers develop a sense of relatedness and compassion.

Photo courtesy of Rachel Cherry, University of Bedfordshire.

Self-Compassion

Self-compassion involves being kind to yourself, forgiving yourself, and not being too self-critical, especially when you are not performing up to your standards or those of anyone else. It is about accepting who you are and realizing that you are a wonderful human being with great potential and fantastic achievements. Self-compassion helps to buffer stress and to counteract negative self-evaluations, self-criticism, and self-blame. For dancers this skill often needs developing.

Like self-esteem, self-compassion is related to many indicators of well-being and positive health outcomes. Having self-compassion can help you bounce back emotionally from negative experiences. Research has shown that self-compassion is related to many health-promoting behaviors, such as regular exercise, better sleep quality, and healthy eating. The good news is that you can develop self-compassion, which can help you become more resilient to the effects of stress.

Body Image

Body image is a multifaceted aspect of the self that reflects how you perceive your body and how it functions. It involves how you feel and think about your physical appearance, including body shape and size. Physical appearance is only one part of you, but it plays a major role in what you think about yourself and others. Body image is particularly important to you as a dancer, because your body is the instrument of your craft. The body is always on display, so naturally it has an important

role in how you feel about yourself. The ways that dancers look and move are always evaluated. A healthy body image involves positive feelings, attitudes, and actions toward the body, whereas an unhealthy body image involves negative feelings, attitudes, and actions. Perceiving your body in a negative light can result from body image disturbances that are driven by unrealistic needs to be thin, muscular, or look a certain way. It is normal to experience some anxiety about how you look and how your physique is evaluated from time to time, but when you have great anxiety about your body to the point that it interferes with functioning, you would benefit from supportive counseling.

EMPOWERMENT

Develop a Strong Sense of Self

You can develop a strong sense of self by recognizing your strengths and your weaknesses. Realizing that mistakes are part of the learning process, you are free to try new things. Use positive statements to yourself, and tell yourself that you are capable, attractive, accomplished, confident, smart, and a good dancer. Dancers deal with a wide range of views about themselves, including self-concept, self-awareness, self-esteem, self-confidence, self-efficacy, and self-compassion. Body image also affects how dancers perceive themselves and, consequently, how they will learn and perform. You can improve your psychological wellness by actively examining these concepts and making positive changes.

Once you have a clear understanding of your motivation, self-concept, and self-image, you can begin to develop strategies to deal with the varied challenges involved in dancing and the dance culture. All dancers experience stress, but how you cope with stress will determine your psychological wellness. The next section teaches you about stress and how to deal with it.

Dealing With Stress

Like everyone else, you undoubtedly have stressful experiences. **Stress** is an emotional experience created by a physical or psychological event that can result in physiological and psychological responses in the body. For example, being chosen for a solo position in the major performance of the year can be a stressful but positive event, challenging you to do your best. In comparison, an injury usually results in a negative experience. Stress can affect your thinking and the way you feel and act. This response is the body trying to change the impact of stress or help you change your response to it. The way you react to and manage stress influences your health and well-being. The body's stress response involves all systems of the body and mind. Psychologists often study stress and how it affects both the body and the mind. This section reviews stress and how to cope with it.

Symptoms of Stress

How the body responds, or what you think and feel in reaction to stress, can be described as symptoms of stress. Physical symptoms include increased heart rate, blood pressure, perspiration, fatigue, and stress hormones (e.g., cortisol levels in blood or saliva). Often when you are under pressure your heart beats faster. Sometimes you can feel your heart pounding. Psychological symptoms include worrying, thinking negative thoughts, and feeling anxious, irritable, or angry. Behavioral symptoms include pacing, eating too much or too little, inability to sleep, overlooking or forgetting something important, and excessive training or practice.

Stress affects what you think, feel, and do in many ways. When checking stress levels it is best to use several markers of stress and not just one. You can experience short-term or long-term stress. Symptoms from short-term stress go away soon after the stress has resolved, but symptoms from long-term stress can be chronic. Short-term stress is not always bad for you; the body needs a certain level of arousal to function at its best. However, long-term stress has negative effects on your immune system and your health. You should manage stress effectively so that you do not develop chronic stress symptoms such as anxiety, constant sleep difficulties, poor eating habits, or illnesses related to chronic stress. Any number of health issues can arise from chronic physical or psychological stress.

Common Stressors

Stressors can be short term (acute) or long term (chronic), external or internal to the person, or positive or negative. **Stressors**, which are stimuli or events that trigger stress symptoms, may include events such as getting a major role in the company or not, changing schools, sitting in a noisy restaurant, arguing with a friend or parent, or experiencing a difficult rehearsal. A stressful experience to one person may not be stressful to another. For example, the lead dancer of a company may look forward to

the hard work of the next 6 weeks of rehearsal, but another dancer in the company may expect to find those weeks grueling while trying to manage the pain caused by a lower leg injury.

Stressful events include negative or uncontrollable events, or those that make you feel uncertain, confused, or overloaded. Stressful life events can be major or minor, positive or negative. Examples of major negative stressful life events include the death of a loved one, changing homes or schools, the breakup of a personal relationship, diagnosis of a chronic illness, or troubles at school. In dance, major negative events may include not getting a particular role, getting chastised in front of others, having a difficult practice or rehearsal, or experiencing injury. Examples of major positive life events may include getting the part you have always wanted, passing a particular test, achieving a certain skill, or heightened fitness. Others may include successfully completing a difficult performance run or learning that you landed a position in a world-renowned company. Minor stressful life events are called daily hassles. They are small annoyances that you manage every day. When they pile up, they can create as much distress as life's major challenges.

Another form of stress is not having enough social support, which can also be unhealthy. It is important to have good friends, family, or other forms of social support around you to help buffer stress. A good social network can help you shake off stress, be comforted in stressful times, and manage your feelings and thoughts.

What you think about yourself and particular situations can be a source of stress. If you believe that you are not good at something or that someone does not like you, you can create internal sources of stress. Your internal self-talk can be positive or negative. The latter sets the stage for a stress reaction. Also, arguing with a friend or worrying about next week's performance can be stressful and make you feel anxious. How you relate to yourself and others can determine how the body responds to stressors. For example, laughing releases hormones into the blood that helps you to feel good, calm, and energized. If you can laugh at minor stressors rather than get upset, then you are helping your body to ward off stress responses that wear the body down. Essentially, you are helping your body to release chemicals that will clear your mind and create a sense of well-being. You could also try relaxation strategies to focus your mind on something else (see table 5.1 later in the chapter). If you are anxious and stressed, your mind becomes clouded and you cannot think clearly. This lack of clarity can lead to more stress because you get frustrated with yourself. Managing what you think and how you behave are not set; you can manage and change your behavior.

Responses to Stress

When stress strikes, the body goes on high alert. The sympathetic nervous system responds. The sympathetic nervous system is one of two parts of the body's autonomic nervous system. It is responsible for the fight-or-flight response through its nerve pathways, and it helps you deal with stressors. It gets the body ready to combat the stressor (fight), flee (flight), seek social support (befriending), or take care of someone (tending or nurturing).

Cortisol is the major stress hormone triggered under stressful conditions. It alerts the body of the need for more oxygen, blood sugar, and energy to cope with the stress. For example, the curtain call and the opening music cue the body to gear up and prepare for the beginning of the performance. The body gets into an action-ready state, addressing the demands placed on it by picking up cues from the familiar environment.

Developing good sleep, eating, fitness, and stress management habits will help maintain health, happiness, and freedom from illness. All dancers can develop good habits when they know how. Learning to cope with stress and creating healthy behaviors and habits are actions within your control.

Coping Strategies

Coping is the deliberate effort to solve personal and interpersonal problems and seeking to minimize or adjust to stressful or challenging experiences. It consists of the thoughts and behaviors used to manage stressful situations. Coping is important for health and well-being. It helps you manage all the stressful life events that come your way. Styles of coping include the following:

> In **approach-avoidance coping**, you either address the stress head on or largely ignore it.

> In **problem-focused coping**, you put in the energy needed to solve the problem.

GOAL SETTING

Set Goals to Deal With Stress

At times you may feel overloaded with various demands. Goal setting can help you to manage your tasks and reduce stress levels. It enhances feelings of autonomy, competence, and control by enabling you to become more self-directed. This, in turn, increases concentration, motivation, and confidence. Goal setting also directs attention to specific task demands, encouraging increased effort, energy, and persistence even when difficulties are encountered. If you are feeling stressed, separate your tasks into those that need to be dealt with immediately and those that can wait. With the tasks that need to be dealt with immediately, set SMART goals so that you can achieve your goals in an effective and timely way. The acronym SMART is explained as follows:

> **S**pecific—What precisely needs to be done?

> **M**easurable—How will you know that you have achieved your goal?

> **A**ction oriented—What actions do you need to take to reach this goal?

> **R**ealistic—Do you have sufficient skills to achieve your goal? Goals should be of moderate difficulty but within reach.

> **T**imed—Set a time by which you want to achieve your goal. It could be a day, a week, a semester, or a year.

For example, you can use SMART goals to help you reduce stress systematically by employing relaxation techniques:

> **S**: Use deep breathing and imagery techniques for relaxation and stress management.

> **M**: Calmer mind (less distractibility or over-activity), lowered heart rate and improved concentration.

> **A**: Practice deep breathing every night for 10 minutes.

> **R**: Nightly breathing practice is an achievable activity.

> **T**: In two months or by the 2-week run-up to a performance it will be easy for me to reduce stress whenever required by taking three deep breaths and focusing on my breathing.

› In **emotion-focused coping**, you become upset, angry, anxious, or uncomfortable about the problem; energy is not invested in solving the problem.

When faced with stressful problems, dancers often use problem-focused coping. They identify the problem and figure out how to solve it. Keep in mind that everyone copes differently, and you might use more than one approach to cope with a problem.

Performance presents its own set of pressures, and you can develop ways to cope with these pressures. In addition, you may be a dancer who becomes highly anxious before performances. Developing certain approaches to performance can relieve some of this anxiety and make performing more enjoyable.

Coping With Performance Pressures

Performance is loaded with expectations from others. The theatrical environment, the critical media, the audience, and your beliefs about what others expect influence how you perform. Performance is infused with certain societal values, dance traditions, choreographic specifications, and aesthetics that often run counter to healthy practices. Teachers, artistic directors, choreographers, other dancers, friends, and family have their expectations too. You have your own expectations. The constant messages about how you should move, look, behave, and perform can influence how you feel and lead to performance pressure and anxiety.

The variety of pressures can cause dancers to doubt themselves and their abilities. Powerful images about the ideal body, the dancing body, or the famous star in the company stand out in everyone's mind. You may start to believe messages in the ever-present images of perfect bodies, such as waiflike female dancers. You may start to question if this is how you should be. You may ask if you should have a perfect body, be a perfect dancer, and always give perfect performances. The world of dance and performance emphasizes this way of seeing the world, which may influence the way you see yourself. While not all schools and companies promote such a view, where it does exist it is detrimental to a healthy approach to dance and well-being. It creates unhealthy pressures, which can be major sources of stress, psychological distress, injury, burnout, unrealistic expectations, strained relationships, self-doubt, disordered eating, perfectionism, or dropping out of dance entirely. You can navigate performance pressures by establishing healthful routines for training, rehearsals, and performances.

Coping With Performance Anxiety

Often considered synonymous with stage fright or "nerves," the familiar sensation of **performance anxiety** is defined as a perceived imbalance between the demands placed on a person and that person's ability to meet those demands. Note that this imbalance is perceived, and it may not be a rational perception. For instance, you might perform a sequence with little concern in the studio, but you are then filled with doubt about performing it in front of an audience. The presence of others watching can suddenly change how capable you feel. Performance anxiety is a situation-specific form of anxiety rather than a more enduring trait or stressor such as those discussed in the previous section, so you may experience it in the run-up to a performance, but it might dissipate quickly during or after the event.

When dancers learn how to cope with stress and anxiety, they are able to perform at their best.

Photo courtesy of Rachel Cherry, University of Bedfordshire.

Causes of performance anxiety tend to center on feeling out of control, and they can result in both cognitive (psychological) and somatic (physical) symptoms. **Cognitive anxiety** symptoms include negative thoughts, worries, self-criticism, distractibility, and negative images. **Somatic anxiety** symptoms include stiff or shaky muscles, needing to go to the toilet often, "butterflies" in the stomach, increased heart rate, and a dry mouth. It is easy to understand why performance anxiety can have a negative impact on performance. For example, muscle stiffness can interfere with precision and control, whereas concentration disruption can result in ignoring important cues or focusing on unimportant ones. However, performance anxiety can also have a positive effect on performance. For instance, an increased heart rate can help you in high-energy parts of a performance. In fact, experiencing a certain amount of anxiety is a key sign of readiness before a performance. Without it, you may feel flat or stale. This fact suggests that, as with stress, the way in which you perceive your anxiety is of critical importance and can have an impact on its intensity and its effects.

When performers perceive their anxiety as being positive and helpful for their performance, they are more likely to feel that anxiety is under their control and they tend to perform better. On the other hand, when performers perceive their anxiety as negative and unhelpful, they are more likely to feel that their anxiety controls them, and they experience poorer performance. Self-confidence can play a protective role in preventing anxiety from being interpreted as negative, so it can be helpful for dancers to work on improving their self-confidence.

The way dancers interpret their anxiety can depend on previous experiences. For example, having had a negative performance experience can make it difficult for dancers to see their anxiety as being helpful. It can also depend on the symptoms themselves; that is, it is easier to perceive somatic anxiety as being more helpful than cognitive anxiety. However, the more you can perceive your anxiety as being helpful, the more in control you will feel, and the more you will enjoy your performance.

Some dancers may want to reduce or remove their anxiety completely, which may be appropriate for those with severe anxiety levels. However, for most dancers, a few changes to the way they prepare for performance can be all they need to find their optimum level of readiness.

If you experience performance anxiety, first, try to see your anxiety in a more positive way. Recognize that a certain level of anxiety is helpful in feeling excited about a performance and in having the energy and determination to do your best. Table 5.1 outlines some simple ways to deal with anxiety by either reducing it or perceiving it as being helpful. Over time, you will find a method that best suits you.

Table 5.1   **Strategies to Cope With Anxiety**

Strategy	Purpose	Description
Deep breathing	Reduce heart rate	Inhale for a slow count of 5, and exhale for a slow count of 6. Try to breathe into the low belly rather than the ribs.
Warm-up	Prepare the body for physical activity and stabilize heart rate	Raise the pulse, mobilize the joints, gently stretch the muscles, and prepare them for physical work.
Progressive muscular relaxation	Reduce excess muscle tension	Maximally tense, hold, and release each muscle group (e.g., gluteal muscles, quadriceps) sequentially starting at the feet all the way up to the face. Repeat 3-5 times.
Mental rehearsal	Enhance self-confidence	Go through the performance accurately in your head, using all of the senses to make the performance as realistic as possible.
Positive self-talk	Reduce negative thoughts and worries, and enhance self-confidence	Replace negative thoughts with positive thoughts that are either motivating (e.g., "You can do it!") or instructional (e.g., "Remember to change the focus here."). Keep the statements concise, and repeat frequently.
Pre-performance routine	Reduce distractibility	Write a list of all the things you need to do before a performance, put them in an order, and time them so that there isn't any spare time before a performance in which doubts can build up. Repeat the routine before every anxiety-inducing event.

Summary

One of the most powerful forces that can influence how well you do in dance is your motivation. Enhancing intrinsic motivation—those internal rewards that make dance so satisfying—can help you persist through challenges and continue to grow. Many aspects of your self, such as your self-concept, self-esteem, and your body image can have a profound influence on how you approach your dancing. Further, the stress and anxiety that can occur with dancing can impede your progress. Developing good coping strategies is the key to success.

Application Activity: **Develop Intrinsic Motivation**

Consider how you might become more intrinsically motivated. Do you rely on the teacher's praise or comparisons with others to feel good about your dancing? You can increase your autonomy by bringing your attention to your personal progress. Set your own goals, and focus on your own progression with the task at hand. If you track your progress over time and recognize your achievements, you can become more confident about your abilities and your work in class. Always being self-critical and never seeing your positive improvements can defeat your sense of self-confidence and self-esteem. At the same time, develop relationships with others that are supportive and not competitive. Instead of comparing yourself with others, think about what you can learn from them and what they can learn from you.

Review Questions

1. What is the difference between intrinsic and extrinsic motivation? Which type of motivation has the strongest influence in your life?

2. Define self-concept, self-awareness, self-esteem, self-confidence, self-efficacy, self-compassion, and body image.

3. Identify which stressors affect you as a dancer. What are the symptoms of stress?

4. What performance pressures do you face? What symptoms of performance anxiety do these pressures cause?

5. How can you develop coping strategies to manage performance pressures, anxiety, and stressors?

 For chapter-specific supplemental learning activities, study aids, suggested readings, web links, and more, visit the web resource at www.HumanKinetics.com/DancerWellness.

Rest and Recovery

Glenna Batson, DSc, and Margaret Wilson, PhD, MS

Key Terms

body–mind
burnout
interval training
marking
non-doing activities
overtraining
overuse
pacing
periodization
proactive
rest
tapering
under-recovery

Photo courtesy of Jake Pett.

After reading this chapter, you will be able to do the following:

› Understand the benefits of getting enough rest.

› Know how to improve your training schedule using methods such as pacing and tapering.

› Describe overuse, overtraining, and burnout and how to avoid them.

› Understand methods of proactive self-care and how to add them to your life.

Dancers are passionate, motivated people whose art places high demands on their whole being. Coping with the stresses of dance training on mind and body requires developing wellness strategies for rest and recovery. Rest benefits the whole dancer, promoting physical and mental well-being. Common wisdom suggests that a healthy balance of activity and rest is a key to overall health and longevity. However, despite the dictates of cultural wisdom, prescriptions for rest and recovery within dance remain elusive. Rarely can dancers point to resting practices, either personal or structured, within training. Yet, the six dimensions of wellness (described in the preface), support the use of rest.

Learning to balance intense physical exercise with rest means addressing daily stress intelligently, mindfully, and practically. Dancers must learn to commit to rest much as they do in learning other motor skills. Treating rest and recovery with the same respect as you do your actual physical practice of dance will maximize the gains in the longevity of your health and career.

This chapter teaches you about the benefits of proper rest and recovery. It summarizes important facts about the positive impact of rest in maintaining energy levels and preventing fatigue. It also explains how rest improves motor learning and performance. In addition, this chapter addresses the downside of neglecting rest to the point of overuse, injury, and burnout. The chapter ends with a proactive approach to rest within dance training.

Benefits of Getting Enough Rest

Rest allows you to retreat into your inner sanctuary, that place of aloneness where you can find a place of true quiet and cessation of activity. Resting requires discipline. **Rest** is a period of no activity and a true break from the current mental or physical tasks. It requires a shift of attention from a busy body–mind to a quiet and calm state of repose. **Body–mind** is the unification of physical and mental function in all activities. It requires going offline, deciding not to engage in the busy world for a short period of time. This disciplined shift requires mindfulness (see chapter 4).

Mindfulness pays off, particularly when it comes to rest. Rest has many benefits and is fundamental to your ability to perform at your best. Rest boosts many healthy processes linked to injury recovery and performance enhancement. Both mind and body benefit greatly from rest, restoring health both physically and psychologically. Mindfulness enhances these benefits and allows dancers to reflect on them, gaining even more from these benefits. Some other benefits of rest include better ability to cope, improved learning of motor skills, and enhanced mind–body harmony.

Rest allows all bodily systems time to repair from the stresses of previous activity. Rest helps muscles adapt to the mechanical stresses from intense physical exercise. After a bout of physical exercise, rest helps accelerate muscle repair and growth between training sessions.

Resting when the body is fatigued is the number one key to injury prevention. Physical or mental fatigue is a major risk factor for dance injury. When resting phases are ignored after a period of intense activity, all body systems are at higher risk for breaking down over time. Injury risk can increase by persistent general tiredness, such as from lack of sleep. The motivation to excel combined with the exercise high (heightened mood) resulting from intense dancing makes it easy to override fatigue signals from the body or the mind, but fatigue is a dancer's enemy.

This dancer is using a wobble board to improve balance, an exercise that requires mindfulness.

Photo courtesy of Jake Pett.

If injury does occur, rest speeds recovery. Rest aids muscle regeneration after injury, bolstering energy stores to build strength and fight fatigue. Rest contributes to overall musculoskeletal health, building tissue that is less susceptible to fatigue. Rest restores and rebalances metabolic levels, such as blood glucose and calcium levels in blood. Balanced body chemistry is vital not only for maintaining the optimal amount of energy but also for absorbing nutrients.

Resting also helps remove toxins in the bloodstream and body tissues, those exercise byproducts that contribute to muscle soreness. Further, a proper schedule of exercise and rest after injury reduces the risk of reinjury from a premature return to dancing. Dancers recovering from injuries need to wait until they get the medical green light from their doctor or other medical practitioner to go back to class and rehearsals. However, the prescription for rest, along with a wise approach to physical rehabilitation, is the key to full recovery and an injury-resistant future.

Optimizing Your Training Schedule

One major way of offsetting stress is through **periodization**, which is the gradual buildup of intensity in physical training through skillful timing and scheduling of workouts. Sport science has focused on many types of training schedules for creating optimal performance for specific sports. With periodization, rest is scheduled at routine intervals to ensure that the ratio between the workload demand and rest is adequate. This approach minimizes the risk of injury.

While dancers have different training needs from other athletes, periodization has value for dancers' wellness. Some examples of periodization for dancer wellness include pacing and tapering, interval training, mental practice, and scheduling.

Pacing and Tapering

Both mental and physical strategies are key elements in periodization. Two of these elements are pacing and tapering activity. **Pacing** is a way of determining a set level of energy expenditure and keeping a balance of energy expenditure and recuperation. Pacing is a distribution of work and energy over a period of time, and it suggests that you have options other than expending the full amount of energy with each repetition of a movement. Pacing strategies allow you to exert a degree of control over external factors. An excellent example of pacing in dance is marking. **Marking** involves doing the movement on a much smaller scale and with less effort. Rather than physically practice a dance phrase full out over and over again, you can mark it. One way of marking is to simply use your fingers to mimic the timing and sequencing of the movements in a dance phrase. Marking helps you conserve physical energy associated with execution. It also helps you focus on qualitative aspects of the movement.

Tapering, or slowly reducing the time or intensity of work, is another practice of reducing the amount of exercise in the days just before an important competition or performance. Tapering is a common practice in endurance athletic events, particularly running and swimming, and it reflects a systematic approach to timing when training athletic skills. For many athletes, a significant period of tapering is essential for optimal performance. The tapering period frequently lasts as long as a week or more. Before an important athletic event, exercise practices are shorter and less intense to preserve the muscle and blood enzymes and hormones and to build in rest for optimal performance. For athletes, this period gives them time to switch from preparation to performance mode. This practice can also work for dancers. As you get closer to performance, one way of tapering is to reduce technical training and classes as rehearsals increase and allow for greater rest time.

DIVERSITY

Learn a New Technique

When you decide to start learning a new technique, such as a tap dancer deciding to try hip-hop dance, you may want to think about tapering in some of your other classes. Each technique makes unique demands on the body. Even if you are used to many hours of training in your chosen form, you may lack the strength and knowledge to tackle this new work. In time, you will be able to add your other classes back into your training regimen.

Interval Training

Other scheduling techniques include scheduling rest following intensive work sessions within a single session, called interval training. **Interval training** looks at the intensity of exercise and recommends a specific rest interval for optimizing recovery for the activity. With power movements, such as intensive explosive jumping, a 1:3 activity–rest ratio is optimal to allow the energy system to recover; that is, 1 minute of intense activity, followed immediately by 3 minutes of rest. Each sport has different activity–rest ratios based on the type of exercise, intensity, and duration, which then determines how much rest will be needed. This idea is also true for dancers. Following a 60- to 90-minute class, a 15- to 20-minute rest period is recommended. For 1 minute of performing a piece of intensely effortful choreography, a 2- to 3-minute rest period is recommended. For rehearsing a 3- to 4-minute piece that has fast and slow sections, 3 to 4 minutes would be a reasonable resting period. The key is to balance the activity and rest to allow for recovery, but not so much time that you lose warmth in the muscles or attention to the task.

Scheduling Considerations

When it comes to dance training and performance, you can monitor your own personal practices of energy conservation, but you are often not in control of scheduling. Ideally, experts recommend that quality, *not* quantity of practice should be the bottom line for dancers. Although you may not necessarily be in control of these schedules, it is important for you to understand how scheduling can affect your performance, health, and well-being.

If possible, you should play a role in planning your training and performing schedules in such a way that you can reach your mental and physical peak in time for performance without making unrealistic demands. Unrealistic demands can harm your physical and mental capacities. Approach any change in routine dance training with caution, ensuring that enhanced artistry and expression are not sacrificed in pursuit of physicality. So, what is an optimal physical workload in dance training, and what kind of training schedule can best optimize performance and offset fatigue? Figure 6.1 shows specific recommendations for athletes that have been adapted to incorporate periodization principles into a dance training schedule.

GOAL SETTING

Incorporate Periodization

Reflect on the nature of what you do in dance practice. Do you take opportunities to rest between classes or rehearsals? Think of strategies you might use to alternate activity and rest. For example, take time for mentally practicing choreography that you are just learning, even preceding performances. Can you think of activities that you might cut back on as rehearsals become more frequent or intense? If you have been doing a conditioning program, intense rehearsal periods might be a time to cut back on this additional stress. Finally, adding new classes or techniques to your training is best done during less active times.

To optimize strategies for work–rest ratio in dance training, try these recommendations, which were originally created for athletes preparing for competition:

> If you are between the ages of 15 and 17, your training intensity should be no more than 2 to 3 hours per day, 4 to 5 days per week. It is recommended that you get at least 1 complete rest day. Build in micro-rest activities while making sure to pursue other healthy habits, such as diet, hydration, and recreation.

> If you are between the ages of 18 and 21, your training intensity should be no more than 4

Figure 6.1   Periodization Strategies

> ❯ At the beginning of the rehearsal process or semester, focus on developing your strength, endurance, flexibility, and skill. Gradually increasing the duration, frequency, and intensity of these elements will best prepare you for optimal performance.

> ❯ The first 7 to 8 weeks are the building phase, followed by tapering, which has greater focus on artistic elements.

> ❯ In preparation for performance, make an effort to decrease training volume and increase focus on quality. During this time you may have to cut back on some of your dance classes or other physical activities.

> ❯ As you near performance, reduce the emphasis on excessive physical training and focus on trying to maintain current levels. The goal of tapering is to maximize performance; once the body has reached a high level of training, you can accomplish this goal with much less repetition.

> ❯ Vary activity; avoid repetitive movements, and engage in non-dance activities.

> ❯ Use distributed practice; when possible, embed a resting phase at least half or equal to the activity phase.

> ❯ Include mental practice; rehearse movements mentally rather than only physically practicing them, especially when you are working privately.

to 6 hours per day, 6 days per week. Add in yoga or another type of somatic practice. Add in mental practice to augment physical practice. Gauge your activity based on your performance calendar; slow and steady to start, build to a peak about 2 weeks before performance, and then taper.

For optimizing your training, you have several choices that involve rest and recovery. Pacing your training and tapering as you near performance will add more periods of rest and reduce the chances of fatigue and possible injury. Further, when your body is rested, your concentration and dancing will be better. Having some control over your schedule, especially in terms of eliminating extra physical work near performance time, can also enhance your dancing. The pitfalls of not paying attention to

your body's need for rest and recovery are overuse, overtraining, and burnout.

Avoiding Overuse, Overtraining, and Burnout

When dancers work smarter, not harder, through periodization, they can stave off the negative effects of overuse, overtraining, and burnout. Unfortunately, at times schedules do not allow either for complete rest or for substituting mental practice for physical practice. When periodization and tapering are not possible, serious consequences can result. Too intense a training schedule without counterbalancing recovery periods leads to a range of negative

Yoga provides an excellent way for dancers to achieve rest and recovery. This dancer is in Savasana (or Shavasana) pose, used at the end of a yoga practice session.

Photo courtesy of Sydney Edwards.

SELF-AWARENESS

Evaluate Your Activities

You can become aware of your needs for rest and recovery by evaluating how you feel during your dancing, especially in the intense time before performances. Log your rest and sleep habits for a week to see whether you're getting enough rest and recovery time. Are you suffering from physical stress? Are you sleeping well? Do you have muscle cramps or other signs of fatigue? Are you dancing without injuries? Do you feel your strength increasing, or do you feel as if you are getting weaker no matter how much you exercise? By answering these questions and evaluating your activity levels, you can decide whether you need to add more rest to your schedule.

physical and behavioral effects. Three major physical consequences of overly stressful training protocols are overuse, overtraining, and burnout.

Overuse

Overuse means using a muscle or muscle group excessively or in actions that are too repetitive. Overuse often results from excessive repetition of movements without adequate intervals of rest or change of movement dynamics. Intentional overuse leads to abuse, the breakdown of the body, and injury. Common sites for overuse are the muscles and joints of the ankle, foot, knee, and hip. Repetitive movement patterns, particularly when adequate variation and rest are lacking, are risk factors for injury. For example, performing too many jumps or repeatedly springing up into relevé might lead to Achilles tendinopathy. Fast, ballistic dynamics taken to end ranges of motion can be harmful if repeated too many times or not counterbalanced with recovery exercises. For example, you might avoid injury by not always practicing a variety of movements en pointe or demi-pointe, or instituting stretching at key points after an exercise session.

Overtraining

Related to the concept of overuse, **overtraining** is a physical, behavioral, and emotional condition that results when training volume and intensity exceed a dancer's capacity to recover. Both overuse and overtraining result from using the same muscles repeatedly, over a prolonged period of time, and without variation in the movement effort. Dancers push themselves too hard physically and mentally

without resting or reducing effort. For example, taking three or more classes in one day followed by 4 to 5 hours of rehearsal is a recipe for stress that can lead to overtraining. Overtraining also can result from rehearsals where the movements are performed full out each time, or adding more frequent or longer rehearsals as performance time nears. Compared to overuse, the signs of stress from overtraining are more severe and potentially more damaging. Characteristically, the dancer not only ceases to make progress but also can begin to lose strength and fitness. Rest can prevent many of the problems associated with overtraining.

SAFETY TIP

Recognize Your Red Flags

Learn to recognize the red flags that signal you are overtraining. Answer these questions: Do you feel as if you are lacking energy during classes and rehearsals? Is your progress beginning to slow down, or are you even losing strength and technique? Are you becoming bored or disinterested, especially during repetitive activities? Are you having difficulty sleeping? If you answered yes to these questions, take them seriously; they are signs of overtraining.

Dance science researchers have noted that continuous training beyond a certain threshold of physical health, without sufficient rest, can impact negatively on both health and performance. The decline in dancers' health over time that starts with overuse and overtraining can lead to burnout.

Another term related to overtraining is under-recovery. **Under-recovery** is the inability to meet or exceed performance in a particular activity. It occurs when the dancer is not attaining sufficient rest or nutrition, and when training variables such as intensity, frequency, and duration are out of balance. This term is new and still under investigation. At the same time, it places more emphasis on the degree of rest needed to recover from exercise rather than on the degree of intensity of the exercise.

Overtraining can lead to chronic periods of too little or erratic sleep, a sense that one is never working hard enough, frequent minor illnesses (colds, flu, menstrual disorders), and chronic irritability. Overtraining can also lead to a greater risk of injury. Injuries are more likely to occur later in a practice session or dance season when you are likely more fatigued. Overtraining also places you at greater risk for burnout. Rather than enhancing performance, overtraining impairs physical ability and negatively alters emotional states. Mere symptoms of stress, the minor warning signs, turn into actual syndromes; that is, they become serious illnesses. If the warning signs of overtraining are left unacknowledged, burnout might result.

Burnout

Burnout is not just a matter of fatigue; it is an illness. At this time, the resulting symptoms of burnout are harder to treat and require more comprehensive and lengthy care. **Burnout** is the negative end result of intense work without sufficient recovery time. The progression from overtraining to burnout occurs over time when training conditions do not change. The time line is important in understanding the shift in the dancer's health from first seeing a decline in performance to eventually experiencing burnout. Often, dancers fail to recognize their lack of intrinsic motivation for dancing and realize—sometimes too late—that they have become burned out. One way you can prevent burnout is by balancing high performance standards with realistic goals, including gradual return to dancing after breaks or injuries. In addition, you can bolster prevention skills by embedding regular rest or recovery time into practice, rehearsal, and performance schedules. Examples for avoiding burnout are suggested in the following section.

As a dancer you should become well aware of the signs and symptoms associated with the continuum of overuse, overtraining, and burnout. If you intensify physical training while ignoring the need to counterbalance exercise with rest and recovery, you place yourself at risk for stress-related injuries and mental strain. You must identify when you are in danger of progressing on this continuum of breakdown; take it seriously. Recovery to bring you back to performance levels again may be long and complicated. Rest is the key to prevention, helping keep you strong, motivated, and free of injury.

Proactive Practice of Self-Care

You must become proactive in taking care of yourself. Incorporate resting practices into your daily dancing life. The resources in this chapter include tips from science and other experts in the field of dance and somatic education. You can understand and embrace a number of ideas and practical strategies for developing a personal program of self-care, and build the necessary skills, simply and easily. The challenge is to keep at it so that you can build a consistent, flexible, sustainable practice of self-care. Attending to a few of these ideas on a daily basis is how a practice becomes part of life.

Steps to Success

You can set specific, concrete goals toward achieving a program of self-care, and learn how to seek and develop a system of outside support. These steps are basic to beginning to build a viable and sustainable practice of rest and recovery, and they can carry you throughout your lifetime. Once you become serious about building a practice of self-care, you will realize you are living a different philosophy. Of course, the actual details of this wellness program are flexible. As you change, your life changes; your program, too, can change. You may frequently add or subtract ingredients from the program, eliminating ones that no longer serve you, incorporating new ideas, strategies, and tasks that work. Starting with these six steps can lead to an excellent program:

The constructive rest position was developed as part of somatic practices and is a well-known strategy to rest the mind and body.

Photo courtesy of Sydney Edwards.

STEP 1: Take responsibility for your own self-care. Adopt the role of a coach, and acknowledge that you are your own best coach. It is amazing how your body has carried you throughout your life, given you all the support and nurturance it has, and withstood the various challenges you have met. Know that you only have one body. Value your physical body and its capabilities, and it will serve you in all of your goals.

STEP 2: Put yourself first. Cultivate care and concern for your physical body, but also have courage and conviction to seek support to meet your needs. Learning to dance smarter, not harder, is the challenge. Rather than finally dropping into bed exhausted after each day of relentless activity, develop an ongoing awareness of your needs and make smart choices to meet them. Building in practices for rest and recovery requires discipline that starts with the motivation to take responsibility and commitment to one's self-worth in being an artist. Remember, life is not a dress rehearsal.

STEP 3: Focus mindfully on the value of rest. Mindful focus on rest shifts your energy from a state of excitability toward a more appropriate level of energetic engagement with the world. Cultivating mindful practice means learning to listen and obey what your body and mind are telling you about your current situation.

STEP 4: Invest in non-doing. Non-doing activities are those that ask you to stop or refrain from your habitual way of doing things. Non-doing requires slowing down, pausing, or stopping your current activity altogether. Recognizing the need to pause or stop alters your sense of timing and effort. A non-doing state requires a mental shift toward openness and ease. It opens you to reflection and to observing just how you are living your life at this very moment of pausing. This practice changes your sense of how much control you can have over your life. It contributes positively to your sense of self-control and autonomy. Cultivating a non-doing state results in becoming more restful, reflective, receptive, and ultimately more responsive.

STEP 5: Practice resting consistently. It takes time to form enough of a memory for an activity to become a habit. If you think your life is too busy for consistency, use a few helpful tips to help you along the way. For example, tape a list of affirmations to your bathroom mirror. Or, try putting colorful notes around your living space to remind you about the need to stop, listen, and reflect. Create a daily resting practice calendar in which you mark each day that you actually practice a few of the ideas mentioned, or add ideas of your own. Note that in only 2 weeks' time, with daily practice you will likely notice improvements in your mood, energy, and ability to focus. You might also notice that these practices have become habit.

STEP 6: Add variability. Any practice can become boring and repetitive. When this happens, take a short break or vary your practice. You can then recommit to the practice or breathe new life into an old practice. The art of practice lies in knowing what elements to keep stable or change, as well as when to change to new tasks.

These six steps are preliminary and basic. Use them to move toward the next phase of developing a disciplined approach to practicing rest—becoming a keen observer of how states of over-activity and states of rest affect your body differently. The importance of this message cannot be underestimated. Learn to stop, listen, and reflect, while you are engaged in activities and tasks that demand your attention; this pausing may at times seem impossible, but it is the necessary skill you must build. Think about your style of being busy. You most likely will feel more tense, stiff, and agitated with a shorter attention span than when you are resting. With rest, you quiet the agitation. Your body lengthens, muscles relax, your world expands, and you become more receptive, accessible, and responsive.

Building a Healthy Approach to Your Training

First, learn to identify when you are fatigued and need a break. This does not mean that you are always exhausted and at the end of your energy. Rather it means you have done a little too much for too long and need a refreshing moment, much the way thirst works. Come to know the sources of your stress and fatigue, such as too little sleep the previous night, too much mental and emotional perfectionism in learning the choreography, or too little hydration. A simple drink of water and 5 minutes of time out might be all you need.

Several strategies can assist in building a healthy approach to your training, including monitoring mental fatigue, keeping a journal, and identifying sources of stress. It is important to monitor your mental fatigue so that you can become aware of it. Remember that mental tasks can be even more fatiguing than physical ones. Digital technology (computer work, mobile phones, and book readers) narrows the focus, negatively affects the eyes, and exhausts brain circuits if tasks become too lengthy. Ergonomic experts (people who prescribe sound working strategies) recommend no more than 30 minutes at a computer without a quick restorative break.

EMPOWERMENT

Journal Your Progress

Keeping a journal or diary is an excellent way to monitor and track your personal habits. Write about how you feel about your dancing and how dancing makes you feel. Record the content of the dance experience, whether you have been learning new movement or rehearsing the same dance over the last 3 months. This exercise is a great way to notice your unique stress patterns over time. To paraphrase somatic movement educator Moshe Feldenkrais, when you know what you are actually doing, you are able to make choices to do what you want. This idea is a key to empowerment.

Finding Outside Support

The need for rest and recovery often is compounded by a variety of factors, both intrinsic and extrinsic, that may happen all at the same time. While we have noted that many of these conditions may be outside your control, you can empower yourself by finding the proper support, whether diet and hydration, psychological support, or other forms of help. Do not wait until you are in a state of despair and exhaustion, but be proactive in building a support network of personal habits, friends/family, medical and fitness personnel, pastoral or other psychological counselors, and a network of other dancers who commit to similar values and practices.

The last element in proactive self-care is finding outside support. You do not thrive in isolation.

Dancers are social beings. You need other people to help your sense of well-being and self-worth. You will more likely thrive in your practice if you also build a community to support it. Find a rest buddy, someone who will meditate with you for 10-20 minutes a couple times a week. Join a meditation class and consider it as important as your dance classes. Some yoga studios offer restorative yoga, where the emphasis is more on resting than on active postures.

You can view these steps as the essential ingredients to learn to cultivate rest in an active ongoing way. These steps are the fundamental underpinnings of learning self-care. The steps combine physical, mental, emotional, and social strategies that provide you with ways of coping with the stresses of dancing and life in general. They can all be customized so that practicing them becomes appealing and pleasurable. Nothing will instill the motivation to practice more than having a feeling of satisfaction that you have done something good for yourself.

Summary

To dance is to communicate art by working the physical body, going beyond pedestrian physical ranges of motion and effort to express artistic meaning. A dancer's drive to commit, improve, and excel in physical expression is extraordinary. Rest provides many benefits that prolong the health and longevity of a dancer's career. However, rest is a not a given in a dancer's life. It is a skill well worth honing. By learning the use of tapering and pacing, and by examining your schedule, you can begin to incorporate rest into your life. Avoiding overuse, overtraining, and burnout is critical to your wellness and your dance career. By building a healthy approach to your training, you empower your dancing through self-care.

Take 20 minutes out of your day for each day that you dance, and set this time aside for rest. Make sure to put away your phone, laptop, or any other devices. The rest should be both physical and mental. Each day write a short section in your journal about how you felt after the 20 minutes of rest and also how you felt at the end of the day. You can also write observations in the morning about your sleep habits, your stress levels, and your energy levels. Do this process for at least 2 weeks, and then note any changes in your daily life. Choose a time of day to journal that seems most beneficial to you, either after the rest period, or before bed when you are reflecting on the entire day.

Review Questions

1. What are the benefits of getting enough rest?

2. Do you know how to improve your training schedule? What are some of the best methods?

3. What are the definitions of overuse, overtraining, and burnout? How can you avoid them?

4. Can you discuss methods of proactive self-care, and how to add them to your life?

 For chapter-specific supplemental learning activities, study aids, suggested readings, web links, and more, visit the web resource at www.HumanKinetics.com/DancerWellness.

Part III

Physical Components of Dancer Wellness

In addition to the training-related aspects discussed earlier in this book, other physical aspects link to dancer wellness. Nutrition for dancers (chapter 7) is not only about the content but also about timing of the intake of various foods, challenges in achieving good nutrition, and issues concerning weight. Bone health (chapter 8) is so important across your lifetime that it has been given its own chapter. Injury risks in dance are high, and you must include injury prevention (chapter 9) in your wellness toolbox. In case you do get injured, you need to know about first aid, the immediate treatment of injuries.

Chapter 7 covers nutrition issues, which include food, timing, costs, and use of supplements. You might think that the main reason you need to eat is for fuel; indeed, providing energy for muscles is important. However, five basic nutrients make up the full palette of what you need (carbohydrate, protein, fat, vitamins and minerals, and water), and each has its own special role in your health. You must listen to the signals you receive about hunger and thirst, and learn how to time meals to best manage performance needs and physical recovery time. You also face many practical challenges, and you have questions about whether or not to take supplements and how to maintain a lean body. All of these issues fall under the broad heading of nutrition.

Chapter 8 discusses bone health, which is of major importance in dancer wellness. You understand that if bones do not develop properly in the teen years, you will suffer over a lifetime. Both nutrition and exercise affect how bones form in these early years. Learning about the structure of bones and joints can help you become aware of the issues and set goals for your development.

Chapter 9 addresses injury prevention and first aid. To prevent dance injuries, you must first be aware of the types of acute and chronic injuries, what predisposes dancers to injury, and what dance activities can result in injuries. Once you have knowledge, you can set goals in your technique and training to aid in injury prevention, such as designing a supplementary conditioning program. You must also recognize how to progress training over time and at what age. First aid is a group of the immediate steps that should be taken when an injury occurs. These steps are defined by the acronym PRICED (protection, rest, ice, compression, elevation, and diagnosis). The other half of first aid is avoiding HARM (heat, alcohol, running and other vigorous exercise, and massage). These elements generally increase blood flow to the injured area and in the early stages cause increased swelling and delay recovery.

Beyond foundations of wellness and mental components of training, the physical aspects of training are very important to dancer wellness. Learning about your personal nutritional needs, how to care for your bones and joints, and injury prevention and care are crucial to the quality and longevity of your career as a dancer.

Optimal Nutrition for Dancers

Derrick D. Brown, MSc, MA, and Jasmine Challis, BSc, RD

Photo courtesy of Jake Pett.

Key Terms

amino acids

calorie

carbohydrate

disaccharides

essential amino acids

essential fatty acids

fat

glycemic index (GI)

glycemic load (GL)

glycogen

high-intensity interval
  training (HIIT)

hydration

insoluble fiber

isotonic drink

macronutrients

metabolism

micronutrients

minerals

monosaccharides

nutrients

protein

saturated fat

soluble fiber

starches

unsaturated fat

vitamins

LEARNING OBJECTIVES

After reading this chapter, you will be able to do the following:

> Define macronutrients and micronutrients, and know the various types of these nutrients.

> Explain the importance of hydration for dancers.

> Recognize the risks of poor nutrition.

> Understand how to develop healthy eating habits.

What do you need in order to optimally fuel your body for dance? Movement is ultimately driven by energy. Muscles need energy in order to produce movement, and energy is at the heart of nutrition. The messages you constantly receive about food and nutrition from media and other sources can be contradictory, misleading, and confusing. Advertisers and marketers may not have the knowledge of a dancer's life or understand the demands placed on the body to excel at this most vibrant art form. This chapter aims to educate you about the steps you can take to maximize your dance practice and performance and get the most from your artistic process. It all starts with good nutrition. A dancer may be blessed with a talent for jumps or be able to execute a beautiful développé à la seconde. He may be the best hip-hopper, or she might be the rising star among b-girls; but without proper nutrition over time, all of a dancer's talents, aspirations, or dreams can come crashing to a halt. This chapter discusses the various factors that comprise maximizing well-being and performance, beginning with a primer of basic nutrition, including hydration and how to regulate your appetite. Next, the chapter examines nutrient timing—what to eat and when. Dietary supplements are also discussed, followed by the importance of promoting good digestive health and weight management. Last, this chapter presents suggestions on how to assess, plan, and personalize your nutritional goals.

Basics of Nutrition

In the study of nutrition, specific terminology is used to categorize nutrients found in food. **Nutrients** are substances taken into the body in food or drink that supply energy or building materials or contribute to body functions. Macronutrients include carbohydrate found in foods such as bread and fruit, fat from foods such as butter and olive oil, and protein from foods such as meat, eggs, and soy. Micronutrients are the vitamins and minerals in your food. Dietary fiber is a type of carbohydrate from plant foods that is resistant to digestion. Finally, hydration is about ensuring that you consume enough water to maintain your health.

Macronutrients

Macronutrients provide energy. They are the building blocks needed for growth, repair, and energy of many bodily functions. A **calorie** is simply a measurement that scientists use to measure different types of energy stored in foods. So, a calorie is no different from a ruler or measuring cup. Calories are found in fat, protein, and carbohydrate. **Fat** is a naturally occurring substance found in animals and also in certain plants. It provides an abundant source of fuel for energy, often in times when the body is doing very little. **Carbohydrate** is a macronutrient broken down in the body to provide a quick energy source to the muscles. **Protein** serves as building blocks. It is found in a variety of tissue from hair, muscle, organs, nails, and even tears. Understanding the functions of these macronutrients will help you make balanced choices about what to eat.

Carbohydrate, fat, and protein supply your body's requirements for energy and repair. The World Health Organization (WHO), the coordinating authority on international health within the United Nations, defines a person's energy needs as the level of calories ingested from the diet needed to balance the energy used. This balance depends on body size, composition, and level of physical activity seen in relation to long-term health. Thus, energy balance occurs when energy intake matches energy expenditure over time. Humans are designed to eat a variety of foods, and food volume can be a helpful part of this variety.

Carbohydrate

Carbohydrate (also called CHO or carbs) is found in a variety of foods and has a variety of structures,

Whole wheat pasta   **Brown rice**

Whole wheat couscous   **Quinoa**

Whole grains provide carbohydrate and also vitamins and minerals.

© Jasmine Challis.

but from a practical point of view it exists as sugar and starch in the food you eat. The WHO recommends that for optimal health at least 55 percent of total energy come from a variety of CHO sources. Carbohydrate represents a rather large collection and variety of foods, such as potatoes, parsnips, beets, kiwi, rice, lentils, cakes, and pastries, to name a few. Sugars include **disaccharides**, which are two sugar molecules linked together, such as lactose, sucrose, and maltose. Lactose is the sugar naturally found in milk, sucrose is the sugar used to sweeten foods and drinks but also found naturally in fruit, and maltose is produced in grain fermentation (not a major part of most people's diets). Fruit and milk products supply both carbohydrate and other essential nutrients. **Monosaccharides**, which are single sugar molecules, include glucose, fructose (fruit sugar), and galactose (found in milk products).

Starches are hugely varied structures of glucose molecules linked together in various ways. Starch can be found in less nutrient-rich foods, such as white bread, cakes, and many snack foods, or more nutrient-rich foods such as whole-grain bread, brown rice, quinoa, buckwheat, whole-grain cous-

cous and pasta, and whole-grain oats. Potatoes also contain starch, and they can be prepared in more healthful ways (e.g., boiled new potatoes) or less healthful ways (mashed with cream and butter). Because the body can carry only a certain quantity of sugar in the bloodstream, it must store some of its energy source in the muscles and liver; in this starch-like form, it is called **glycogen**.

A variety of factors determine which types of nutrients the muscles utilize during physical activity such as dance. However, it has long been established that performing athletes will need to use carbohydrate as a primary energy source more than those leading an inactive lifestyle. The three key physical moments in your life as a dancer are class, rehearsal, and stage performance, and all usually entail physical movement that is brief in duration and high-intermittent intensity. Accordingly, these characteristics place dancers in the category of athletes that have been recommended to consume 55 percent or more of daily intake of carbohydrate to perform the varied demands in their daily dance activities. This percentage roughly translates to at least 4.5 grams (g) of carbohydrate per kilogram (kg) of body weight (1 kg = 2.2 pounds), which is at least 200 grams per day spread over the day from good quality foods as much as possible.

Ingesting quality carbohydrate from a variety of sources, in particular before any of the key physical moments, provides a steady flow of nutrients to your body to fuel the muscles for performance. Fruit such as a banana or dried fruit with nuts can be a valuable energy boost an hour or less before dance, but earlier in your schedule it is important to supply the body with a steady source of glucose. For most dancers this glucose should come from whole-grain carbohydrates. (See the section titled Dietary Fiber for additional information.) Although not all whole-grain carbohydrates release slowly into the bloodstream, they are generally slower than the white versions. Al dente pasta (pasta that is firm to the bite) always releases slowly because its structure is more resistant to digestive enzymes than other white carbohydrates. In addition to carbohydrate, whole-grain foods supply useful amounts of vitamins and minerals together with some protein and fiber. This combination of nutrients assists in appetite regulation. Sources of whole-grain carbohydrate are oats, quinoa, rice (with the bran and germ intact), and wheat (in the form of whole-grain breads and pasta). New potatoes and sweet potatoes are also good slower-releasing carbohydrate sources. Other potatoes release more quickly and therefore have a slightly higher glycemic index (discussed next).

The **glycemic index (GI)** factor is a ranking of foods based on their overall effect on blood sugar levels. Low-GI foods, such as whole-grain oats, are slow release; the carbohydrate is released into the bloodstream over a longer time than high-GI foods, providing sustained energy. High-GI foods, such as jellybeans, tend to give a short, sharp boost to blood sugar levels, which will then fall again; this pattern is less helpful for sustaining energy demands in dance.

The **glycemic load (GL)** is another way of estimating how much a certain food will raise your blood glucose level by combining GI with portion size. GI and GL might seem too technical, but these numbers can provide you with easy ways of manipulating your carbohydrate intake for optimal health and performance. The goal is to get the most out of foods at different times of the day and different times of the year in which demands on your body differ, such as performance times.

SAFETY TIP

Beware of Carbohydrate Supplements

Carbohydrate supplements, packaged as powders, energy gels or shots, must be treated with great caution for a number of reasons. They are highly refined and contain an extremely high GI and GL. They contain various types of carbohydrate, many of which are likely to cause spikes and dips in blood sugar levels. In addition, they can use up a large amount of the food budget, and they may be contaminated in the manufacturing process. It is best to avoid these supplements and rely on food to meet your carbohydrate needs.

Fat

Fat is classified into two types according to its chemical structure, saturated and unsaturated. **Saturated fat** contains as many atoms of oxygen as possible in the fat molecule, which makes this form of fat highly solid at room temperature; examples include butter, lard, meat fat, and cheese. **Unsaturated fat** contains one or more spare spaces on the fat molecule, making it liquid at room temperature; examples include olive oil and other vegetable oils, and fat in fish such as salmon. Saturated fat has been linked to heart disease (although it is not clear whether this correlation varies with the food source), whereas unsaturated fat seems to be more useful to health if consumed in the recommended amounts.

A subgroup of unsaturated fat, **essential fatty acids** are those fatty acids that humans need to eat because the human body cannot make them from other types of fat. They come from two sources. The first is omega-3 from alpha-linoleic acid, found mostly in oily fish, linseed or flaxseed, pumpkin seeds, walnuts, pecans, hazelnuts, canola oil, and soybeans (fortified). The second is omega-6 from linoleic acid, found in vegetable oils. Omega-3 fatty acids may enhance aerobic metabolism, so dancers are advised to include foods rich in omega-3 fatty acids. There are some indications of deficiency in athletes, and this might suggest that dancers could also be deficient.

Fat is the fuel used in low-intensity, long-duration exercise such as middle- and long-distance running or low-intensity aerobic exercise. The mechanism regulating which fuel, fat, or carbohydrate the body chooses is not well understood, and much debate exists about how to change the combination used by the body. What is certain is that if the fuel intake does not match the fuel needed, you will be subject to fatigue and increased risk of injury and illness. Dancers will usually get around 20 to 30 percent of their energy from fat, and a rough guide is around 1 gram per kilogram (2.2 lb) of body weight from

Include oily fish twice weekly in your food plan if possible.
© Jasmine Challis.

good quality foods, which should include oils, nuts and seeds, and if possible, oily fish twice weekly.

Protein

Protein is a major functional and structural component of all cells. While you probably think of muscles when you think of eating protein, it is also found in enzymes, hair, fingernails, and many hormones. An adequate supply of dietary protein is essential for the body to function.

Protein is made up of **amino acids**, which are compounds that contain carbon, hydrogen, oxygen, nitrogen, and sometimes sulfur. Twenty amino acids are required in order for human life to exist. Nine are **essential amino acids**, which means that humans cannot synthesize them but must get them from the foods eaten. You cannot adjust completely to low protein intakes. Although the body will try to recycle amino acids where possible, muscle will be lost. Protein is found in many foods. High-protein sources of animal origin include meat, seafood, eggs, and dairy products. Plant-based high-protein sources include beans and lentils, nuts and seeds, and soy products.

The body has no reserve or store of protein. All protein in the body is functional protein, which means it is part of body tissues such as muscles, or it is part of metabolic systems such as transport systems or hormones. Any extra protein you consume is broken down; the nitrogen is excreted with urine, most of the remainder is used immediately for energy, and a very small amount may be metabolically converted and stored as either glycogen or fat.

If you are deficient in protein, levels of hemoglobin

in blood may fall. Hemoglobin carries oxygen around the body, so a low intake of protein can reduce energy production and reduce capacity for endurance exercise (stamina). The immune system will also be compromised, as will the production of enzymes. A low carbohydrate intake will result in greater nitrogen losses, so an adequate intake of both carbohydrate and protein is vital.

Previously people thought that 0.75 to 0.8 grams of protein per kilogram of body weight is enough for most people, but this recommendation is now being reviewed. People under 18 years old need more protein to allow for growth. The recommendation for dance and sports is 1.2 to 1.6 grams per kilogram for men, and 0.9 to 1.2 grams per kilogram for women. These figures are derived from studies on athletes. Note that one kilogram is equal to 2.2 pounds; for example, if you weighed 120 pounds, you would weigh about 56 kilograms.

Eating protein with carbs immediately after strength training results in greater muscle hypertrophy (growth) compared to carbs alone. Eating protein alone after training can also result in hypertrophy if a large enough amount is consumed, but carb intake at the same time causes insulin release, which minimizes muscle protein breakdown and therefore is more helpful overall. Moderate amounts of protein are needed for best effect within 30 minutes after exercise. The recommendation is 20 to 30 grams of protein and 20 to 35 grams of carb, although more carbs are needed to optimize glycogen recovery. Dancers should choose from a variety of protein-rich foods at two or three meals per day.

Foods such as fish, tofu, and Quorn (a meat substitute) that provide 18 to 20 grams of protein provide a good basis for a main meal.

© Jasmine Challis.

DIVERSITY IN DANCE

Accommodate Your Unique Dietary Needs

You may have a varied or restricted diet for medical or personal reasons. For example, you might embrace a vegetarian or vegan lifestyle. You need to be particularly aware of the sources you can use to make sure you are getting enough protein. If you are lactose intolerant and you have no dairy in your diet, find out how to get adequate amounts of calcium and vitamin D from plant sources or supplements. A registered dietician or nutrition specialist can help you find out what to add or change in your daily food intake to make sure you have a complete and healthy diet.

Micronutrients

Micronutrients are also found in food, and they are commonly called vitamins and minerals. They consist of natural elements or substances needed in small or micro amounts for development and maintenance. Contrary to what many people believe, vitamins and minerals do not provide energy but assist in releasing energy from food.

Vitamins

Vitamins are organic substances essential to normal metabolism, found in small quantities in natural foodstuffs and sometimes produced synthetically. They affect a variety of bodily functions, and they are required only in trace quantities (milligrams or micrograms). Most vitamins were first identified during the early part of the 20th century, between 1906 and 1939. Initially each was given a letter, and once the chemical structure was identified, each was given a name.

Fat-soluble vitamins are dissolved in fat and can be stored in the liver, so they do not need to be eaten daily. Although both fat-soluble and water-soluble vitamins are essential to a dancer's health, the only fat-soluble vitamin of concern is vitamin D. Provided that you follow the advice in this chapter with regard to the appropriate daily amounts of healthy foods, you will get enough of the other fat-soluble vitamins—vitamin A (important for your immune system, vision, and skin, and is also an antioxidant), vitamin E (an antioxidant; it helps to slow down or prevent processes that damage cells), and vitamin K (important for normal blood clotting). Few foods are naturally rich in vitamin D (e.g., oily fish, eggs), although some foods are fortified with it; and most vitamin D in the body is produced as the result of sunlight acting on the skin. Research shows that many people, including dancers, have low levels of vitamin D. Ensuring some sunlight exposure (15 minutes per day from late spring to early autumn without sunscreen) before 11 a.m. or after 3 p.m. will provide much of what is needed. Always avoid sunburn. If you are concerned about your vitamin D level, ask your doctor for a blood test; if your level is low, then take a supplement as advised by the doctor and work on improving your nutrition habits.

Other vitamins are soluble in water, and they are absorbed into the bloodstream dissolved in water. Water-soluble vitamins are excreted in urine and cannot be stored in the body, so they need to be consumed regularly. Vitamin C is an antioxidant (like vitamins A and E) that is also important for maintenance of healthy connective tissue, wound healing, and to help iron absorption from plant-based foods. Vitamin C is found in many fruits and vegetables. Dancers are advised to include at least three different vegetables and at least two different fruits per day to get sufficient quantities of both vitamin C and other antioxidants. The B group of vitamins is also water soluble. This group is shown in detail in table 7.1.

Minerals

Many minerals are essential to human health. **Minerals** are nonliving natural substances of definite chemical composition. Your body needs to regulate the amounts of minerals so that it has neither too much nor too little. Most cannot be stored and therefore are needed on a daily basis. For example, sodium and potassium help in muscle function and fluid regulation. They are constantly being adjusted by the kidneys to make sure the levels in the cells and blood remain at healthy levels. Thus sodium and potassium, as well as other minerals, are tightly regulated by the body. Calcium, which is the most abundant mineral in the skeleton, is also vital for a number of other functions. The absorption of calcium from the small intestine is regulated by way of vitamin D, so low levels of vitamin D will have a negative effect on bone health. Chapter 8 explores this topic further.

Iron is of particular concern to dancers, because it is needed to help transport oxygen through the body. Low iron levels result in tiredness and early signs of fatigue when dancing. Iron from animal sources such as meat and fish is more easily absorbed than from vegetarian sources. Vitamin C helps with the absorption of iron from grains,

Table 7.1 Sources and Functions of Vitamins

Vitamin name	Alternative names	Sources	Function/Role
Vitamin A	Retinol; beta-carotene can also be converted into vitamin A.	Yellow and green vegetables and fruits, oily fish, cheese, milk, yogurt, eggs, liver	Immune system, vision, skin, normal growth and development
B vitamin group:			
Thiamin	B_1	Many foods, including milk, vegetables, pork, whole grains	Metabolism of carbohydrate
Riboflavin	B_2	Many foods, including milk, eggs, yeast extract	Utilization of energy from food
Niacin	B_3	Many foods, including meat, grains, milk	Utilization of energy from food
Pantothenic acid	B_5	Many foods, including meat, grains, vegetables	Metabolism of fat and carbohydrate
Pyridoxine	B_6	Many foods, including whole grains and protein-rich foods	Metabolism of protein, production of hemoglobin
Folic acid/folate		Many foods, including fruits and vegetables, brown rice, bread	Normal red blood cell production, spinal cord development in early pregnancy
Cobalamin	B_{12}	Foods of animal origin including milk, cheese and yogurt, and fortified plant foods, such as fortified cereal and fortified yeast	Prevention of anemia
Biotin		Meat, eggs, vegetables, dried mixed fruit	Metabolism of fat
Vitamin C	Ascorbic acid	Most fruits and vegetables	Wound healing, antioxidant, iron absorption
Vitamin D	Cholecalciferol, ergocalciferol	Oily fish, eggs, fortified foods, action of sunlight on skin	Absorption of calcium, immune system
Vitamin E	Tocopherol	Plant oils, nuts, seeds, wheat germ	Antioxidant, anti-inflammatory, immune system
Vitamin K	Phylloquinone	Dark green leafy vegetables, olive oil, soybean oil, green beans, cauliflower, cucumber	Blood clotting, bone health

beans, and vegetables. Female dancers need about 50 percent more iron in their diets than male dancers to replace losses from menstruation, and they are advised to check their meal plan regularly to ensure they have included enough iron-rich foods. Many minerals are found either in protein foods or in nuts, seeds, and vegetables. Therefore, a diet including adequate protein will automatically provide more essential minerals than a diet based on refined carbohydrate such as cakes, cookies, and candy. Table 7.2 provides an overview of the main minerals needed for a healthy dancer's body.

Dietary Fiber

The digestive system is supremely well set up to extract the nutrients from food and to absorb fluids, and amazingly it is around 6 to 7 meters (20-23 ft.)

Table 7.2 Sources and Functions of Minerals

Mineral name	Sources	Function/Role
Sodium	Salt, soy sauce, preserved foods—canned, smoked and salted, meat and fish, cheese, bread, most cereals, and many other manufactured foods	Maintaining the water balance of the body, muscle and nerve activity, regulation of blood pressure
Potassium	Fruits and vegetables, chocolate, coffee, nuts, cereals, meat, milk	Maintaining the water balance of the body, muscle and nerve activity, regulation of blood pressure
Calcium	Milk, cheese, yogurt, fortified soy products, nuts and seeds, green vegetables, dried fruit	Bone/tooth structure, nerve conduction, blood clotting
Phosphorous	Grains and cereals, milk, cheese, yogurt, green vegetables, meat, nuts	Bone/tooth formation, energy metabolism
Iron	Red meat, eggs, cereals, green vegetables, pulses	Hemoglobin/myoglobin formation (to transport oxygen around the body), healthy immune system
Magnesium	Green vegetables, meat, dairy products, cereals	Muscle and nerve activity, bone formation, enzyme reactions (energy metabolism)
Zinc	Meat, seafood, green vegetables, seeds	Prevent low mood, allow normal wound healing, involved in the immune system, appetite regulation, enzyme synthesis
Copper	Shellfish, organ meat, pulses, nuts, cocoa	Enzyme synthesis
Iodine	Seafood, eggs, dairy	Thyroid function
Fluoride	Seafood, water, tea	Tooth structure
Manganese	Nuts, dried fruit, cereals, tea	Enzyme synthesis
Chromium	Meat, whole-grain cereals, beans and lentils, nuts, dairy, eggs	Glucose/insulin metabolism
Selenium	Brazil nuts, fish, offal, meat, grains, eggs	Antioxidant, electron transfer

long packed intricately into the abdominal cavity. It has a large number of nerves connected to it, and anxiety and stress can affect the gut significantly. While a high-fiber diet is generally the best choice, you will need to consider whether this choice is appropriate for you. Dietary fiber comes from plant foods. Two types of dietary fiber exist, soluble and insoluble fiber. Most fiber-containing foods have a combination of both.

› **Insoluble fiber** is indigestible matter that passes through the digestive system almost unchanged. It is found in the skins of vegetables and fruit and the bran portion of whole grains. Insufficient insoluble fiber may be a cause of constipation and is linked to a less healthy bowel in the long term.

› **Soluble fiber** turns to a gel during the digestive process and helps regulate blood glucose levels. It can be found in some vegetables, fruits, and legumes, such as dried beans and peas as well as in oats. It also contributes to regulating cholesterol levels as well as supporting the "good" bacteria in the gut.

GOAL SETTING

Improve Your Nutrition

Once you have taken a look at your daily food intake, think about how you might improve your nutrition. Set some short-term goals. For example, if you are not eating enough fruits and vegetables, give yourself a couple of weeks to increase your intake of these important items to the recommended quantities. In the long term, can you reduce the foods you eat that are less nutritious and replace them with healthier choices? Give yourself 6 months to replace donuts with fruit, fast-food dinners with cooked meals, and soft drinks with water or fruit juice. Be patient; making changes can at first be difficult, but with time you can arrive at a healthy, nutritious diet.

To make sure you get enough fiber in your diet, have at least three servings of vegetables or salad every day and at least two servings of fresh or dried fruit. Choose whole-grain breakfast cereals or oats, and use whole grain instead of white bread. Brown rice and pasta will give you more fiber and more vitamins and minerals than the white versions. Peas, beans, and lentils not only provide protein and carbohydrate, they are also very good sources of fiber.

Hydration

Simply put, **hydration** is the introduction of water into your diet. It can be in the form of water or fluid from the foods you eat. The human body is around 50 to 75 percent water, depending on factors such as age, weight, and percent body fat. Men have a higher water content than women; women have a higher body fat content than men. When you consume too much water, the kidneys work efficiently to lose this excess water in urine. However, this regulatory system has limits, so extreme hydration is dangerous. In contrast, dehydration caused by consuming too little water or not including fluid-rich food daily means that the body is not able to function as it should and needs this imbalance corrected for optimal functioning. Fruits and vegetables are at least 80 percent water, so you may need a little less fluid if you have a high intake of fresh fruits and vegetables.

Thirst is one of the most primitive mechanisms that the body has for self-protection. It should guide you to replace fluid when necessary, but for many reasons it is not always reliable. If you have a good sense of thirst and make sure you have fluid available, then thirst should help keep you hydrated. Fill up a water bottle before class or rehearsal, and check that it holds enough water given your gender and activity requirements. For men, a 0.5-liter (17-oz.) bottle is not enough for a difficult 90-minute class. For women, a minimum of 0.5-liter (17-oz.) bottle might be sufficient for a high intensity 90-minute class. Dancers usually have a good idea of the teaching style of the class so when in doubt plan for more rather than less hydration. For many people thirst is not a reliable mechanism; they need to consciously make a plan to drink at regular intervals, usually around 150 to 200 milliliters (about 5-7 oz.) every 20 to 30 minutes. If you know you need more, then drink a little more at each drink break. It can be a strange sensation at first if you are not used to drinking regularly, but it pays off over time. You may need to take more bathroom breaks while your body adjusts to more frequent hydration, but it does adjust over time. You may need to experiment with the type of fluid that works best for you; keeping some notes can be useful.

For example, your notes may indicate that you find it easier to drink enough when the water is colder or if you add a little fruit juice for flavor. Perhaps you have a milkshake during a break and notice that it takes much longer than water to leave your stomach; every time you jump, you feel it splashing around.

Around 1.5 to 2.5 liters (6-10 cups) of fluid per day (lower amount for smaller, lighter females; higher amount for taller, heavier males) spread over the day will keep most people in fluid balance for day-to-day living. You will need to replace the additional fluid that is lost in sweat from dance. The amount can vary from around 0.5 liters (2 cups) per hour for smaller, lighter female dancers to 1 liter or more (4+ cups) for taller, heavier male dancers.

All fluid will hydrate, except alcohol, which dehydrates. Caffeine has been the subject of much debate and discussion, but it seems that if you drink moderate amounts of caffeine (normal-strength tea and coffee, up to 4 cups per day) then you can count it as part of your day's fluid intake. If you increase your caffeine intake, you may notice fluid passes through your body more quickly, which is less helpful in class, rehearsal, or performance if you have to take many breaks. It also means the fluid can't be used to produce sweat and regulate your temperature. Some people are more sensitive to caffeine than others. If you struggle with sleep, it is best to avoid caffeine after midday, because it takes several hours to leave the system. For most people water is a great choice; it is readily available, quickly absorbed, and will not damage teeth or studio floors.

Some people may find isotonic drinks useful. An **isotonic drink** has a composition similar to that of body fluid, such as blood and saliva. These drinks have around 4 to 8 grams of sugar per 100 milliliters (about 3 oz., or 0.4 cups); the hydrating effect seems to be the same whatever the type of sugar. They also have some salts to replace salt lost in sweat. Isotonic drinks can be made from diluting fruit juice or squash, a concentrated syrup that is usually fruit-flavored; following a recipe with glucose and salt; or you can buy a commercial drink. Table 7.3 describes some classic sports drink recipes. You can easily find variations online; just check that the ratios of ingredients are similar, then see what works for you.

Isotonic drinks can be useful for people with higher energy needs or those with diabetes who need to keep blood sugar levels steady in classes

Table 7.3 Isotonic Drink Recipes

Type of drink	Ingredients	Instructions
Lemonade/cordial or fruit-flavored drink	200 ml (about 7 oz.) ordinary (not low-calorie) fruit lemonade/cordial 800 ml (27 oz.) water Pinch of salt	Mix, cool, and drink.
Fruit juice	500 ml (about 17 oz.) unsweetened fruit juice (orange, apple, pineapple, or a combination) 500 ml water Pinch of salt	Mix all ingredients in a jug or bottle; if time allows, refrigerate.
Glucose/sugar	50-70 g sugar or glucose powder 1 liter (about 2 cups) warm water Pinch of salt Up to 200 ml (about 7 oz.) sugar-free squash/cordial/lemonade, or 1 drink flavor sachet if preferred	Mix, cool, and drink.

or rehearsals where the intensity can be difficult to predict in advance. Use isotonic drinks with caution. They affect dental health, so you should also have water available and keep your mouth as clean as possible.

Some of the beverages that dancers consume are too high in sugar. Above 8 grams sugar per 100 ml (about 3 oz.), the rate of absorption slows down. The sugar will need to be absorbed ahead of the water, so most juices and carbonated drinks are not good choices before and during any dance or training activity. Sugary drinks also pose a risk to dental health. So-called energy drinks are very high in sugar (typically around 17 teaspoons in a 500-ml/17-oz. bottle) and often have added caffeine; this combination is not a great way to stay hydrated or keep energy levels steady.

In summary, a healthy diet requires a range of nutrients. Macronutrients include carbohydrate, fat, and protein, and they are essential for energy and building a healthy body. Micronutrients include vitamins and minerals, and they are necessary to support the function of all of the organs of the body. Dietary fiber and hydration are important dietary components for every dancer.

Risks of Poor Nutrition

Poor nutrition and hydration can have a number of effects. In the short term, dehydration results in you feeling more tired than expected, potentially leading to physical discomfort such as a headache. Blood is made up of more than 90 percent water. In a dehydrated state, blood flow is less efficient, so muscles receive less oxygen and nutrients than usual, and

waste products of metabolism are removed more slowly than usual. The immune system also does not function as well, so when you are dehydrated you are at increased risk of becoming sick. Your mood is less than optimal, so you get less enjoyment from the efforts. In short, poor nutrition and hydration leave you at risk not only for poor performance, but also for increased risk of injury from enhanced effort to sustain physical, mental, and artistic performance. When aiding your body in repair and recovery, consider these three key points:

1. Eat meals and not just snacks. Eating too little does not allow your body to repair after a hard day of dancing.

2. Fats are your friend. Good fats have many benefits, such as keeping inflammation under control.

3. Eat a meal after training or performing. Eating after exercise increases your chances for repair and recovery.

SELF-AWARENESS

Track Your Nutrition Habits

For 1 week, record everything you eat and drink. At the end of the week, review your record, evaluating whether you are getting all of the nutrients you need and in their proper amounts. What are you missing? What are you eating in excess? Make any adjustments needed, and track your nutrition habits for another week. Make note of how you feel and whether these adjustments to your food intake change your energy or other aspects of your health.

Cultivating Healthy Eating Habits

Today, the word "diet" is synonymous with "sacrifice" and "rumors." For example, some people give up carbohydrate because they heard that everyone might be gluten sensitive. Some people scorn fat, hearing it makes them fatter. Some people eat only animal protein because they heard someone figured out exactly all the foods humans consumed two million years ago. Others eat only salad because they heard it's good for dancers who want to lose a few pounds. These attempts at sacrifice and deprivation are short lived, for key logical reasons. First, your metabolic systems have evolved to fight against food deprivation and starvation. More important, your brain, a primary organ for survival, fights to ensure that appropriate levels of nutrients are available to keep you functioning. This evolutionary efficiency is one that diet companies either forget or omit when convincing you that your diet will help you lose unnecessary pounds. The reality, however, is profoundly different.

A healthy metabolism actually burns more fat reserves quickly when quality nutrients are ingested. **Metabolism** is a term used to describe all biochemical transformations in the body necessary for sustaining life. Conversely, when insufficient food is ingested, metabolism works more slowly. For performers this metabolic rate could have many more negative consequences than a pound here or one less there. Poor metabolism offers a host of problems for performers from insufficient heat to keep the body warm internally (without leg warmers) to an inability for nutrients to aid quickly in healing damaged muscle.

The first step in developing healthy eating habits is to understand the nutrients that your body needs. The next step is to adopt a lifestyle that supports meeting your body's needs. To adopt this lifestyle you need to create a positive environment for eating, pay attention to your body, and recognize the effect that food has on your level of performance. Each of these aspects will help you move toward a daily pattern of healthy nutrition.

Create a Positive Environment for Eating

Aside from the fast-food habit of eating on the run that has become a part of the Western way of eating for about seven decades, many people generally eat in a social setting. At least once or twice a week since your childhood, usually with your family, later perhaps with friends, you laugh, cry, argue, discuss, and love—all while sharing a meal. This almost innocuous event has shaped your early memories of food and of food choices. A meal with perhaps fewer flavors than you would like when shared with friends in a relaxed and friendly setting is enhanced in your perception of its quality.

In contrast, the most meticulously prepared meal with only the best ingredients, perfectly seasoned, but presented in the company of strangers or in an unsafe and hostile environment, simply does not sit well. Thus, thoughts surrounding food and eating can elicit a change in mood and arousal before, during, and after eating a meal. Before the onset of meals, animals (including humans) tend to be aroused, alert, and even irritable when hungry. These signals encourage the instinctive search for food. Most animals become calm, lethargic, and restful upon meal completion, generally displaying a more positive than negative mood. Research on negative mood or stress related to eating in humans and animals finds a clear interface between stress levels and how people choose what and when to eat. When stressed you may tend to either eat too much or not at all. You may choose more savory salt-laden dishes or syrupy sweet dishes to sooth your stress levels, which only offer a temporary fix. Real-life stressful situations, such as exams, dance recitals, and rehearsals with a high workload, potentially provide situations where high stress will occur.

When choosing what to eat, it becomes paramount to also consider where and with whom you eat. Try not to eat alone. When a break is given, take the break. While eating, simply eat; don't do a mental run through of the repertoire piece just rehearsed, sew ribbons on pointe shoes, or schedule a costume fitting. If your dance company gives a lunch or dinner break, pause to share a meal with a close and trusted colleague or friend. Even a quick lunch where you can laugh, cry, or let off steam with a friend changes your perception of the meal and eating. Finally, cook with a friend. It does not matter what your current skill level is. Start small; you can make great snacks without starting a fire! Be creative. Combine flavors you have never tried as well as your old trusted combinations of ingredients. Try to see cooking as a fun event and not one that must be controlled or, far worse, perfect. Some of the most delicious dishes came about because of mistakes. So don't be shy; be as creative in the kitchen as you are in the dance studio.

Listen to Your Body

Your body has amazing feedback systems to detect the nutrients it has received in any meal or snack. It will know if it needs more protein, chromium, or thiamin. However, because your access to precisely what you need is not guaranteed, when your body needs something it sends this general signal to you regardless of the specific need: *Eat food!* These signals are elegantly choreographed by the nervous system and by the body's key messengers, hormones. From the moment they are born, humans cry as an indication that they are hungry. Once fed they are perfectly content to play, drool, and watch the world unfold—until they receive signals again that it is time to eat, and they scream to be fed again. As children develop, this early instinct to scream when hungry changes according to the culture in which they grow up. An example would be children who are forced to finish their food in one sitting when they feel full, or toddlers in impoverished families who become accustomed to eating less.

To ensure that your nutritional needs are met, the best way to eat is to provide a range of nutrients at each of three meals each day, adding one or more nutritious snacks if needed for your schedule and workload. The subject of how to meet your nutritional needs is covered in the next section. If you override or lose touch with your sense of appetite, you can reprogram it with a system of regular meals and snacks. However, it isn't this simple; often your dance schedule can be out of sync with your normal meal pattern. If you have back-to-back classes with only a small break, consuming regular meals and snacks can be challenging. Humans also develop likes and dislikes and often fall victim to preferred foods that may not provide them with all that is needed to dance long and hard and then recover properly. Appetite is often reduced after intense activity, probably a response to increased body temperature. It generally returns around 15 to 20 minutes after stopping exercise, just at the point when the next class or rehearsal begins. So, you may have to put in food when you need it rather than when you want it. Good-quality snacks, such as nuts with fresh or dried fruit, or snack bars (check the label to make sure the main ingredients are grains/nuts/fruits rather than sugar), can help you meet your needs.

Finally, be aware also that fatigue from lack of sleep or insufficient rest can result in overeating. When your body is not being allowed to rest, it may demand increased fuel from food in an attempt to restore energy levels. Poor fluid intake can also result in overeating. Some people do not easily differentiate between hunger and thirst. If you are aware that you have a poor sense of thirst, pay particular attention to your fluid intake; otherwise, you may be eating when you need to be drinking instead.

Your surroundings can be almost as important as what you eat. Consider what works for your body as you are unique, and take time to consider how to fit the food and fluid you need into your schedule. Taking a break is not a waste of time; it is a moment to rest, replenish, and recover even if you have a packed schedule with irregular breaks.

Recognize Food's Impact on Your Performance

In most living situations, it is possible to live your entire life without ever thinking about what happens to food once it has been eaten. For nonathletes or nonperformers, the concerns may be centered on pleasure of foods liked or loved—and pain when too many of these foods start to increase the waistline. As a career, dance requires more care in understanding the relationship between food and performance. This section discusses how dietitians, nutritionists, and performance specialists assess nutritional requirements for dancers. It provides you with basic ideas behind the science of nutrition to manipulate the timing of foods to enhance both performance and recovery.

EMPOWERMENT

Use Nutrition to Enhance Your Performance

Consider ways that you might improve your levels of performance through better nutrition. Perhaps you need to add more carbohydrate to give your body more energy when dancing. Or you may need to add more protein to enhance muscle repair. These changes may include evaluating the timing of your meals. You may want to increase your hydration for better muscle function. You are now empowered with knowledge that you can use to enhance your dancing simply by paying attention to what you eat and when you eat it.

Fuel to Burn

The science behind dance has revealed a great deal about what happens when dancers dance. How energy is expended depends greatly on the intensity of activity. Chapter 3 provides more detailed information about the anaerobic and aerobic systems. A practical way to think of intensity is that the more intensely you work, the more energy is used that needs to be replenished at some point. Even when you have just finished an intense dance class and are either cooling down or relaxing, your body can use energy reserved in muscle tissue. A key reason that emphasis is placed on eating enough relates to the energy reserves that can be used to help restore the body to work in the coming hours or the next day. If you miss too many meals and snacks throughout a day, an energy deficit occurs, and it can create problems in the long run. In order to keep the body running, you need to think of different foods providing different functions when you dance.

Dancing is an act of physical, mental, and emotional integration. When strictly observed from a physical perspective, distinct differences are apparent in dance genres. Within genres, different times of a class can impact a dancer in different ways. This timing also has a connection to how dancers can learn to manipulate diet to match the physical demands of dance. Figure 7.1 presents a way to categorize the differences in terms of intensity. For example, the beginning of a traditional ballet class comprises movement combinations that start off simply but grow in complication as the class progresses. Plié combinations are followed by tendu and dégagé combinations, which are all designed to warm up the lower extremities. Such actions can be categorized as shown in the smallest bar in figure 7.1. Consider the largest bar in the figure. In dance performed over hours (e.g., matinee followed by evening performance, or dance marathons

and jams) dancers juggle many different physical intensities over long periods. In a 2-hour *Swan Lake* performance, a dancer may enter and exit the stage several times and be required to attend to many complex movement components in choreography, such as going from duet to trio to ensemble sections.

The majority of dance classes and some performance can be categorized as **high-intensity interval training (HIIT)** movement sequences which is represented by the middle bar in figure 7.1. For example, most classical syllabi combinations are constructed such that more complexity is established toward the end of the barre in preparation for chains of movement phrases in the center. Thus the end of the barre might contain a combination containing rond de jambe en l'air; a series of large leg movements of the gesture leg at a medium tempo might be followed by a batterie phrase that demands quick movements. A couple of combinations later, there might follow large full-leg movements such as grand battements. These combinations of low intensity followed by quick, high-intensity kicks are indicative of HIIT, especially when repeated several times on each leg. Ballroom dancing, fast-paced tap routines, as well as urban dance competitions are other examples of HIIT in dance. The intermittent nature of dance requires a high capacity for both aerobic (oxidative) and anaerobic (nonoxidative) energy expenditure.

Although fatigue has many factors, high- and low-intensity physical activities can deplete more rapidly the energy stored in skeletal muscles than activities with a more continuous nature. For example, short warm-ups of 30 to 45 minutes are unlikely

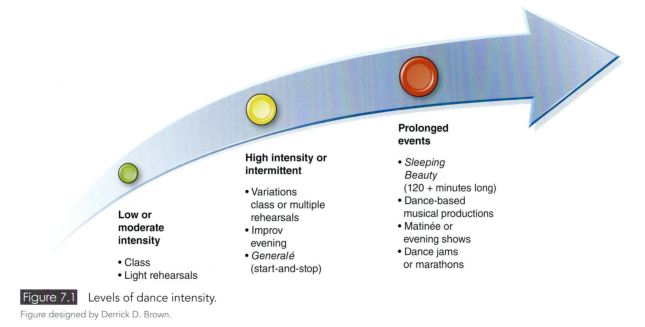

Prolonged events

- *Sleeping Beauty* (120 + minutes long)
- Dance-based musical productions
- Matinée or evening shows
- Dance jams or marathons

High intensity or intermittent

- Variations class or multiple rehearsals
- Improv evening
- *Generalé* (start-and-stop)

Low or moderate intensity

- Class
- Light rehearsals

Figure 7.1 Levels of dance intensity.

Figure designed by Derrick D. Brown.

to have an immediate impact on energy reserves. However, on days containing full technique classes and multiple rehearsals throughout the day, energy levels in muscles are quickly depleted. Figure 7.2 provides a quick reference of energy use. As you can see, the two key energy burners for dance are fat and carbohydrate (in the form of glucose), and both are equally important for fueling the dancer's body to match the demands of dancing. Energy use is a cycle; by continually fueling the body you have fewer opportunities to deplete the system. It is important to note that while everyone has enough fat to keep going at lower-intensity exercise for hours, carbohydrate stores are very limited and will be exhausted by around 1 1/2 hours of high-intensity exercise.

The performance is finished. Adrenaline is surging through your body. During the buzz, you are also processing many emotions, memories, and reflections about what you just experienced. Some dancers, especially professionals who perform several times a week, develop a habit of living off the post-performance buzz and, either intentionally or not, forgetting to eat. However, as a dancer, this is a time to place more effort on getting energy in your body as quickly as possible. For dancers, this timing becomes necessary not only for topping up energy reserves just lost, but most especially for muscle repair and future performance.

During this post-performance time, carbohydrate is crucial. How much to eat depends on many factors, such as amount of food and liquids ingested throughout the day, intensity of the dance day, injury status, and the schedule for the following day. Ingesting carbohydrate as soon as possible after a performance, in particular, helps the body create energy from energy stored. Delaying too long can slow down this process. In addition, adding some protein will help quicken recovery and aid with muscle repair. One caveat would be to limit intake of fructose-based carbohydrate sources (e.g., fruit juice, fruits) to avoid potential gastrointestinal distress. A guide when choosing your food is a carbohydrate-to-protein ratio of 3:1. The following section addresses possible post-performance food intake.

Timing of Food Consumption for Performance Needs

Dancers can follow certain guidelines for food intake during the entire day of performance. You should consume carbohydrates regularly. If possible, your carbohydrate intake should be from whole-grain sources, and the amount needed will vary according to the day's schedule. Eat breakfast. If you do your first classes or rehearsals without eating, you may limit your energy levels, especially when the intensity of the class or rehearsal increases. Lunch and dinner should both contribute to your totals of protein, carbohydrate, and fat, but you may need to combine them differently depending on the time you have for lunch: it takes around an hour for food to start to leave your stomach, so very short breaks may limit how much you can eat and still dance comfortably. Training does help you to cope

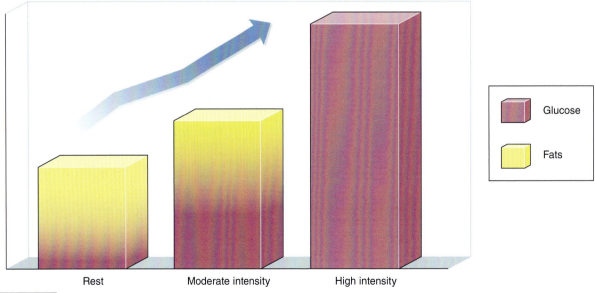

Figure 7.2 Relative relationship between intensity and energy use.

Figure designed by Derrick D. Brown.

with dancing soon after eating, but if you know it will be very high intensity, expect that digestion will slow until intensity reduces again.

For preclass and performance periods, follow these guidelines: If possible allow at least an hour between eating and class or rehearsals. For performances it is better to have a relatively empty stomach, but not be hungry, thus for most people the ideal time to start a performance will be between 2 and 4 hours after a meal.

Finally, guidelines also exist for post-performance recovery strategies; in particular, these guidelines have a protein focus. Refuel with both carbs and protein after intensive classes, rehearsals, and performances, using the first 45-minute window. One option is to use milk, yogurt, or soy equivalents together with a fruit and, if needed, also add some whole-grain bread to get the refueling process underway. It is best at this point to use foods that will be digested quickly enough to fuel the muscles while they are still most receptive, but still maintaining good quality. You should not eat empty calories such as candy at this point. As a target try to take in 1 gram of carbs per kilogram (2.2 lb) of body weight from the day's total carbohydrate intake, plus around 20 grams of extra protein after a difficult class or rehearsal. You can get 20 grams of protein from a piece of chicken or fish or about 500 ml (17 oz.) of milk. Table 7.4 provides information to help you make choices about different types of carbohydrate for the activities you undertake.

This section has examined the relationship between energy use and dance. The need to prefuel and refuel as well as the intensity of your activity will influence how you time your meals for dance events throughout your day so that intake and output are kept in balance.

Challenges to Maintaining Good Nutrition

When discussing health and nutrition, often people do not equate it with money. Yet for most students, lack of sufficient funds for nutritious meals can be a real problem. Students living at home while studying simply rely on home-cooked meals and may not have considered nutritional value or cost. Those living away from home have it harder; many might have only learned to make toast or boil an egg. Most dancers face the dual challenge of limited budget for buying food and little time for preparing good food. The wise dancer will protect the food budget when money is tight, and get skilled at cooking speedy but nutritious recipes in several portions so as to freeze several portions for a future date. Table 7.5 shows 5 days of sample meals that are both easy to make and economical. Portion sizes are not defined; they depend on the individual dancer.

Dietary Supplements

Use of dietary supplements is common in the general population. Research has revealed that at least half of the population in the United States and Europe uses some kind of supplementation. Similar trends have been seen in athletes and in dancers. In

Table 7.4 Practical Guide to Maintaining Energy Levels: Carbohydrate Choices

Carbohydrates	Hydrating drinks	Simple carbs	Starchy foods	Fruits and vegetables
When	Toward the end of dance class; during heavy rehearsals; or during long demanding performances	Sparingly	As part of each main meal—1/4 to 1/3 of your plate or within an hour after a large dance event	Recommended serving sizes: At least 1-2 types per meal with each meal
Example	Water, low-sugar or sugar free noncarbonated drinks with added electrolytes are suitable for drinking at all times. If rehearsals, performances, or classes are long and demanding consider isotonic (sports) drinks to sustain energy.	Sports drinks Commercial breakfast cereals Soda Fruit Juice Table sugar Sugary desserts Ice cream Muffins, bagels, sugar rich snacks	Breads Pasta (whole grain) Rice (whole grain) Potatoes (including sweet) Oats (whole) Cereal grains (wheat, rye, etc.)	Spinach Carrots Tomatoes Broccoli Cauliflower Apples Oranges Avocados Berries

Table 7.5 **Sample Economical and Balanced Meals**

	Day 1	Day 2	Day 3	Day 4	Day 5
Breakfast	Oat porridge made with milk or milk substitute together with fruit or dried fruit, and nuts/nut butter/seeds	Polenta-style porridge (grits) made with milk or milk substitute together with a tablespoon of Greek-style yogurt with fruit or dried fruit, and nuts	Skinny egg sandwich: 1 whole egg, 1 egg white, mushrooms, onions, tomatoes seasonings, rolled in a flour or corn tortilla for easy transport	Rice porridge made with milk or milk substitute together with fruit or dried fruit, and nuts	Nut/seed butter with whole-grain toast, a banana, and a glass of milk or milk substitute
Lunch	Whole-grain pasta salad with tuna and egg / Fruit and yogurt	Rice salad with egg and mixed beans / Fruit and yogurt	Whole-grain cheese salad sandwiches with vegetable soup / Fruit	Quinoa salad with chicken / Fruit and yogurt	Homemade lentil and vegetable soup with whole-grain bread / Yogurt
Dinner	Chicken stir-fry with brown rice and vegetables / Fruit and yogurt	Mackerel or salmon with potatoes and vegetables / Fruit and yogurt	Baked potato with chili con carne / Side salad / Fruit and yogurt	Omelet with baked sweet potato and vegetables / Fruit and yogurt	Pasta Bolognese with vegetables or salad / Fruit and yogurt

some cases, temporary use of supplements might be warranted. In other situations, continued use of certain supplements can have long-term consequences that may compromise health and well-being.

A study of dancers and their supplement use revealed that the major motives for supplement use were to improve health, boost immunity, and reduce fatigue. However 45 percent believed that dancing increased the need for supplementation, while 30 percent recognized that risks were associated with nutritional supplementation. Supplements were mainly obtained from pharmacies, supermarkets, and health food stores. With regard to getting information about which supplements to use, many dancers received their information from either colleagues or their teachers. While friends and teachers may offer good advice, professionals with training in the field of nutrition can provide a more comprehensive overview of supplementation. For example, a sport nutritionist may provide information on supplements that may work for performance. Always check on the background of a nutritionist. While a registered dietitian will always be fully qualified (although not many will be specialized in dance), the word "nutritionist" is open to use by anyone in many countries. In addition, some are actually employed by supplement companies, so they are likely to be biased and not use the best research to advise you. In contrast, a clinical dietitian can provide an in-depth assess-

ment of how supplementation works in relation to general health both on- and offstage. Supplements can be particularly important in dancers who are recovering from injuries or young dancers who are still in their growing years.

In terms of motivation for dietary supplementation use, the study suggests that a large majority of dancers ingested supplements for general health: 81% of males versus 79% of females. Males to a greater extent than females perceived that supplementation improved performance, citing the benefits as energy improvement (60%). Female dancers perceived benefits focused more on compensation for an inadequate diet (24%) and as a weight or fat loss mechanism (14%). Elite dancers would no doubt benefit from individual consultations with health care professionals who are knowledgeable in dietary supplementation specific to dancers.

Keep in mind that supplementation is not without risk. Recent investigation into supplements found that only one out of five products contained what the label mentioned. So, you might be ingesting more or less than you bargained for. Contamination is perhaps the most dangerous problem, especially when purchasing products that are cheap or from companies with substandard quality control. These examples provide more reasons to seek out a health care professional if you believe you have a health-related reason to start supplementation.

Maintaining a Healthy Weight

From the moment you were born, you were weighed, and thus your preoccupation with weight might be forgiven, as it has become a natural part of your life. It is, however, important to recognize that worrying about your weight is at best a nuisance and at worst a disease. As difficult as it is to believe, the number you see on the scale is just a number. For this reason, many professionals speak of body composition and not body weight. They are interested not just in weight but also height, frame size, and how the body is functioning. The body is composed of no fewer than five components that go into weight: water, fat, protein, glycogen, and minerals (mainly calcium and phosphorous, mostly in bone). Humans are complex and need not be reduced to one type or one number.

The first question to consider is whether weight is really what you need to think about. There are no weight categories in dance as there are in sports like judo or rowing, in which you need to be under or over a particular weight. In dance you need a fit, healthy body that can perform the dance style of choice. If looking in the mirror makes you think you need to be thinner, first check with a trusted teacher or medical practitioner who is familiar with dance and discuss whether or not you are being overly critical of your body. It may be that you need more muscle, in which case you would need to review your exercise program overall. If you tend to build overly bulky muscles, losing pounds will not achieve your goal. In this case, you would need to get advice on working differently to reach your goal. If after careful consideration and taking suitable advice you are sure you need to see the number on the scale change, then there are further points to consider before changing your food and fluid choices.

It is normal for your weight to vary by a few pounds from one day to another without the amount of muscle or fat changing significantly. This variation occurs because of water fluctuations and changes in the glycogen (carbohydrate) content of the body. It is normal to weigh less first thing in the morning, before eating and drinking, and for weight to increase through the day. To get a true view of what is happening if you do feel it is necessary to step on a scale, you will need to compare your weight from one day to another at the same time of day. Later in the day the heavier weight just reflects food and drink that have yet to be processed by the body, not a gain in body fat.

It might be useful to note that 2 pounds (0.9 kg) of body fat is the equivalent of around 7000 calories (kcal). So, to lose 1 pound (0.45 kg) in a week means burning off around 500 kcal per day more than you take in (adding up to 3500 kcal in a week). This energy is the equivalent of 25 teaspoons of sugar each day. In food terms, it would be a very large piece of cake or a sandwich and a yogurt each day. You can achieve weight changes while staying healthy, with good enough energy levels and without lacking in minerals such as calcium and iron, but it requires education, planning, and patience. When making changes to your food intake, always look to cut out less helpful high-sugar/high-fat foods such as candy, chocolate, cake, cookies, sugary drinks, and crisps (chips), and avoid fried foods and other high-fat choices as well as alcoholic beverages before reducing other foods. If you find it difficult not to look for progress on the scale, keep weighing to a maximum of twice a week or you are likely to become disappointed with the fluctuations.

The issues of weight and health are important topics for dancers, as the culture and aesthetic of dance often makes dancers believe that they are overweight. Managing your weight, and arriving at a lean body composition, is possible within a healthy nutritional intake.

Summary

Your nutrition is as important to your development as a dancer as your classes and your outside conditioning program. Nutrition affects every aspect of you, including physical, psychological, and emotional health. You need to take in all of the macro- and micronutrients that have been described, as well as enough calories to have energy for your dancing. You may decide to take dietary supplements, but seek advice from a qualified professional before making that decision. If you think intelligently about your food choices and maintain a healthy body composition rather than a specific weight, you will have a healthy, strong body for dancing.

For 1 week, observe and record the food that you see others around you eating. At the end of the week, place the food items in various categories, such as protein, carbohydrate, and fat. Then go back and look at the recommended amounts of these foods discussed in this chapter that people should be eating. Do you see any general deficiencies? Do you think those you are observing eat a balanced and nutritious diet? Remember that peer choices can be very powerful in influencing your choices, so this activity may help you realize some of the potential barriers to achieving a healthy diet.

Review Questions

1. What are macronutrients and micronutrients? Describe the various types of these nutrients.

2. Why is hydration important for dancers?

3. What are the risks of having poor nutrition?

4. How can you develop healthy eating habits for your body's needs?

 For chapter-specific supplemental learning activities, study aids, suggested readings, web links, and more, visit the web resource at www.HumanKinetics.com/DancerWellness.

Bone Health

Shannon Sterne, MS, and Christina Patsalidou, MFA

Photo courtesy of Thomas Sawyer.

Key Terms

anorexia nervosa
articular cartilage
bone marrow
cancellous bone
cartilage
cartilaginous joints
collagen
compact bone
endosteum
epiphyseal plate
epiphyses
fibrous joints
flat bones
interosseous membrane
irregular bones
joint cavity
joint stability
kinetic chains
long bones
medullary cavity
ossification
osteoblasts
osteoporosis
periosteum
remodeling
sesamoid bones
short bones
synovial fluid
synovial joints

LEARNING OBJECTIVES

After reading this chapter, you will be able to do the following:

> Describe the various bone structures and joints of the body.

> Understand the elements and physical activities that enhance bone formation.

> Identify elements and dance activities that may negatively impact bone and joint health.

> Discuss why warming up and proper stretching are important for joints and bones.

The body's ability to bend at various sites, stand upright, and twist the spine allows dancers to create complex shapes and movements such as balance on one foot, extend a leg in various directions, turn in various positions, and jump in the air. The architecture of the human skeleton enables dancers to show extraordinary lines onstage, to communicate meanings without speaking, and to express emotions that no words could describe. Bones, joints, and muscles are structured in a magnificent way that allows you endless possibilities for movement choices.

This chapter outlines the structure and function of the skeletal system, with emphasis on bone and joint development and maintenance in relation to health. Additional topics include key components of bones and joints, along with main factors and elements that affect their health, such as a nutritionally balanced diet and the role of physical activity. Further, the chapter explains how these subjects relate directly to dancers and their physical needs. Finally, the chapter helps you appreciate the main risks along with required strategies needed for the wellness of dancers' bones and joints.

Bone Structure

Your body has fewer bones today than you had when you were born. At birth, the human skeleton is composed of nearly 300 soft bones. During childhood and adolescence, these bones grow in size, change shape, and harden, and many of them fuse together. The resulting adult human skeleton consists of 206 individual bones, as shown in figure 8.1, and throughout life they change size and shape in order to better serve their functions.

Functions, Categories, and Structures of Bones

Bones have five different functions:

1. support,
2. protection,
3. movement,
4. blood cell production, and
5. mineral storage.

Bones provide the structural framework to give the body form; without the supportive structure of bones, the body would collapse. Some bones protect internal organs and other tissues. For example, the rib cage protects the heart, and the pelvis protects the reproductive organs. Bones also allow for movement by serving as attachment points for muscles. When muscles contract, they can move bones, thus producing movement. Many bones contain a specialized tissue called red bone marrow, which is responsible for the production of red blood cells. These blood cells are responsible for transporting oxygen to tissues throughout the body. Finally, because bones are made primarily of minerals, they can be broken down to provide these minerals to the body when dietary intake is low. While most bones share these generalized functions, the unique shape and size of each bone helps it to serve particular needs in the body.

Bones are classified into five categories according to their shape, as seen in figure 8.2. Each shape allows the bone to function in a particular way in the body. These categories include:

1. long,
2. short,
3. flat,
4. irregular, and
5. sesamoid bones.

Long bones are longer than they are wide, and they are important in allowing for movement. The bones of the legs, arms, fingers, and toes are examples of long bones. Because they must support the entire body when standing, the bones of the legs are larger and stronger than those of the arms. **Short bones** are shaped like small dice. They are found in the wrists and ankles, and they allow for complex and detailed

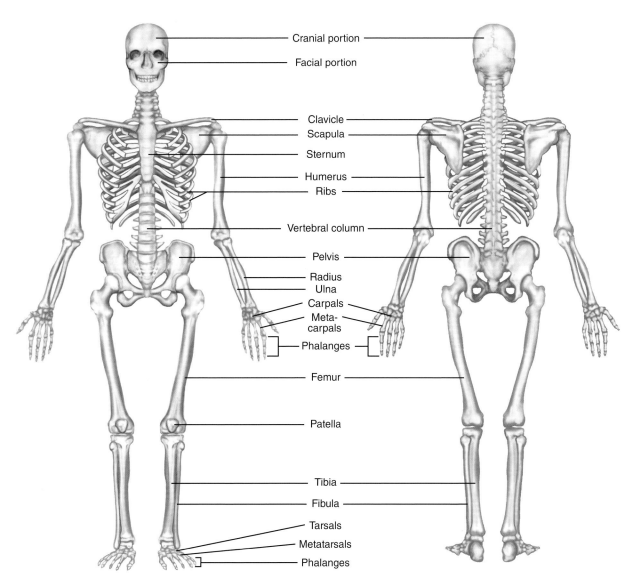

Figure 8.1 The human skeleton.

movements. **Flat bones** typically surround and protect organs. For example, the flat bones that form the skull protect the brain, and the ribs protect the lungs. **Irregular bones** have complex shapes, and they do not fit into any of the previous categories of bone. Their shapes are specialized for specific purposes. For example, the vertebrae protect the spinal cord while allowing for complex movements ranging from a cambré to an arabesque. **Sesamoid bones** are unique because they are embedded within tendons. They help to protect the tendon and to make movement more effortless. The patella (kneecap) is an example of a sesamoid bone. Two additional tiny sesamoid bones are located under the ball of the foot near the big toe.

Although bones vary tremendously in their shapes, they share a similar and complex internal structure. Most people see bones only in museums or in photographs. Often the bones you encounter have been fossilized; they appear dead, rigid, and unchanging. They are rigid because of their high mineral content. Although it may be difficult to imagine, bones are in fact living tissues undergoing continual changes in response to dietary intake, the body's needs, and the demands placed on the body.

The main structural components of bone are **collagen** (a type of connective tissue), which holds the internal structure of the bone together, and minerals, such as calcium, phosphorus, and magnesium, which provide bones with their strength and rigidity.

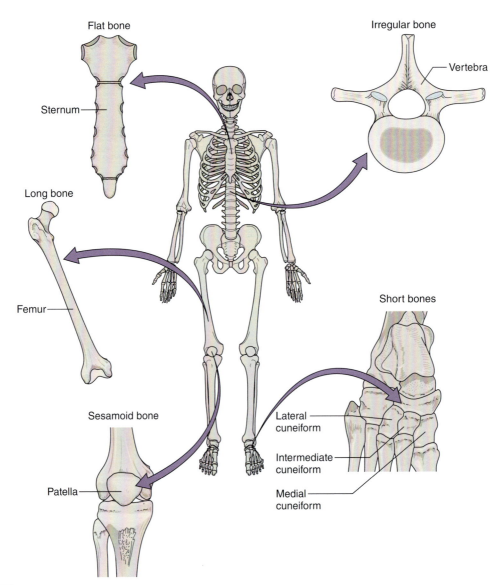

Figure 8.2 Five categories of bones by shape.

© 1999-2016, Rice University. Except where otherwise noted, content created on this site is licensed under a Creative Commons Attribution 4.0 License. http://cnx.org/contents/8x7YlLHu@4/Bone-Classification

Bones consist of several layers, which are shown in the cross-section of a long bone in figure 8.3.

A thin, slippery layer of specialized connective tissue called **articular cartilage** covers the ends of the bones where they come into contact with other bones. The articular cartilage allows the bones to glide more smoothly when moving. With the exception of the cartilage, the entire bone is covered in a hard, dense outer shell made of **compact bone** (also called cortical bone), providing the bone with strength and stiffness. Covering the compact bone is a very thin membrane called the **periosteum**, which contains specialized cells that create new bone. The periosteum also contains numerous blood vessels, which supply the bone with oxygen and nutrients. A similar lining, the **endosteum**, lines the open space inside the bone, the **medullary cavity**. The ends of long bones are filled with **cancellous bone** (also called trabecular bone). This spongy tissue has open spaces that allow the bone to absorb shock and to be more lightweight. If the skeleton were made entirely of compact bone, it would be far too heavy to move! Both the medullary cavity and the cancellous bone are filled with a soft fatty tissue called **bone marrow**. Red bone marrow is responsible for making new red blood cells.

Long bones have these two distinct regions: the shaftlike diaphysis made of hard compact bone

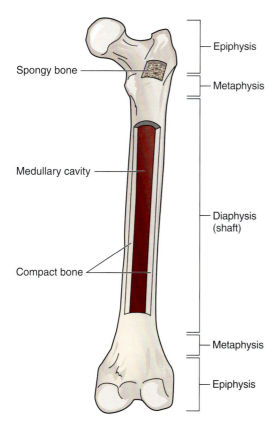

Spongy bone

Epiphysis

Metaphysis

Medullary cavity

Diaphysis (shaft)

Compact bone

Metaphysis

Epiphysis

Figure 8.3 Cross-section of a long bone.

https://commons.wikimedia.org/wiki/File:Structure_of_a_Long_Bone. png. Blausen.com staff. "Blausen gallery 2014". *Wikiversity Journal of Medicine.* DOI:10.15347/wjm/2014.010. ISSN 20018762

18; however, ossification slows down significantly, and new bone formation essentially stops after age 30. Thus, the adolescent dancer must build up strong bones early in life. Consider bone health as a retirement plan; build up bone tissue and deposit minerals into the bone when you are young and the process is very rapid, so that after age 30, you have a high peak bone mass to sustain strong bones for the remainder of your life.

EMPOWERMENT

Build Strong Bones

You can take charge of your bone health through some simple and practical strategies. Make sure your diet is built on sound nutritional information, including the nutrients your bones need, such as certain vitamins and minerals. Stay physically active during the times you are not dancing between seasons. If you smoke, find a program that will assist you in quitting. Limit your daily intake of caffeine, including coffee, tea, and caffeinated soft drinks. The practices you develop today will have a huge impact on your bone health later in life.

Elements That Enhance Bone Formation

Many factors, including genetic and environmental factors, can influence bone health. While genetics are largely responsible for determining the size, strength, and quality of bones, environmental factors such as diet and physical activity also impact bone growth and development. You can modify many of these environmental factors, including dietary intake, energy availability, and physical activity, in order to enhance bone formation during childhood and adolescence.

Vitamins and Minerals

Bone is composed of mainly the minerals calcium and phosphorus. Approximately 98 percent of the body's total calcium and approximately 90 percent of the body's total phosphorus are stored in the bones. When a short supply of calcium exists in the blood because of insufficient consumption through diet, the body can remove calcium from its stores in bone. Too many withdrawals can weaken the bone, thus making it vulnerable to stresses that can cause fractures.

Calcium intake during all ages is of critical importance. For the adolescent dancer, calcium intake of 1,300 mg per day is necessary in order to assure a

and the **epiphyses**, which are the enlarged ends of the bone made chiefly of cancellous bone. The two regions are separated by **epiphyseal plates** (also called growth plates). During childhood and adolescence, these plates are made up of cartilage, which allows the bones to grow in length. Toward the end of puberty (between ages of 15 and 25), the cartilage is replaced with bone, effectively closing the growth plates and preventing further growth in height.

Although bones cease to grow in size after about age 25, they do continuously undergo a lifelong process called **remodeling**, in which old bone tissue is removed from the skeleton, and is recycled and replaced by new tissue. During childhood and adolescence, new bone is formed by a process called **ossification** at a much faster rate than it is broken down. Ossification continues to outpace bone breakdown until peak bone mass (maximal bone size and strength) is reached. Approximately 90 to 95 percent of peak bone mass is attained by age 18 in females and 20 in males. Bones will continue to harden and increase in density after age sufficient supply of calcium in the blood. Vitamin D is another micronutrient that plays a significant role in bone health. Other important vitamins that play a key role in bone health are vitamins A, C, and K. Vitamin A plays an essential role in the development of the bone-building cells, called **osteoblasts**, and in the process of calcium absorption and metabolism. Low vitamin A levels are associated with poor bone growth and increased risk of fractures. Vitamin C is also essential for healthy bones. It assists in the formation of collagen, stimulates the cells that build bone, and enhances calcium absorption. Vitamin K contributes to the production of collagen, which is a component of cartilage, connective tissue, and bone.

The minerals that play a significant role in bone health are phosphorous, potassium, magnesium, zinc, and manganese. Phosphorous, often adequately taken through the diet, affects bone health because of its role in the mineralization of the soft osteoid bone. Potassium also affects bone health. It is a key mineral for dancers with eating disorders; if inadequately taken through diet, bone loss and cardiac problems can occur. Therefore, dancers should include in their diet enough fruits, vegetables, and legumes to assure the proper intake of potassium. Magnesium also has a role to play in supporting bone health. Magnesium is essential for the absorption and metabolism of calcium and helps in the preservation of bone mass. Adequate magnesium intake through the diet thus is essential, because it is also needed for the conduction of nerve impulses to the heart and other parts of the body. In bone metabolism, zinc is needed for the production of the collagen protein and is also necessary for the production of enzymes that degrade recycled worn-out bits of bone protein. Proper calcium absorption and bone healing also depends on zinc. Like zinc, manganese is a trace element that can profoundly affect bone health. Recent research has indicated the special role of manganese in the formation of bone cartilage, bone collagen, and bone mineralization. **Osteoporosis** is a condition in which bones become weak, porous, and brittle due to a loss of calcium and other mineral components, and fractures become much more likely. It is a progressive disease and is often referred to as the silent thief, because bone loss occurs without initial symptoms. Early detection of bone loss through screenings and medical checkups is critical. Results can lead to changes in diet and exercise that focus on increasing bone strength and lower risk of fractures. For additional information on sources of vitamins and minerals and how they are used in the body, see chapter 7.

SELF-AWARENESS
Know Your Bone Health
Are you at risk for weak bones and osteoporosis later in life? Can you take steps now to become aware of the possibility of developing this condition? First, explore possible family history of osteoporosis. To find out if it runs in your family, begin with information about your biological grandparents. Did they have osteoporosis? Second, if you are a woman experiencing delayed or irregular periods, see a doctor; a dietary or hormonal reason could exist for this condition. Delayed periods are related to a lack of estrogen, which is necessary for calcium absorption and therefore important for bone health. Third, did you have incidents of childhood fractures or do you currently have stress fractures? The answers to these questions could be warning signs of bone issues. The more aware you are of your potential for problems, the more you can do now to prevent them.

Hormones

Various hormones control or influence the metabolic activity of bones. Three calcium-regulating hormones are instrumental in producing healthy bone. *Parathyroid hormone* maintains the level of calcium and stimulates both breakdown and formation of bone. In addition, *calcitriol* (the hormone derived from vitamin D) stimulates the intestines to absorb enough calcium and phosphorus and also affects bone directly. Finally, *calcitonin* inhibits bone breakdown and may protect against excessively high levels of calcium in the blood.

Along with calcium-regulating hormones, sex hormones have been known to affect the bone mineral density directly and indirectly according to fluctuations in their levels. Both the female hormone estrogen and the male hormone testosterone have direct effects on bone growth and development. Produced by the ovaries during childhood and early puberty, estrogen can increase bone growth. This process is impaired when a dancer has low weight resulting from intensive exercise and calorie restriction, and it is particularly pertinent to an adolescent dancer who has disordered eating. Sometimes an aesthetic that emphasizes thinness is imposed on a dancer, and it can lead to extreme dieting and weight loss regimens. Consequently, depending on age it may cause menstrual dysfunction in the form of delayed menarche, which is also known as primary amenorrhea; secondary amenorrhea is the absence of menstrual cycles lasting more than 3 months, and oligomenorrhea refers to infrequent menstrual cycles over a period of time. The window of maximizing peak bone mass during adolescence is diminished in such circumstances. Particularly, evidence shows that delayed menarche, frequently seen in dancers who start intensive training in childhood, has an effect on bone growth in the spinal column and increases the risk of developing scoliosis.

Physical Activity

Physical activity plays a critical role in bone health. Specifically, the shape of bones is determined by the pull of the attached muscles and the density, and strength of the bones is largely impacted by the mechanical stresses of physical activity. Bones respond to the stress of physical activity by increasing ossification, and thus increasing bone mineral density. High-impact activities, including dance, provide mechanical stress to stimulate bone growth. Conversely, when little or no stress is applied to the skeleton, bone breakdown occurs at an increased rate. For example, astronauts may lose as much as 10 percent of their bone mineral density in just 6 months living in zero-gravity environments. Bed rest and inactivity take a similar toll on the body and cause bone strength to diminish rapidly.

Most dance activities stress the bones of the lower body, pelvis, and legs. Therefore, bone strength and density are more developed in the lower limbs compared to the spine and upper extremities. To increase total body bone density and to strengthen all of the bones of the body, dancers should cross-train with activities that impact the upper extremities. Gymnastics, martial arts, volleyball, and strength training with weights or resistance bands are examples of activities that have been shown to improve total-body bone density. For more information on conditioning and cross-training, see chapter 3.

Elements That Diminish Bone Mineral Density

Dancers often engage in behaviors that can counteract the benefits of their physical training on bone health. Insufficient caloric and nutrient intake associated with patterns of disordered eating result in low body mass. Smoking, high caffeine and alcohol intake, and some medications can also negatively affect bone mineral density. Controlling these factors is essential to improving bone health. Even small changes in bone density can significantly reduce risk of bone diseases and fractures.

Restriction of energy over a prolonged period of time is responsible for health problems such as pubertal delay and irregularities in the menstrual cycle. When the body weight is extremely low, the regulatory systems of the human body are impaired and can lead to insufficient bone growth and weakening of the bones.

Low caloric intake usually includes insufficient amounts of other vitamins and minerals important in the bone modeling and remodeling process. Thus, dancers who are engaged in a vigorous training regimen and restrict their nutrient intake have a higher risk for diminished bone mineral density and an increased risk for bone fractures. Dancers who are prone to disordered

The dance skills using the arms for weight bearing in street dance help build bone density in the upper extremities.

Photo courtesy of Jake Pett.

eating or have eating disorders are the most susceptible to impairing bone health.

Some medical conditions influence bone health because of either the medical disease itself or the medication prescribed for the disease. Diabetes mellitus (type 1 and type 2 diabetes), a chronic disease associated with abnormally high levels of glucose in the blood is one condition that can influence bone health. Another example is **anorexia nervosa**, a complex eating disorder characterized by excessive dieting that results in an abnormal low body weight. Use of glucocorticoids (often used for the treatment of asthma and arthritis) has been identified as a cause of bone disease.

Smoking can have detrimental effects on your health as a dancer. In relation to bone health, smoking decreases bone mineral density in various ways. Among others, smoking can have indirect effects on bone health by lowering the amount of calcium absorption in the body, altering the handling of vitamin D, and by influencing estrogen and other hormone metabolism necessary for the healthy process of bone breakdown and formation. Smoking can also have a direct toxic effect on bone cells. If you are a dancer you are highly encouraged to quit smoking to improve general health and reach optimum performance. Research has shown that smoking cessation can partially reverse the negative effects of smoking on bone health. For similar reasons, high consumption of alcohol can inhibit the bone remodeling process, thus making the bones weaker and vulnerable to stress fractures later on in life. Therefore, lowering alcohol consumption is recommended for dancer wellness. Check to see if there is a counseling center at your school that can assist you in changing these habitual behaviors.

Physical Activities That Enhance Bone Formation

Physical activity plays an important role in bone health. Physical activity can influence peak bone mass during adolescence and has a protective effect in all ages. Research indicates that childhood and adolescent years give opportunities to maximize bone mass and strength. Exercise during these periods, particularly weight-bearing and muscle-strengthening activities, increase bone mineralization over a short term and, if sustained, it may lead to higher peak bone mass in young adults, reducing fracture risks in later life.

The following exercise guidelines, based on recent scientific evidence, can help you enhance bone formation and lower the risk of developing osteoporosis later on in life:

> Bone density is affected by the mechanical stress produced by the forces generated during the various physical activities. The bones respond directly to the mechanical stresses placed on them by laying down more calcium and becoming stronger. For example, for a tennis player the arm bones of the dominant side most likely show an increased bone density. Runners and dancers may show an increased bone density in the lower leg bones.

> Research shows that in order to increase bone mass, these mechanical stresses need to be greater than the ones bone usually experiences. Thus, an increase in load during weight-bearing activities should be done at frequent intervals. For example, if dancers include weight training in their supplemental activities, the weights should be gradually increased over time.

> High-impact, high-intensity weight-bearing activities such as jumping, jogging, and hiking have been proven beneficial for developing and maintaining strong bones. Fortunately, jumping is always included in a dance technique class. Evidence has shown that even 5 to 10 minutes of jumping can increase bone mass. To create even increases in bone mass, a jumping sequence on the right side always needs to be repeated on the left. Cross training with high-intensity, weight-bearing activities such as jogging or climbing stairs will improve both cardiovascular fitness and bone density. Aim to engage in such activities for at least 30 minutes, 5 days per week.

> Because physical activity only affects bone at the skeletal sites that are stressed or loaded by the activity, dancers need to include in their training regimen weight-bearing activities that are usually not emphasized in the dance technique class. Because jumps are always within the structure of a typical dance class and are proved to be as effective as any activity that imparts impact, incorporating weight-bearing activities stressing the bones of the upper body is beneficial. It is not to say that a complete regimen will only involve upper body, it has to include stressing the bones of the whole body. Pilates, yoga, or tai chi classes not only make your bones and muscles stronger but also improve your balance, coordination, posture, and flexibility as well as reduce stress and anxiety.

> Endurance activity still plays a significant role in skeletal health by increasing muscle mass and strength, balance, and coordination. These skills and characteristics are already major concerns for improving technique. However, the risk of fractures during class and rehearsals still exists, especially if you are stressed, undernourished, dehydrated, or

fatigued. Therefore, protect the health of your bones by taking precautions to prevent falls during training sessions. Get enough rest and proper nutrition, and stay aerobically fit.

› Complete lack of activity, such as during illness or a period of recovery following an injury, causes bone loss. Therefore, you should still be engaged in daily weight-bearing movements when capable without stressing the part of the body that is injured. For example, if you sprain an ankle, you can still perform movement that does not require standing or using the injured leg; lifting weights while seated or using elastic bands for your arms and noninjured leg are good examples.

The human skeleton provides the body with a frame that allows for mobility and for protection against injury. Each of the 206 bones in your body changes size and shape throughout your life in order to better serve its function. Although bones make up the rigid structure of the body, their architecture as a whole provides the body with mobility. It is of crucial importance that you know how to keep your bones healthy. Optimizing peak bone mass during childhood, adolescence, and early adulthood can provide long-term prevention of stress fractures during your dance career. When designing a personalized wellness plan, consider these guidelines that contribute to bone health:

› Consume a well-balanced diet with enough calories and nutrients. See chapter 7 for more information about maintaining a well-balanced diet.

› Increase your calcium bank account in your bones by consuming at least three servings of low-fat or fat-free dairy products, such as 1 cup of milk or yogurt, 30 grams of hard cheese, and 60 grams of soft cheese. In the case of a vegan dancer, consume other foods that are high in calcium such as spinach, tofu, broccoli, kale, edamame, figs, oranges, fortified cereal, and almonds. If you and your doctor determine that you need a calcium supplement, choose one that contains vitamin D, which aids in absorption of calcium.

› Make sure you get at least 15 minutes of sunlight exposure every day. In addition, include in your diet some foods containing vitamin D such as salmon, canned tuna, trout, mackerel, and egg yolk, as well as fortified milk, orange juice, and cereal.

› Dancers with very low weight or disordered eating should seek advice from a dietitian and a physician in order to safeguard bone health. In addition, consult a doctor if you do not menstruate properly; a dancer who has not had a period for 6 months, or has had irregular periods for over a year, should also seek medical help.

› Limit your caffeine intake to one cup of coffee per day. Avoid smoking, and limit alcohol intake. If you have a medical condition or you are taking medication that may affects bone health, seek help from a health professional.

› Physical activity plays a significant role in bone health. Include activities that involve impact three to five times a week, because they are most useful for increasing or maintaining bone mass. Weight-bearing activities should be included in the training regimen two to three times per week by increasing weight loads at different sites of your body. High-intensity cardiovascular exercise sessions should also be included in your training

The high-impact steps of tap dance enhance bone density in the lower extremities.

Photo courtesy of Jake Pett.

regimen. Complete lack of activity causes bone loss. When it is not possible to avoid immobility, even brief daily weight-bearing movements can help to reduce bone loss.

Healthy bones are important to your overall wellness as a dancer. How you eat, rest, and move contribute to the health and development of your bones. Disordered eating is particularly harmful to bones in the early and adolescent years. As you read the next section on joints, continue to think about how your personal habits might be improved to enhance the health of your skeleton.

SETTING GOALS

Improve Your Bone Health

Think about your daily food and beverage intake. Are you getting enough of the necessary nutrients for bone health? What might you add to your diet to ensure enough calcium and vitamin D? Over the next several weeks, make it a goal to monitor your nutrient intake and ensure enough of the necessary foods and liquids are in your daily dietary plan. Second, if you are not doing enough weight-bearing exercise, particularly for the upper extremities, make it one of your goals to add these exercises to your conditioning plan.

Joint Structure

Bones provide rigid structural support for the body, and they are connected to one another in a variety of ways to provide a framework for the body and allow for purposeful movement. However, bones cannot create movement on their own. All human activities, including dance, rely on the effective interaction of bones, muscles, and connective tissues to move the joints optimally for dance activities.

Components of Joints

Muscles connect bones to one another through specialized connective tissues called tendons, and muscle contractions provide the force necessary to move the bones. The movement itself occurs at the connection between the bones, called a joint (or articulation). The body has many types of joints; some allow a great deal of movement, and others permit almost no movement but rather are designed for stabilization and shock absorption. The joints that allow the greatest range of motion are called **synovial joints** (also called moveable joints).

In synovial joints, the bones are not directly connected to one another. Instead, they have a small space between them, called a **joint cavity**, surrounded by a synovial membrane, which is filled with fluid to lubricate and nourish the joint. This **synovial fluid** has a consistency similar to egg whites, and it responds to temperature changes in the body. When the body is at rest, the fluid is thickened and range of motion is reduced. Warming up the body raises the heart rate, muscle temperature, and core body temperature. In addition, it thins the synovial fluid, allowing the joint to move with less resistance. A brief warm-up before any physical activities is beneficial for this and many other reasons.

Inside the joint cavity the ends of the articulating bones are covered with **cartilage**. Cartilage is a hard, slippery layer of tissue that allows the bones to glide smoothly over one another and prevents the bones from rubbing directly against each other. Healthy cartilage is well-lubricated, durable, and somewhat elastic for shock absorption.

In addition to the cartilage covering the ends of the bones, some joints have other specialized structures in place to help stabilize the joint or absorb shock. Such structures include the labrum (found in the hip and the shoulder) and the meniscus of the knee. Both of these structures help the bones fit together correctly, adding to the stabilization of the joint. Located outside of the joint cavity, bursae help to protect the tendons around a joint. These specialized pads reduce friction and prevent tendons from being irritated as they pass over bones.

The bone structure of most joints is reinforced by ligaments, specialized connective tissues that directly connect bones to one another. Ligaments are strong, nonelastic bands of tissue that limit range of motion in order to stabilize the joint. The knee is an example of a joint that relies heavily on ligaments to stabilize the joint.

Types of Joints and How They Function

You may notice that some joints move more freely than others, and that some joints can move in multiple directions while others have limited actions. Consider the movements possible by your elbow. You can bend (flex) your elbow, and you can straighten (extend) it. Now consider your shoulder. The shoulder joint allows motions in virtually all directions. These differences in range of motion are largely due to the structure of the bones and how they fit together. Synovial joints are classified by the shape of the joint and the range of motion permitted at the joint. For a review of the six types of synovial joints, see chapter 2.

In addition to synovial joints, the body contains two other types of joints: fibrous joints and cartilaginous joints. **Fibrous joints** allow little or no movement. These types of joints hold together the bones of the skull and also serve to connect, reinforce, and strengthen bones. For example, the two bones of the forearm are held together by a specialized fibrous joint called an **interosseous membrane**. **Cartilaginous joints** act as shock absorbers. The discs between the vertebrae of the spine function in this way and also allow for increased movement in the spine.

While much of the function and stability of a joint is dictated by the shape of the bones, other factors also influence the range of motion allowed at a joint. **Joint stability** is the ability to control joint range of motion or position. Both an arabesque turn and a leap require control of multiple joints to maintain the clarity and form of the movement and to execute the step without faltering. Without appropriate control of the joints, the leg may drop in the arabesque turn or the ankle may twist landing the leap. In dance classes, muscles are strengthened and neuromuscular control is developed to improve joint stability, but dancers are also encouraged to perform movements at extreme range of motion. Because extreme range of motion is desired for many dance forms, dancers frequently stretch to increase flexibility. Range of motion may be limited by a number of factors. You can safely alter some of these factors with stretching and training, but other restrictions to range of motion cannot be changed without causing damage to the body's tissues.

Joint stability and mobility are related, such that an increase in stability results in a decrease in range of motion, and excessively mobile joints may be difficult to stabilize. The relationship between stability and mobility is impacted by many factors, including the structure of the bones and the joint, ligament length, muscle length, muscle extensibility, and joint capsule tightness. Some, but not all of these factors can be changed over time, leading to increases in range of motion.

The bony architecture of the joint can limit movement and provide structure and stability. For example, when bearing weight on the hips, gravity pushes the head of the femur into a relatively deep socket, the acetabulum. These bones are configured and positioned so that standing enhances the closeness of their fit.

Joint movement can also be limited by soft tissues such as ligaments and muscles. Short ligaments hold bones tightly in place, protecting the integrity of the joint. Ligaments that have been elongated by incorrect stretching or injury do not return to their original length and thus joint stability is compromised; if you have experienced such elongation, you may be at risk of repetitive injuries. In some cases, you can strengthen the muscles surrounding the joint to compensate for the slackness in the ligament. Some people, such as contortionists and flexors, are born with very long ligaments, and developing appropriate muscular strength to protect and stabilize joints is essential for them.

The ability of a muscle to stretch and lengthen is termed muscle extensibility. Most muscles can extend one and a half times their resting length. Short, tight muscles can be trained to improve extensibility. These improvements in flexibility require gentle 30-second stretches, and for optimal effect they should be repeated three times. For more about flexibility training, see chapter 3.

Some joints are tight because of immobility of the entire joint capsule. This immobility is common after injury in which immobilization of the joint is required for recovery. Joint capsule mobilization is often a part of the rehabilitation process following certain types of injuries.

Standards for normal range of motion in each joint have been established in the general population, but researchers are still investigating normal and optimal ranges specific to dancers. Genetics plays a big role in determining the degree to which range of motion may be safely increased. Some people are born with short ligaments and tight muscles that do not extend well. These dancers have the advantage of having very stable joints, which is desirable for partnering and high-impact work such as large jumps.

Other dancers have bodies with joints that can readily move to extreme ranges of motion. Such dancers may have joint hypermobility, sometimes called hypermobility syndrome. They have connective tissue that is structurally different from that of people with typical range of motion. While hypermobility may seem like a great asset in dance, moving beyond anatomical neutral can compromise strength and stability, and very few elite level dancers are hypermobile.

Most professional dancers have ranges of motion that are greater than that of the general population; and many dancers have hypermobility on some of their joints, but are not systemically hypermobile. It is important to know whether you (or your dancers, if you are a teacher) are hypermobile, because stretching and strengthening needs will vary by body type.

Dance Activities That Can Negatively Impact Joint Health

Choreographic demands for greater range of motion appear to be a trend in many dance genres, but pushing too hard to increase range of motion can damage soft tissues and bones alike. The joint problems that dancers experience may be short term, resulting from new choreography or from an acute injury, or they may be chronic and long term. Dance training can result in many chronic joint problems, which may set you up for greater injury or chronic pain. A number of factors can contribute to joint damage.

Joint problems affecting dancers include arthritis; bony deformations such as bone spurs, subluxations, and dislocations; and inflammation of the soft tissues such as bursae and tendons. Joint capsules can be overstretched, and ligaments can be sprained. These injuries are discussed in more detail in chapter 9.

Instability or problems in one joint can lead to problems in other areas of the body. This is because many of the joints of the body are connected by way of **kinetic chains**, which are a combination of a number of joints arranged in a sequence, forming a complex motor pattern. An example of a kinetic chain is the joints involved in a demi-plié: the hip, the knee, and the ankle. All three joints must flex (bend) to create the movement. Because the joints are linked together, a problem in one joint can negatively impact another joint. In the demi-plié, insufficient strength in the muscles that externally rotates (turns out) the hip can lead to inward rolling of the ankle and twisting of the knee. This particular cascade of problems is common in dancers who are required to stand in 180 degrees of turnout regardless of their individual hip structure and muscular strength.

Demanding that dancers attempt to conform to certain technical standards without consideration for individual body type, structure, strength, and physical development can lead to many problems, including damage to joints. Forcing 180 degrees of turnout is one example, but many others exist. Forcing the body to sit in fourth position on the floor in a modern dance class with both sitting bones touching the floor can stress the knees. Beginning to work en pointe before the body and the technique are fully developed can potentially damage growing bones. Pointe work and criteria for starting pointe are described in chapter 9. Some dance technique teachers have traditionally required dancers to stand up so tall and straight that they minimize the naturally occurring curves of the spine and neck. The elimination or minimization of these curves prevents the vertebrae from articulating properly with one another and can lead to overuse of the back extensor muscles, which can lead to back or neck pain.

A posture similar to slouching that is commonly assumed by hypermobile dancers is fatigue posture. In this posture, the dancer leans back while thrusting the hips forward. The result is that instead of using the postural muscles of the core and the spine to hold the torso upright over the pelvis, the torso hangs by ligaments. This error puts undue strain on the ligaments, the vertebrae, and the discs between the vertebrae.

Excessive strain on the ligaments and tendons of the knees may develop in dancers with hyperextended knees if they lock their knees. Hyperextended knees and other misalignments are discussed in more detail in chapter 2. Extreme stretching can damage joints and the surrounding soft tissues and is discussed in detail in chapter 3.

One of the most common and noticeable joint issues is popping and cracking in the joints. This sound is usually nothing to worry about unless the popping is accompanied by pain. The cracking sound occurs when the joint capsule is stretched, and the gasses present in the joint come together to form bubbles. You will notice that you cannot immediately pop that joint again but must instead wait for the gas bubble to dissipate.

Although it is a popular myth, cracking these joints does not lead to arthritis. However, popping and cracking sounds may be the result of arthritis or other damage to the joint. Arthritic joints may crack and grind as a result of the unevenness and roughness of the joint caused by the deterioration of the cartilage. Unlike the popping that results from the gas bubble formation, the popping in arthritic joints usually occurs each time the joint is moved. Other joints may lock up and pop intermittently because damaged tissues get caught in between the joint surfaces. Torn cartilage or a torn labrum may get stuck in this way. If pain or limited range of motion is associated with the movement that produces the sound, then it may be an indication that something needs to be addressed.

In dancers, two very common popping or snapping sounds occur frequently at the hip, called anterior and lateral snapping hip. Both may be associated with pain, and both are caused by tight muscles and therefore readily prevented and treated. These two conditions are described in detail in chapter 9.

Ways to Enhance Joint Health

The best way to ensure healthy joints for years to come is to minimize undue stress on the joints. For dancers, undue stress is a gray area. High extensions, inversions, and contemporary choreography can place the body into positions that stress the joints, and performing these movements may be necessary to fulfill class and rehearsal demands. However, forcing range of motion beyond what is normal for your body will eventually deteriorate the cartilage and other delicate tissue in the joint.

SAFETY TIP

Protect Your Joints

You can take several steps to protect your joints. First, make sure you always warm up. Even on a hot day, joints must be properly lubricated. Second, avoid stretches that tend to stretch ligaments rather than muscles. Remember that once you overstretch a ligament, it will not go back to its original length, leaving the joint unprotected. Third, make sure you have adequate muscle strength, particularly in the upper extremities, to protect your joints during difficult choreography.

There is no substitute for working smart, knowing your body, and understanding its limitations—and everyone has limitations. Even when choreographic demands are not optimal for joint health, you can take steps outside the dance studio to help minimize stress. Following are some additional guidelines for keeping joints healthy.

Use Correct Technique

The normal range of motion for every joint in the body is dictated by structural elements such as bone and joint shape, ligament length, and muscle tightness. Correct technique and biomechanics both in the studio and out keeps joints working within their normal range of motion. This idea applies regardless of the style of dance; you could be doing a brush of the foot to the back in ballet class or extreme spine articulations in street dance. In either situation, poor technique and biomechanics could lead to acute or chronic pain in the low back.

Maintain Proper Posture

You could negatively impact your posture with poor furniture design as well as with postural habits outside of the studio. Many dance instructors forbid leaning on the barres during class for a number of reasons, one being that leaning on the barre promotes slouching when you can be standing tall to strengthen your postural muscles. Check your standing and sitting posture periodically throughout the day to make sure you are not slouching or falling into fatigue posture.

Relax

While fatigue posture can be bad for dancers' bodies, relaxation and restoration are essential. Dancers work their bodies hard, and sore muscles come with the territory in the dance world. Take time to pamper yourself. A bath with Epsom salt not only soothes sore muscles, it can help reduce stress on joints, too. Regular massages have been shown to slightly improve muscle soreness and to profoundly ease stress levels. The stimulation of the relaxation response can also relieve joint stress. Some studies have shown that massage therapy and acupuncture both improve symptoms of osteoarthritis. Chapter 6 provides extensive information on rest, relaxation, and restoration.

Always Warm Up

A proper warm-up is essential for maintaining the normal functioning of joints. A warm-up can be a light jog around the dance studio. If jogging gets boring, mix it up with prances, chassés, squats, and lunges. Start small, and make the movements progressively larger and deeper as you get warmer. Warming up in this way increases the temperature of the active muscles and of the synovial fluid inside the joints, making the fluid less viscous (thick). Warm muscles and joints move more easily. Chapter 3 includes important information about warming up.

Use It or Lose It

The old adage *Use it or lose it* applies to joints, too. If you are not taking regular dance classes over the summer or other seasonal break, be sure to include some form of daily activity. Also, joints move readily when you are young; as you age, they can become stiff and range of motion can decrease. This natural aging process can be amplified with reduced physical activity. To help keep those joints pliable, keep moving—even if you do not specifically do dance training. Cross-training with other activities, such as swimming and yoga, can help maintain healthy range of motion.

Cross-Train

No single dance genre or class can provide a dancer with technique training that results in perfect balance among all muscle groups. The muscular imbalances inherent in dance training stress the joints. Therefore, all dancers can benefit from engaging in activities that work muscles and joints in ways that traditional dance classes do not. Cross-training can take on many forms, as described in chapter 3. These training techniques can be invaluable in correcting muscular imbalances caused by traditional dance training, and they help to strengthen and stabilize the muscles around the joints. Alternatively, a physical therapist or an athletic trainer who understands the needs of the dancers and the demands of the profession can design a strengthening and conditioning regimen to address individual needs. Various somatic techniques can help you identify areas of unnecessary tension that may be pulling on bones and stressing joints.

Summary

The human skeleton provides the body with a frame that allows for mobility and for protection against injury. Each of the 206 bones in the body changes size and shape throughout life in order to better serve its function. Although bones make up the rigid structure of the body, their architecture as a whole provides mobility. This chapter discussed the elements that enhance bone formation and the factors diminishing bone mineral density. It has particularly described the effects of nutrient intake, energy availability, and physical activity on bone health. Research suggests that childhood and adolescent years give opportunities to maximize bone mass and strength. It is extremely important for you to understand that optimization of peak bone mass during childhood, adolescence and early adulthood can provide long-term prevention of stress fractures during your dance career. A well-balanced diet with enough calories and nutrients will strengthen your bones and lengthen your career. Limiting smoking and alcohol consumption will benefit your overall performance and dancer wellness. Finally, you should participate in bone strengthening activities, such as weight training, activities that involve impact, and exercise with high cardiovascular intensity, 5 days per week for at least 30 minutes. Bones, joints, and muscles are structured in an extraordinary way that allows you many possibilities for movement in dance and other activities; taking care of your bones and joints is essential.

Application Activity: **Cross-Train for Bone Health**

Over your next break from intensive dancing, explore some ways to work on upper-extremity strength for your bone health. Classes in yoga, aerial work, street dance, and gymnastics all use movements and skills that place the body weight on the arms. You can also think about using weights, exercise bands, kettlebells, and medicine balls to do resistance training. These activities will not only give you the strength you need for today's choreography, they will help you develop strong, healthy bones.

Review Questions

1. What are the various bone structures and joints of the body? Describe them.

2. What are the elements and physical activities that enhance bone formation?

3. What elements and dance activities have potential negative effects on bone and joint health, and why?

4. Why are warm-up and proper stretching important for joints and bones?

 For chapter-specific supplemental learning activities, study aids, suggested readings, web links, and more, visit the web resource at www.HumanKinetics.com/DancerWellness.

Injury Prevention and First Aid

Jeffrey A. Russell, PhD, ATC, Marika Molnar, PT, LAc, and
Brenda Critchfield, MS, ATC

Photo courtesy of Jake Pett.

Key Terms

acute injuries

avulsion

chronic injuries

doming exercises

heel clocks

hypermobility

injury

injury signs

injury symptoms

meniscus

myofascial pain

sprain

stress fractures

tendinopathy

LEARNING OBJECTIVES

After reading this chapter, you will be able to do the following:

> Define and recognize acute and chronic injuries.

> Understand the genetic factors, bad habits, and muscle imbalances that can lead to chronic injuries.

> Describe ways to prevent dance injuries.

> Explain common dance injuries to the upper extremities, hip and pelvis, knee, foot and ankle, and spine.

> Define first aid, and know how to apply it to an immediate injury.

Dance is an intense, competitive physical activity. Training requirements increase as dancers progress through their years, in turn increasing the tendency of dancers to overtrain. Regardless of the warning signals their bodies send, factors such as overtraining lead to a high percentage of injuries; some studies place as high as 95 percent of the dancers injured in a given season. While it may be a shocking statistic to some, anyone involved behind the scenes in the dance world readily recognizes the rigors of dance, especially the long hours and the repetitive nature of learning and rehearsing choreography. In spite of this understanding, many dancers do not yet readily embrace that prevention is much preferred over treatment. Such a thought seems logical—even intuitive—yet in the face of the realities of dance practice, this idea is frequently ignored. The large percentage of dance injuries reported in research studies suggests that it is a matter of *when* a dancer will be injured rather than *if* a dancer will be injured.

This chapter holds many keys to success for those ready to reduce their chance of injury. To help you best understand and practice injury prevention, the chapter focuses on the fundamental concepts underlying injuries, prevention techniques for common types of injuries, and specialty discussions about topics such as injury prevention and dancing en pointe. Finally, this chapter addresses the procedure for what to do if you get injured.

Common Dance Injuries

An **injury** is a physical impairment that requires you to take at least one day off from normal activity beyond the day the injury began. Dance injuries are numerous, but many of them are preventable. If you learn to recognize factors that contribute to dance injuries, you can become more aware of your own potential for injury and design suitable prevention practices.

Dance injuries are categorized as either acute or chronic. **Acute injuries** occur essentially in an instant; they could be called accidental. Dancers can usually identify a point in time when the injury occurred; a specific unfortunate event resulted in the injury. The injured body tissue is unable to withstand an instantaneous force placed on it. Examples of acute injuries are sprained ankle ligaments, a fractured fifth metatarsal (also known as a dancer's fracture), and a dislocated patella.

On the other hand, **chronic injuries** occur over a period of time; they build up to the point where injury symptoms and signs become problematic and affect your dancing. **Injury symptoms** are the sensations that one feels, such as pain. **Injury signs** are the outward evidence of a limitation from an injury, such as decreased range of motion or inability to complete a specific movement. These injuries are sometimes called overuse injuries or repetitive strain injuries. Dancers cannot pinpoint a specific event or moment when the injury occurred, although they typically can identify the activities that created the symptoms or worsen them.

In such cases, the affected tissues are unable to withstand the repetitive demands placed on them. Examples of chronic injuries that commonly affect dancers are Achilles tendinopathy, flexor hallucis longus tendinopathy (also known as dancer's tendinopathy), stress fractures, and myofascial pain of overused muscles. **Tendinopathy** is the term for injury to a tendon, sometimes incorrectly called tendinitis. **Stress fractures** are small fractures caused by excessive repetitive impact of bones, such as the metatarsals. **Myofacscial pain** is a type of pain rooted in overuse of the muscles and the connective tissue (fascia) that surrounds and runs through the muscles.

Acute Injuries

An acute injury is the result of sudden trauma, and infinite ways exist to sustain one. It can be anything—a rolled ankle, a strained muscle, or something else. Acute injuries are often difficult to prevent, but if they are minor and are treated promptly and correctly, they have a good chance of full and speedy recovery. Nevertheless, an acute injury can take time to heal. If you sustain an acute injury, you should take some time off to allow the injury to heal correctly. You should also consult a health care professional when the injury occurs. First aid, such as ice and rest, will help reduce pain and time away from dance and other activities, but it will not replace proper medical attention for injuries. First aid is discussed in detail later in the chapter.

SAFETY TIP

Prevent Acute Injuries

- Make sure all equipment, props, and wardrobe are in proper working order and are being used as they were designed. Make sure the dance surface is clear of debris and obstacles. For additional information about the dance environment, refer to chapter 1.

- Develop proper alignment and well-executed movement patterns in your dance training (see chapter 2).

- Warm up before all dance activities, and avoid static stretches before dancing. For more information about warming up, refer to chapter 3.

- Develop strategies to reduce stress and anxiety, and to promote psychological wellness (see chapters 4 and 5).

- Avoid dancing in states of fatigue or without sufficient sleep (see chapter 6).

- Get enough nutrients to support your body's needs (see chapters 7 and 8).

Chronic Injuries

Chronic injuries are more typical for dancers than acute injuries, and they result from repetitive use,

stress, and trauma placed on soft tissue structures of the body without proper time for healing. Many of these injuries are preventable with a little understanding of how they occur, and they take longer to heal because they take longer to develop. Typically, these types of injuries develop slowly over a long period of time—months or sometimes years. The pain is usually low level but long lasting, and often it is overlooked and dismissed as normal or expected pain until the body can no longer adapt to the stress. Many times, symptoms of chronic injuries are vague and difficult to pinpoint. Some dancers experiencing chronic injuries unknowingly might say, "My knee just aches most of the time" or "I have a little pain on the bottom of my foot when I first walk on it after sitting" or "I have shin splints, and I get them all the time." If not treated or taken care of, a small, nagging pain can turn into a major debilitating injury.

Genetic Predisposition for Chronic Injuries

Chronic injuries can occur for a variety of reasons. They can be genetic or structural, such as hyperextended knees or scoliosis. These conditions are not injuries in and of themselves, but they can lead to chronic injury if the dancer does not know or understand how to mitigate the effect of the structural deficiency. For example, a young dancer with scoliosis should see a physician or a rehabilitation specialist, such as a physical therapist or athletic trainer, to monitor the progression of the curvature and make sure it is not getting worse. A rehabilitation specialist can provide exercises to help correct the curvature or slow down the progress. With permission of the health care professional, the dancer would most likely still be able to continue to dance with or without some modifications based on the medical advice. Without treatment, the dancer could sustain a major deformity if the spine continues to curve, which would rotate the rib cage, cause extensive muscle tightness on one side of the spine, and elevate one shoulder or one hip higher than the other.

Bad Habits

Bad habits developed over time are another source of chronic injuries. One common problem is pronation of the feet (when the foot is constantly rolling toward the medial aspect). Some possible injuries from chronic pronation include knee pain, shin splints, hip or pelvic dysfunction, and low-back pain.

Another common bad habit is standing and walking in full turnout. Standing and walking with the hips externally rotated creates unnatural stress on the medial knee, lateral hip, low back, and feet. Likewise, it creates muscle imbalances in all those structures as well. These stresses and imbalances can turn into a debilitating injury. Turnout is important in most genres of dance, but it should be used when dancing, not in daily locomotion.

DIVERSITY

Different Dance Forms, Different Injuries

Think about the various dance forms and styles that you do. If you are taking many ballet classes each week, check that you are not walking and standing in turnout in your daily life. If your dance form involves doing repetitions of lumbar hyperextension, make sure that you stretch your low back, and walk and stand in good alignment during the day. If you are a ballroom dancer and work in high heels, be sure to stretch out your calf muscles and work on rolling through the feet in ordinary walking. Each form of dance has its own potential injuries, and you can take preventive measures related to your form.

Another bad habit is standing or walking with an extended (arched) back. When a dancer stands for long periods of time in an arched position, it has a cascade effect on the rest of the body; it can create anterior pelvic tilt, which can shorten the hip flexor muscles and weaken the abdominal muscles, leading to chronic injury of the hips, pelvis, and low back. It is often seen in conjunction with hyperextended knees, placing undue stress on the back of the knee (which can lead to knee pain), and weakness in the hamstrings. It can also contribute to tendinopathy in the hamstring tendons, popliteal (the muscle behind the knee) strain, Achilles tendinopathy, and plantar fasciitis. Having the muscles on stretch for long periods of time while consistently standing or walking with an extended back weakens them, making them more prone to injury. Again, back extension is needed for performing certain dance moves, such as an arabesque; however, in standing or walking, the spine and pelvis should be in neutral alignment.

Outside Influences

A huge contributor to chronic headaches, neck pain, shoulder pain, and mid-back pain is the use of handheld electronic devices for a good portion of a day. While not specifically a dance-related cause of injury, these devices have affected many dancers. A huge increase has been observed in chronic injuries of the neck and upper back caused by texting, gaming, and Internet use on handheld devices. Instead of having the screen at eye level like a normal computer or television setup, the majority of people look down at the screen because they are holding the handheld device at around chest level. This habit places up to 60 pounds of pressure on the neck and upper back. It's like walking around with four bowling balls or an average 8-year-old child sitting on your neck. Unfortunately, these injuries are increasingly common in many dancers as well as the general population.

While general pain and headaches make up the majority of the complaints, some have been as serious as herniated discs that have required neck surgery. This is a relatively easy fix. Avoid spending extended periods of time looking down at the phone when texting, watching a movie on a handheld device, or reading emails on a phone. If possible, use a computer that has a screen at around eye level. Another way is to hold the phone or handheld device at eye level so that the spine can be in neutral position.

Muscle Imbalances

Chronic injuries can also be caused by muscle imbalances, weak muscles in general, or lack of control. While having a dominant side is normal, as a dancer you should avoid developing muscle imbalances, which can happen when the movement requires a repetitive motion, such as in ballroom dancing. The ballroom expression *holding frame* includes holding the arms at shoulder level, slightly arching the back, and turning the head. Sometimes this pattern can lead to muscle imbalances, which can lead to neck and upper-back injuries.

Ways to combat these chronic injuries (if specific repetitive movements are necessary for the dance genre) are to make sure you are creating the movement with the correct musculature, as instructed by your teacher, and to do cross-training that encompasses the whole body, as explained in chapter 3. Also, determining which muscles are underdeveloped and focusing on exercises that will strengthen them will help prevent and even treat these injuries. The significant disadvantage with repetitive movements is that unless you actively work on not developing a muscle imbalance, the injury has a high likelihood of occurring again.

Holding frame for ballroom dance. Notice the extended back and turned head for both partners.

© Brenda Critchfield; Dancers: Sterling and Nicole Stolle

General Weakness

General weakness in muscles can also be a source of chronic injury. Often dancers try to do a movement that they might not be strong enough to perform at the time. While they may be able to re-create the movement for a while, if they don't strengthen the musculature, the body will begin to fatigue, resulting in an injury. For example, weak hip muscles can cause knee pain in many dancers. This weakness is most notably seen when doing a plié, especially when doing grand pliés. The knee needs to be centered over the foot when doing demi- or grand pliés. When the hip muscles are weak, the knee can move slightly medially, and over time this misalignment can create some serious knee injuries, including patellofemoral tracking problems (how the kneecap aligns on the femur) and tendinopathy. If you experience knee pain during knee flexion, such as doing demi- or grand pliés or walking up and down stairs, you can look in the mirror and do a plié, or ask someone to observe. See where the knee is aligning as the knee flexes; if it is falling medially, start working on hip strengthening exercises to avoid a more debilitating chronic injury.

Lack of control for body movement can also lead to chronic injuries. Many dance styles involve very specific movements that, if done correctly, are generally safe and will probably not cause injury. However, some dancers may not understand the movement, and they try to imitate what the instructor or choreographer is doing. This imitation can lead to poor movement patterns and chronic injuries. For example, a contemporary dancer in a musical whose choreography involved him being jerked around as if he were a puppet, didn't engage the correct core muscles to stabilize his spine and pelvis. After 4 to 5 months of rehearsals, he started to have mid-back and hip pain, almost to the point of inability to dance during the performances. Once the initial problem was addressed and corrected, the debilitating pain abated and rehabilitation was successful. To avoid injury, you must understand how to correctly align and move the body.

Predisposing Factors of Common Dance Injuries

Several factors inherent to dance provide an environment in which injuries can occur. In addition, some aspects of a dancer's body can make injuries more likely. Overall it should be the goal for dancers, dance educators, dance health care professionals, and caregivers (in the case of young dancers) to

Other ways that muscle imbalances develop are from the dancer's bad habits. Most dancers feel more comfortable learning and practicing certain movements on a specific side. Once they feel comfortable with the movement on one side, they practice it on the other side. You need to be aware of how you are learning and rehearsing various movements, and make sure you are equally working both sides.

work as a team to reduce the likelihood that these factors result in an injury.

Characteristics of dance or the dance environment that may predispose you to injury include the following:

› Long training hours
› Choreography that is too complex or physically demanding for you
› Dance floors that are too hard or too soft
› A change in surface from one level of firmness to another, where your body is not able to adequately accommodate to the surface

Other characteristics are long class and rehearsal hours; unreasonably demanding educators, choreographers, and artistic directors; and climatic considerations such as the studio temperature. For more information on environmental factors in dance, see chapter 1. Virtually all of the factors listed are modifiable in order to ensure that dance training contributes as little as possible to injury risk.

Internal factors (facets within a dancer) that can lead to injury include ignoring symptoms that suggest injury, an unwillingness to rest, poor nutrition, inattention to physical training that can prepare the body for the demands of dancing, beginning dance without a proper warm-up, poor alignment, and rehearsing with improper or forced technique. Atypical anatomical features of a dancer's body also can make injury more likely. Examples include the presence of an os trigonum (an extra bone that can be present behind the ankle joint), pes planus (flat foot), genu valgum (knock-knees), relative inflexibility of the body's connective tissues (tissues such as ligaments and fascia that hold the body together), and **hypermobility** (a condition of greater than typical extensibility of the connective tissues). When confronted by any of these conditions, it is essential that you have supportive teachers and qualified health care providers to care for you properly and steer you away from potentially injurious practices.

Common Dance Activities That Can Cause Injuries

Several activities that dancers do in the course of training can lead to injury. Rehearsing with improper or forced technique is a significant culprit in dance injuries. For example, forcing one's turnout is a common tendency, and it can lead to injuries from the low back all the way down to the foot. When dancers do not naturally exhibit the turnout

they desire or are asked to attain by a teacher, they sometimes use various tricks to squeeze every last degree of turnout from the body. They may include tactics such as tilting the pelvis forward and bending the knees to turn out, then straightening the knees once in position. However, these efforts place undue stress on the tissues of the low back and lower extremities that can have undesired injury consequences. For more detail on these compensations regarding turnout, refer to chapter 2.

Poor jumping habits, careless alignment, and insufficient stabilization of the core (the musculature that maintains the position and causes movement of the trunk and hips), are three other aspects of dance training that can negatively affect a dancer. Particularly in view of the extremely repetitive nature of many genres of dance, any movement, jumping or otherwise, that is performed incorrectly and repetitively is likely to result in pain and injury. Because body alignment is so aesthetically crucial to dance, it must be rigorously developed and maintained. If a starting or ending position is not aligned, or if the required alignment is not maintained throughout a movement, a risk of overuse injury exists from the poor biomechanics (the mechanical principles that govern the actions of biological tissues). In addition, imbalances in muscle strength and unwanted shortening of certain tissues may result, thus accentuating faulty technique and further leading to symptoms of injury.

Interestingly, the support of the core musculature, including the muscles that attach the hips to the trunk, plays an enormous role in executing proper dance technique, especially jumping and alignment. The core muscles must not only support the trunk in the correct position for each variation or exercise, they also must act as the foundation from which the extremities operate (see figure 9.1). Poorly conditioned core muscles, and resulting inadequate core stability, lead to an increase in injuries in virtually all types of physically active people, including dancers.

The earlier in a dancer's career that poor technique is eliminated, the better. With young dancers, parents often are unaware of the differences between good and poor dance teaching, so a local community studio is the convenient choice. However, parents should be encouraged to engage with their children's dance teachers as they would with academic teachers in order to assess the care with which the teachers instruct dancers. Ultimately, children depend on their parents or guardians to ensure their well-being, so these caregivers must become knowledgeable enough about dance to make wise decisions related to instruction for their

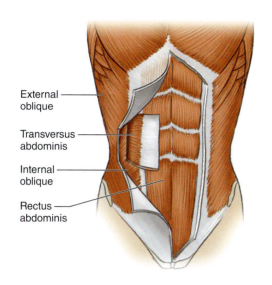

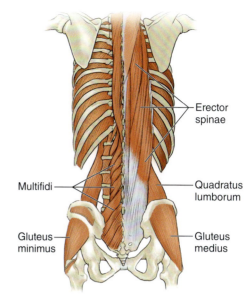

Figure 9.1   The many muscles of the core both stabilize and move the trunk, as well as form a foundation for movements of the extremities.

young dancers. This attention will assist in reducing the likelihood of injuries related to poor technique. Chapter 2 further discusses the anatomical and technique foundations of dance.

SELF-AWARENESS

Poor Alignment and Technique

Consider your alignment and your technical habits. Are you aware of any patterns that may be leading to possible injuries? Is your core adequately conditioned, and do you recruit it when you are dancing? Examine your jumping habits. Notice how you use your feet and pliés to absorb the shock of the landing. When you develop heightened awareness of your alignment and habits, you can intentionally develop technique to help you prevent injuries.

In summary, whether the injuries are acute or chronic, many factors can lead to injury. Predisposing factors (both environmental and anatomical), certain dance activities, and age-related factors can lead to serious injuries in the life of a dancer. Fortunately, many injuries can be prevented.

Preventing Dance Injuries

Prevention of dance injuries is a shared responsibility. Dancers, dance teachers, health care providers, and parents must all take part. One of the best overall preventive measures in dance is conditioning. Many studies demonstrate the value of proper conditioning not only for prevention of injuries, but also to lessen injury severity and increase the speed of recovery. Chapter 3 contains information about this facet of injury prevention.

Many risk factors can increase the likelihood of injuries in dance. While injuries cannot be entirely prevented, this section identifies ways to deal with these risk factors in order to minimize risk.

Several physical characteristics predispose a dancer to injury. These characteristics are primarily musculoskeletal conditions that a health care practitioner or other appropriate professional should address. Once you have identified these characteristics, you should seek sound advice about whether or not your chosen genre of dance is appropriate given the risk factors present. These conversations are difficult to have, but they are necessary for your benefit. Screening is one way to discover these parameters; guidelines for screening appear in chapter 10.

Another important risk factor is the speed with which the duration, frequency, and intensity of dancing increases. If you go from taking 5 classes a week over the course of a spring season to 15 classes a week during a summer intensive without a gradual buildup to that workload, the increase will take a toll on you. The physical and mental overload of such a scenario will cause excessive fatigue that reduces the force-absorbing qualities of muscles, stresses the joints, and diminishes your ability to focus on skill acquisition. Rest is an important component of injury prevention; see chapter 6 for more information on rest and recovery.

Muscle imbalances during a growth spurt cause certain muscles to tighten and others to weaken. The resulting unequal forces can change the alignment of joints due to tightness and decrease their stability due to weakness. Alterations in the biomechanics of the joints also can alter the information sent to the brain; this miscommunication may bring about deficits in proprioception. For example, you maintain spinal support and stability by correctly recruiting the abdominal and the gluteal muscles to counterbalance the tension from the lumbar extensors, hamstrings, and hip flexors. Daily flexibility, strengthening, and stabilization programs can maintain correct spinal alignment and reduce the likelihood of injuries to these specific areas of concern.

EMPOWERMENT

Use Your Knowledge to Prevent Injury

Consider what you know about injury prevention and your specific physical capabilities. Learning about conditioning and methods of gaining strength, flexibility, and core support can give you the knowledge you need to prevent injuries and sustain long hours of dancing and rehearsing. Increasing numbers of dancers are participating in supplemental training programs for injury prevention. You, too, can empower yourself with this knowledge.

Working with his physical therapist, this dancer is using a gym ball to work on balance and proprioception.

Photo courtesy of Kyle Froman. Physical therapist: Marika Molnar. Dancer: Robert Fairchild.

Focusing on a daily injury prevention routine is important for all dancers. Aspects requiring continual attention include the following:

› **Postural training:** Body awareness education in combination with appropriate lengthening, strengthening, and stabilizing.

› **Healthy gait patterns:** Reestablishing a normal walking pattern without turning out the feet.

› **Shoulder girdle, pelvic, and core stability:** Training for proper lifting strategies, especially emphasizing the deep antigravity muscles for core support and lifting the limbs while maintaining postural form.

› **Muscular and ligamentous tension:** Deep abdominal and pelvic floor education for lumbar stability; flexibility programs done daily to minimize the effects of tension on bone, especially for the hamstrings, tensor fasciae latae, iliotibial band, and lumbar extensors.

› **Proprioception and balance exercises:** Variations of standing on one leg with the eyes open and closed while changing the position of the leg and foot from relevé to plié.

› **Taping as necessary:** Assist control and proprioception of specific body regions.

› **Stress reduction and recovery skills:** Dynamic rest and decompression activities, such as controlled breathing and other calming methods for stress relief; postexercise relaxation and flexibility exercises to restore length in tight structures, and lying supine (on your back) with the legs supported on wedges to allow the lumbar spine and hip muscles to relax.

Pointe Work

Originally no more than satin slippers darned at the toes, pointe shoes were developed in the 19th century by the father of ballerina Marie Taglioni to showcase her talent and to make her appear weightless and sylph-like onstage. Those early performances used a system of guide wires to move the ballerina up, down, and across the stage surface to create the desired illusion of floating on her toes.

Construction of modern pointe shoes is often attributed to the 20th century Russian ballerina Anna Pavlova; she made modifications such as adding toughened leather soles for extra support and flattening and hardening the toe area to form a box. With the exception of two or three manufacturers, modern pointe shoes are not substantially different from those of Pavlova's day. They still are constructed largely from materials such as satin, muslin, burlap, cardboard, and glue. The majority of today's professional ballerinas usually order their pointe shoes from a custom maker who tailors the shoe to their individual specifications. They also engage in highly individualized rituals that transform a new pair of pointe shoes into shoes that give them the feel they desire.

Dancers who love ballet and have been studying it regularly for 3 or 4 years often progress to wearing pointe shoes in class. It is an exciting time for young dancers; however, it also can be a time that leads to injury if proper precautions are not taken. A crucial method for minimizing injury risk during the transition to dancing en pointe is for a dance teacher to train his or her pre-pointe dancers with progressive strengthening exercises for the feet, legs, and trunk (core). In addition, some girls benefit from wearing special demi-pointe shoes as an intermediate step between soft ballet flats and pointe shoes, although the teacher must not see these shoes as a replacement for proper strengthening and careful attention to technique.

The rest of the body balances on the feet, so fitting correctly in pointe shoes is one measure for preventing injuries. Stress reactions of the metatarsals can occur when the shoe is too narrow, compressing the metatarsals together and possibly causing neuromas (enlargements of the nerves between the toes) and soft corns in the web spaces between the toes. When pointe shoes are too wide or too long, the foot has reduced support and can slip forward. This improper fit may lead to hallux valgus, an outward angulation of the big toe that is associated with bunions at the first metatarsophalangeal joint where the big toe meets the foot. Other results of ill-fitting pointe shoes include increased strain across the midfoot and weakened ligaments.

Once en pointe, the dancer must have strong enough ankle stability to not sickle (bear weight on the lateral side of the pointe shoe box). This position increases susceptibility to ankle sprains. It can also cause cuboid subluxation, a malalignment of the cuboid bone in the foot as it sits between the calcaneus, or heel bone, and the metatarsals on the lateral foot.

Similarly, a dancer en pointe must not bear weight on a foot in a wing position (bearing weight on the medial side of pointe shoe box). This position may lead to a Lisfranc sprain; the Lisfranc joint and its supporting ligaments that cross the midfoot are crucial for dancing en pointe.

Young girls who are considering the transition to pointe shoes typically experience individual physical differences, including in the feet, which must have both sufficient strength and flexibility for pointe work. Therefore, age is not the sole criterion to determine whether a dancer is ready for pointe work. Rather, it must be a careful, informed decision that the teacher makes in cooperation with the dancer and the parents. Consultation with a health care provider who is knowledgeable about the demands of pointe work may also be helpful.

Following is a list of factors that should inform any decision for a girl to begin pointe work. In the event that a young dancer does not exhibit the characteristics needed for clearance to go en pointe—and she no doubt will be disappointed with such a decision—the teacher and parents should not change their minds under pressure. At the same time, they must remain supportive and provide further training to equip the dancer for success when she finally is released for pointe.

› **Overall body alignment and postural control:** Can the dancer control the trunk and pelvis in static balance and complex movements?

› **Strength of the lower extremities:** Can the dancer maintain the turnout of her hip joints as she moves up to full pointe? Can she relevé without her feet and ankles wobbling? Is she able to confidently bear weight and control her lower extremities to work safely en pointe?

› **Flexibility of the lower extremities:** Can the dancer's ankles and feet achieve a fully plantar flexed position with her knees straight?

› **Hypermobility:** Is the dancer hypermobile with loose joints in the foot and ankle and an overpointed foot? Is the knee excessively hyperextended, causing an even greater degree of plantar flexion at the ankle and foot?

> **Hypomobility:** Is the dancer's foot hypomobile at the ankle or foot? If one extends a line from the tibia (shinbone), is it parallel to a line from the top of the foot to the floor, or does the dancer need to slightly bend the knee to achieve the pointed foot position?

If you are excessively hypermobile, you will require strengthening exercises for all the muscles of the foot and ankle, as well as improvement in your ability to balance and to know where you are in space when your heels are not on the ground. This type of exercise for proprioception is beneficial to all dancers, not just those preparing for pointe. However, in the typical pre-pointe period, marked by a time of rapid growth spurts with lots of physical and psychological changes, heightened proprioception is especially necessary.

If you have insufficient range of motion, you may need extra stretching for the top of your foot and ankle, done carefully so as not to injure any tissues or force any joints beyond their safe range. It is often difficult to continue pointe work if sufficient range cannot be achieved.

Proper Stretching

Before class, rehearsal, or performance the body must be prepared for the work it will be required to do. Most dance genres require large ranges of motion at the joints (e.g., grand battement in ballet and jazz, and shoulder joint range in flamenco), one of the most efficient ways to prepare the body for these activities is to perform dynamic exercises during the warm-up time. These exercises activate all the muscles that dancers need to use. It is not beneficial to do static stretching exercises (e.g., sitting in splits while conversing with friends) before any event. Static stretching has its place at the end of the dance session, during the cool-down period; at this time it serves to gently lengthen the muscles that have been working and relieve them of tension. The various forms of stretching, their timing, and their applications are explained in detail in chapter 3.

Stretching can either prevent or enable injury, not only based on the type and timing of stretches but also based on a dancer's body type. Dance's unique demands on range of motion means that dancers who are relatively tight are prone to certain types of injuries if they do not stretch regularly. Tight muscles can tear and develop scar tissue with repetitions of movement beyond their range. Hamstrings, calves, spinal muscles, and quadriceps are examples of muscles that tight dancers frequently injure.

On the other end of the spectrum, dancers who are hypermobile, especially those with great flexibility but without sufficient strength and motor control, are equally susceptible to injury. These dancers should not spend much time stretching; instead they should work on core support and strength. Because they possess such extreme ranges of motion, the stabilizing structures of the joint (e.g., ligaments) are so extensible that they have difficulty providing the necessary joint stability and are vulnerable to injury. For example, dancers with vary lax knee ligaments can sprain these structures more easily. Similarly, these dancers may be more predisposed to ankle sprains or low-back problems than dancers who are not hypermobile.

The logic of trying to prevent injuries to reduce the need for treating them is sound and includes obvious benefits for dancers. Overall a team approach involving you, your dance teachers, health care professionals, and other personnel such as exercise instructors, all adhering to well-founded principles of performance physiology and psychology, yields the greatest chance of success in keeping you in the studio and on the stage.

It is clear that you and your teachers must take into account various factors in determining when you should begin certain activities, such as pointe work, and when you should modify activities, such as height of extension and jumping. In the next section we will discuss the prevention of specific dance injuries.

Preventing Specific Dance Injuries

Dancers can incur a large variety of injuries because they are so physically active. Virtually every genre of dance requires repetitive actions, motions through large range, maintenance of unusual postures, and movements of varying speeds through intricate and carefully choreographed patterns. The possible disruptions to dancing are virtually limitless. However, certain injuries are more common in dancers than others. This section defines many of these injuries and provides appropriate preventive methods. For a review of the anatomical structures described, refer to chapter 2. The section also covers upper extremities; hip and pelvis; knee, ankle, and foot; and finishes with the spine, the area of the body that ties the upper and lower extremities together.

Upper Extremities

While most dance injuries tend to be in the lower extremities, dancers do experience injuries to the upper extremities (the arms and shoulder blades).

GOAL SETTING

Design a Plan for Injury Prevention

As you read the next section, think about what aspects of your physical capabilities or technique might predispose you to any of these injuries. To prevent these injuries, set specific goals in terms of conditioning and realignment that will make you less susceptible. If you lack flexibility in your muscles and joints, you can plan a regular program of stretching. If you are a hypermobile dancer, you can work on strength, balance, and core support. Be proactive; set goals for a healthy approach to injury prevention.

With the increasing amount of choreography involving aerial work, partnering lifts for both men and women, and increasing weight bearing on the arms, it is likely that injuries to the upper extremities will be more common in the future. Some of these injuries currently seen are lateral epicondylitis, shoulder dislocation, shoulder impingement, rotator cuff tears, and acromioclavicular (A-C) joint sprain.

Lateral Epicondylitis

Often called tennis elbow, lateral epicondylitis of the humerus is an overuse injury of the lateral (outside) aspect of the elbow. Repeated contractions of the muscles that extend the wrist cause an inflammatory reaction where the muscles insert into the bone. Dancers who sustain this injury typically do styles of dance that require repetitively using their upper arms in weight-bearing maneuvers or holding partners, such as modern or contemporary dance or street dance.

Prevention of lateral epicondylitis calls for stretching and strengthening exercises of the hand, wrist, elbow, and shoulder muscles. Whereas most partnering occurs with the wrist extended and the fingers either flexed or extended, these muscles must be stretched carefully so that they have their full range of motion when called upon. Strengthening the forearm pronators and supinators both concentrically and eccentrically will increase the workload of the tendons at their insertions so that they can manage more force. Strengthening the extensor-supinator muscles (located on the outer surface of the forearm with the palm facing forward) will help avoid tension buildup at the origin of these muscles at the lateral epicondyle.

Shoulder Dislocation

Shoulder dislocation is a serious traumatic injury that must be managed urgently and properly. The ball of the humerus slides from its very shallow socket. If it is lodged in the dislocated position, several complications can occur. Physician consultation is a necessity; only qualified medical personnel should relocate the joint. Once a shoulder dislocation occurs, it is likely that subsequent dislocations or partial dislocations will occur, because the stabilizing tissues around the shoulder joint are stretched. This injury is most likely in dancers who perform choreography requiring upper-extremity weight bearing, such as in modern or contemporary dance, street dance, or contact improvisation.

Shoulder dislocation is an acute injury and usually occurs during an accidental slip and fall on an outstretched arm. Especially in females, hypermobility or instability of the shoulder joint often make the injury more likely. Strengthening and stabilization exercises of the shoulder girdle are required in dancers with these predisposing factors.

Shoulder Impingement

Shoulder impingement is an overuse injury caused by repetitive movements of the upper extremities at the level of the shoulders or higher. The rotator cuff is a group of four deep muscles that surround the shoulder joint. A portion of a tendon in one of these muscles gets pinched between the humerus and the underside of the acromion of the scapula during this type of upper extremity movement. Repeated enough times, the tendon can become painful, inflamed, and, if not cared for properly, torn. This type of injury can occur in any dance genre where the arms move above the shoulders.

Shoulder impingement is often accompanied by poor posture and alignment of the shoulder joint complex. Certain muscle imbalances can cause incorrect movement of the humerus. Maintaining proper alignment of the shoulder girdle on the trunk is an important consideration in prevention. Muscles such as pectoralis minor and levator scapulae should be gently stretched while serratus anterior, middle and lower trapezius, and biceps brachii are strengthened. The thoracic spine should be able to move fluidly and not be stiff. Squeezing and separating the scapulae will stimulate the muscles in that area and will allow the rotator cuff to perform as it should, helping to maintain proper positioning of the humerus as the shoulder joint moves.

Rotator Cuff Tears

Rotator cuff tears occur usually because one or more of the tendons of the rotator cuff around the shoulder joint becomes weakened and gives way when the muscles attached to the tendons exert enough force. The likelihood of this type of injury increases with age, because tissue strength decreases with age; it also increases with untreated shoulder impingement. It can be quite painful and limiting, so appropriate health care consultation is advised. To help prevent this injury, you can strengthen the muscles of the rotator cuff with light weights or exercise bands.

Acromioclavicular (A-C) Joint Sprain

Acromioclavicular (A-C) joint sprain is a traumatic injury that typically occurs when a dancer falls on the point of the shoulder. It can occur during an accidental fall, or when choreography requiring a roll or similar action is completed incorrectly. The ligaments that hold the outer end of the clavicle to the acromion (a protrusion from the upper part of the scapula) are stretched or torn. A shoulder separation occurs when an A-C joint sprain is severe enough to allow the clavicle to move from its position against the acromion. Medical consultation is required in this instance. Because A-C joint sprain is an acute injury caused by an accident rather than overuse or poor technique, no exercises can assist in preventing it, although learning correct falling techniques can be a useful aid in prevention.

Hip and Pelvis

Injuries to the hip and pelvis are more common in most dance forms than are injuries to the upper extremities, and studies suggest that some of these injuries are more frequent in adolescents. The use of the hip and pelvis in large range of motion can increase the chances of these injuries. Hip injuries include avulsion injuries, stress fractures, snapping hip, hip arthritis, bursitis, sciatica, and acetabular labral tears.

Avulsion Injuries

Avulsion injuries occur when tissue pulls away from its attachment to a bone, either with or without a piece of bone attached. These injuries are relatively uncommon in dance except in the pelvis and hip of skeletally immature dancers. They occur because the apophyses (singular, apophysis) are generally weaker than the muscles and tendons that attach to them. The apophyses are growth areas of bones other than those that create long bone growth. Examples are the anterior superior iliac spine (ASIS), the iliac crest, and the ischial tuberosity. Thus, when a muscle contracts with enough force, its tendinous portion can avulse (detach) the edges of the bone in these areas as the growth area in the bone separates. If the muscle is stretched when it contracts,

the force is compounded. Usually the separation at the growth area is either not complete or not wide, so with proper care the injuries heal well. Physician consultation is essential for properly managing this type of injury.

Preventing avulsion injuries is a matter of not using momentum or performing highly ballistic movements in positions where the muscles that attach to the pelvis are able to generate enough force to create an avulsion. In the legs, the hamstrings, the rectus femoris, and the sartorius are the most likely contributors, as are the trunk muscles such as the obliques that attach at the iliac crests. Limiting the height of battement or arabesque will be helpful until the skeleton matures sufficiently for those bony areas to strengthen.

Stress Fractures

Stress fractures are overuse injuries where an area of bone is weakened by repetitive force being applied to it. It starts with fairly subtle changes in the bone structure, then small cracks may develop in the bone. Left untreated, it is possible for a stress fracture to become a complete fracture, so early and proper care is warranted. In the hip region, the most common place to see a stress fracture is in the portion of the femur closest to the hip joint, either right below the trochanters or at the neck of the femur.

The main strategy to prevent stress fractures is to be aware of the importance of recovery time. Dance training that requires repetitive, low-load stresses may cause muscle fatigue when not enough recovery time is allowed during or after activity. This situation is most common during rehearsals when certain choreographic routines are repeated over and over, or when back-to-back classes are scheduled. A stress fracture is a process, not an event; thus, you will have many clues alerting you that you need rest before you continue dancing. For example, sudden onset of pain with a recent change in frequency or duration of dancing, pain while weight bearing that is relieved with rest, or point tenderness over the affected area can all be early indicators of a stress fracture developing.

Because muscle fatigue causes heightened strain on the bone, it is prudent to stop dance activity before the muscles are overly tired. Relaxing and elevating the legs during class breaks or rehearsal breaks, and upon arriving home at the end of a day, should be part of a dancer's daily rest and recovery routine. In addition, walking with a normal gait, rather than in external hip rotation with the toes pointing outward, is important for the health of your lower extremities, because the muscles will be most efficient and the least stressed and the joints will be optimally positioned for movement. It also allows the force of gravity and the reaction force from the ground as the foot strikes it to be absorbed and dispersed correctly by the body.

Snapping Hip

Snapping hip has two varieties: anterior (internal) snapping hip and lateral (external) snapping hip. Internal snapping hip occurs when the tendons of the psoas major and iliacus muscles, together called the iliopsoas, snap across part of the pelvis. This snapping can occur because of poor movement patterns or tightness and possibly weakness in this muscle. Another cause of internal snapping hip is a torn acetabular labrum, which is discussed later in this chapter. External snapping hip occurs when the iliotibial (IT) band is tight and snaps over the trochanter of the femur during movement.

Preventing snapping hip can be quite challenging. Motor control (the ability of the nervous and musculoskeletal systems to work together to produce coordinated, efficient movement) is important in the muscles that stabilize the pelvis. The tensor fasciae latae (TFL), hamstrings, lumbar erector spinae, and quadratus lumborum muscles are usually tighter, and the abdominal and gluteal muscles are usually weaker in young dancers. However, this injury is not confined to young dancers. Flexibility exercises for the tight muscles and tendons that create the snapping bands will help the pelvis remain in its neutral alignment when the legs are moving on a stationary trunk. Learning how to dissociate movement of the legs from movement of the pelvis and lumbar spine will allow for safer, more productive mobility without compromising the structures in the region that may give rise to snapping hip.

Hip Arthritis

Hip arthritis most commonly occurs when there is a degenerative breakdown of the smooth cartilage surface that covers the head of the femur, the inside of the acetabulum, or both. It is usually a result of either a traumatic injury to the hip joint itself or a long-term cumulative effect of forcing the hip joint to beyond its typical range of motion or loading it beyond its capacity. Without that smooth covering, the joint becomes increasingly painful and irritated. At this time, no known method of preventing arthritis exists, nor is it fully understood why some dancers develop it and others do not.

Bursitis

Bursitis is an inflammation of a bursa, which is a lubricating sac located between two adjacent anatomical structures that tend to rub together. The anatomical arrangement of the hip is such that tendons can rub across other tendons and across bony structures. In these areas, bursas provide lubrication to make the rubbing as smooth as possible. However, if they are overused, bursas may become inflamed, swollen, and painful.

You can help prevent or alleviate bursitis with daily routine of stretching and every-other-day strengthening of all the muscles of the hip and pelvic girdle. When resting, you can reduce compression on bursas caused by weight bearing by lying on your back with a roll under your knees rather than lying on one side. If you must lie on your side, put a pillow between your knees so that the top leg remains parallel to the floor and the muscles are not in a lengthened position. Stretching muscles and tendons that press over bursas is usually helpful both for prevention and relief.

Sciatica

Sciatica is a painful condition of the sciatic nerve. The sciatic nerve comprises nerve roots that start in the lumbar spine and join to form a large nerve that passes under the buttocks and into the thigh. This nerve travels underneath one of the main muscles used for turnout, the piriformis. When the piriformis is tight or well developed, it can press on the sciatic nerve, causing pain or radiating symptoms that travel into the posterior thigh.

During growth spurts, spinal alignment can alter because of tightness in the lumbodorsal fascia and the hamstrings. Therefore, a daily program to maintain flexibility will be helpful in preventing sciatic pain. Maintaining a neutral position of the spine during everyday activities such as sitting is beneficial, as is concentrating on walking with a gait pattern that is not turned out. The position of turnout naturally shortens the piriformis and, consequently, it becomes tight when not in turnout; consciously working on flexibility of the hips into internal rotation is one key to the prevention of sciatica. When standing on one leg, the pelvis should not tilt to one side or the other; this action puts unnecessary tension on the piriformis, as does sitting with the legs crossed. Maintaining normal range of motion in the lumbar spine and hip joints will help preserve the necessary length of the nerves and allow them to be mobile during movement. If you always maintain a turned-out position at the hip joint, the piriformis muscle will shorten and tighten, and it will put pressure on the sciatic nerve.

Acetabular Labral Tears

The acetabular labrum is a ring of cartilage located around the edge of the acetabulum (or hip socket). Tears of this structure can result from a single traumatic event or, most commonly in dance, by repeated rubbing of the femur against the labrum. It is one cause of internal snapping hip. If you have a torn labrum, you must have it evaluated by a medical professional to ensure that it does not worsen and cause hip arthritis.

A hypermobile dancer with excessively lax ligaments in the anterior hip joint may experience movement of the head of the femur too far forward when the hip joint is externally rotated or the hip joint is extended. This position puts pressure and compression on the labrum and may cause it to tear. Maintaining the femoral head in its stable position in the acetabulum requires excellent motor control, development of which must be part of the hypermobile dancer's daily routine. One method of working on this control involves assuming a position on the hands and knees with the hip starting at 70 degrees of flexion (with the trunk positioned toward the head), and then shifting toward 90 degrees of hip flexion by pushing the trunk backward with the hands. This procedure helps restabilize the head of the femur in the acetabulum. A good daily strengthening program for the psoas major, iliacus, and deep abdominals, as well as the gluteus maximus and deep external rotators, will help train the musculature to maintain this stability.

Knee

The structure of the knee joint is not particularly stable, especially considering the amount of weight the knee joint must bear. Unlike the hip joint that has a deep socket, the tibial plateaus that support the femoral condyles are very shallow. Knee injuries and knee pain are unfortunately common in dance. They include meniscal injuries, patellofemoral pain syndrome and chondromalacia, patellar subluxation and dislocation, ligament ruptures, strains, patellar tendinopathy, knee bursitis, and Osgood-Schlatter's disease.

Meniscal Injuries

Meniscal injuries are caused by twisting trauma to the knee. A **meniscus** (plural: menisci) is a circular piece of cartilage that forms a spacer pad in the knee joint. Both medial and lateral menisci are present in the knee joint. Injury to these pads may cause clicking and pain in the knee. They must be cared for properly to reduce the chance that they lead to arthritis in the knee.

While traumatic injuries are difficult to completely prevent, you can lessen the chance of meniscal injuries by strengthening the muscles that surround the knee joint. An exercise for strengthening these muscles involves standing on one leg, with the supporting knee straight, and then lowering the body by bending that knee. Maintaining proper alignment from the hip down to the toes will help recruit the appropriate muscles to protect the joint. Adding weights (handheld or placed in a backpack) or using an elastic resistance band (placed under the supporting foot with one end held in each hand) will allow increased intensity of the exercise. Use caution especially when performing dance activities requiring weight bearing in knee flexion, because greater knee flexion places increasing pressure on the menisci, particularly the posterior portions.

Patellofemoral Pain Syndrome and Chondromalacia

Patellofemoral pain syndrome and chondromalacia are related conditions that occur under the patella (kneecap). They can cause pain and grinding of the patella as it slides up and down in its groove on the femur. The PF pain syndrome is typically a tracking problem where the patella slides toward the lateral side instead of sliding in the middle of its groove. This misalignment can happen because a dancer is relatively knock-kneed, has a tight iliotibial band, or turns out below the knee. Ignoring the symptoms and not engaging in proper rehabilitation can lead to a condition known as chondromalacia patella; the term means "bad cartilage", but the condition is a softening and degeneration of the smooth joint surface (cartilage) on the posterior patella.

Using correct knee mechanics is an essential part of preventing patellofemoral pain syndrome. For example, turning out from below the knee puts extra stress on the patella to move laterally. This technique fault can be corrected with proper training. Stretching the lateral quadriceps and lateral hamstrings reduces tension on the IT band. This tension causes increased external rotation of the tibia and applies a lateral pull on the patella that tends to increase the likelihood of patellofemoral pain. Rolling the IT band on a foam roller is also helpful for lengthening that structure. Specific strengthening of the vastus medialis oblique muscle, while challenging to fully isolate, will help draw the patella medially (toward center) during knee extension.

Patellar Subluxation and Dislocation

Patellar subluxation and dislocation are two degrees of a traumatic injury in which the patella moves out of the groove on the femur in which it rests. It is a very painful injury if the patella does not return to its normal position. Straightening the knee usually helps the patella slide back where it should be. The difference between a dislocation and a subluxation is that in a dislocation the patella comes completely out of its groove, while with a subluxation it comes partially out of its groove and often goes back to where it belongs spontaneously. A dislocated patella is a significant injury that a medical professional should evaluate as soon as possible; it is more likely to recur after it has occurred once. Note that a dislocated patella is not a knee dislocation.

Ligament Ruptures

Four main ligaments are primarily involved in ligamentous injuries of the knee: anterior cruciate (ACL), posterior cruciate (PCL), medial, or tibial, collateral (MCL), and lateral, or fibular, collateral (LCL). The ACL is the main stabilizing ligament of the knee. The ACL is the most widely known ligament of the knee because it is commonly torn in sports, especially in females. Fortunately the incidence of ACL rupture is much less in dancers; however, it is a significant injury that usually requires surgery and several months of rehabilitation.

Knee ligament injuries are not easily preventable because of their instantaneous traumatic nature. However, research shows that dancers have far fewer ACL injuries than sports participants do. This lower incidence is attributed primarily to the very specific jump landing training that dancers receive in order to aesthetically accomplish their work. It may also be because unlike athletes, most of what dancers do is preplanned and controlled. Overall, a daily program of stretching and an every-other-day strengthening program for the muscles of the core, pelvic girdle, hips, and lower extremities will help maintain adequate muscle balance and stability around the knee joint.

Strains

Strains are injuries to a muscle, and they are one of the most common injuries in physically active people. In the lower extremities they occur most often in the quadriceps on the anterior thigh or the hamstrings on the posterior thigh. They are traumatic injuries caused by a muscle that is stretched quickly beyond its limit or when it contracts against too much resistance. The pain of most muscle strains is from overstretched muscle tissue or slight tears in the muscle. They respond well to rest and standard first aid for dance injuries. You can review the topic of rest and recovery in chapter 6, and first aid is covered later in this chapter.

Most strains occur at the musculotendinous junction, the transition zone where muscle becomes tendon. Due to the changes in tissue structure at this location, there is relative weakness of the tissue to withstand the forces generated in the muscle–tendon unit. Warming up before any activity to increase the blood supply to the area is warranted, as is daily work on strength, endurance, power, coordination, proprioception, and flexibility. The best time for stretching to ensure good flexibility of these areas is after a class or rehearsal when the tissues are warm.

Patellar Tendinopathy

Sometimes called patellar tendinitis or jumper's knee, patellar tendinopathy is a painful condition of the patellar tendon that connects all four of the quadriceps muscles in the anterior thigh to the proximal tibia. It is easy to find this tendon; it is a prominent band right below the patella. In fact, the patella is embedded in the patellar tendon. The term *tendinitis,* which means "inflammation of a tendon," is an incorrect term for this injury in most cases because research shows that no inflammation exists in a tendon with tendinopathy. It is simply a painful condition caused by overusing a tendon or putting too much strain on it.

Tendons are best prepared to withstand the demands that cause tendinopathy when their muscles are worked eccentrically, as described in chapter 2. It allows training to withstand higher loads than concentric training. The places where tendon attaches to bone are susceptible to injury if you are not warmed up and trained properly for much the same reason as musculotendinous junctions; the tissue between tendon and bone is transitional, so it may be less able to handle forces across it.

An example of eccentric proprioceptive training to prevent patellar tendinopathy is lunging forward onto a single leg from standing on two feet. In this exercise, the patella tendon absorbs the stresses of load bearing and, with the quadriceps, decelerates the knee and adapts to the forces of the limb planting on the ground with the knee moving into flexion. You can do this type of exercise from a step to increase the height from which the landing occurs and, over time, train the tendon to absorb more force. Changing the speed and direction of tendon loading are other elements used to progress this type of training.

Knee Bursitis

As noted in the discussion on the hip, bursas are lubricating sacs that help prevent undue friction in structures that rub across one another. Bursitis in the knee is usually a traumatic injury rather than an overuse injury. It occurs when a dancer falls with the knee directly striking the floor. The sign of this injury is a jellylike swelling on the anterior knee in front of the kneecap, or directly below the level of the knee joint. A common term for this injury is *water on the knee*. This sensation comes from fluid building up in one of the bursas because of the force of the injury. Although they sometimes swell a lot, traumatic bursitis is not particularly serious. Nevertheless, a medical professional would be helpful in managing it.

Osgood-Schlatter's Disease

Osgood-Schlatter's disease is seen in adolescent dancers and other athletes who jump repeatedly. It is characterized by a tender area on the anterior tibia where the patellar tendon inserts. Usually a small prominence of bone exists in this area, but with Osgood-Schlatter's disease this prominence is often enlarged because the contractions of the quadriceps muscles pull on the patellar tendon which, in turn, pulls on the bony area where it attaches. This is a place of relative weakness in the growing bone. Once a dancer's skeleton matures, the symptoms of Osgood-Schlatter's disease subside, but the added prominence on the tibia may remain as the bone solidifies.

Ankle and Foot

The incidence of injury to the ankle and foot is exceptionally high in dancers. Several factors contribute to this problem, including repetitive jumping without supportive footwear, alignment issues in the lower leg and foot, and long hours of classes and rehearsals. Injuries to the ankle and foot include lateral ankle sprains, medial ankle sprains, fractures, posterior ankle impingement syndrome, anterior ankle impingement syndrome, flexor hallucis longus (FHL) tendinopathy, Achilles tendinopathy, hallux limitus and hallux rigidus, hallux valgus, and Morton's neuroma.

Lateral Ankle Sprains

Lateral ankle sprain is far and away the most common injury in physically active people. A **sprain** is an injury to a ligament. In the lateral ankle, a sprain is often caused by a dancer catching the side of the foot on the floor, or by having his or her foot come down on another dancer's foot. The foot then turns inward, causing the sprain. Sprains can range in severity from a stretched ligament to a complete rupture of a ligament. They also can occur to several ligaments on the lateral ankle. One of these in particular, located slightly above the ankle joint and called a high ankle sprain when injured, can create long-term problems if not treated correctly. Usually ankle sprains increase in likelihood after their first occurrence, and if the ligaments are stretched out enough, this injury can result in significant ankle instability. Proper diagnosis, treatment, and rehabilitation are important for returning to dance. Because these injuries are due to accidents, the main prevention is to be careful! However, there are also certain measures that can assist in prevention, such as correct alignment of the subtalar joint, the talocrural joint, and the cuboid bone, usually by manual manipulation or mobilization. Also, when dancers cannot relevé correctly on half pointe, they usually sickle to get higher, which can lead to ankle sprain. Therefore they can reduce the risk of sickling by making sure that the first metatarsal joint has good range of motion. Finally, improving proprioception by challenging single leg stance (standing on one leg) in many different ways can reduce sprain risk.

Medial Ankle Sprains

Medial ankle sprain is a similar, but less common, injury than lateral ankle sprain. This is because the outward turning movement of the foot required to cause it is less likely to occur and the medial ligament complex of the ankle is stronger than the lateral ligaments. This injury generally requires more recovery time than a lateral ankle sprain.

Fractures

When fractures occur in the ankle region they often accompany a ligamentous injury. Fractures may occur to the medial or lateral malleolus when the foot tilts during a ligament injury. In severe cases of sprain, one or both of the malleoli can sustain a fracture. Another type of fracture in the foot is the avulsion fracture, which can occur when the proximal end (closer to the midfoot) of the fifth metatarsal located along the side of the foot is avulsed by a tendon that attaches to it. One of the most common fractures seen in dancers is a fracture of the shaft of the fifth metatarsal, called dancer's fracture. It is caused by twisting through the middle portion of the foot during a fall. A key finding of many fractures is crepitus, a crunching sensation caused by the broken pieces of the bone rubbing together. Fractures should not be managed without proper medical care. Preventing avulsion injuries in the foot and ankle is similar to what was described for avulsion injuries in the hip and pelvis.

Stress fractures are different from the fractures just identified, because they are caused by repetitive strain on a bone instead of by a traumatic incident that causes a bone's structure to break. In dancers, stress fractures around the ankle and foot most commonly occur in the metatarsals, especially the second, third, and fourth, and in the fibula. They are accompanied by tenderness on the bones in very localized areas.

Prevention of stress fractures requires strengthening of the intrinsic muscles of the foot (the small muscles between the metatarsals). **Doming exercises**, which involve contracting the muscles of the arch and the flexors of the proximal phalanges, and toe extension exercises are part of this routine (see figure 9.2). Prevention also includes general calf stretching to help ensure that weight bearing is not only on the balls of the feet but shared equally by the forefoot and heels when standing. Other ways of reducing the chance of stress fractures in the feet include avoiding rapid increases in the intensity or duration of footwork or pointe work and being sure that pointe shoes are properly fitted. Tucking the tied strings of pointe shoes under the vamp can put increased extrinsic pressure on the metatarsals, as will overly narrow shoes that compress the metatarsals.

Posterior Ankle Impingement Syndrome

Posterior ankle impingement syndrome can be caused by several factors, all of which are the trapping of soft tissue or bone behind the ankle joint. This is most common in genres of dance that require extreme plantar flexion, such as ballet, particularly ballet en pointe. Ligaments or other soft tissues can be pinched by the bones coming together during plantar flexion, but the most common type of posterior impingement is attributed to having an extra small bone, called an os trigonum, behind the ankle. Many dancers can participate fine with an os trigonum, but when symptoms associated with it or other types of posterior ankle impingement become too burdensome, they should seek a medical consultation.

It is impossible to prevent the types of posterior impingement that are congenital, such as the presence of an os trigonum. However, some helpful measures exist for reducing the chance that these types of conditions become problematic to dancers. The posterior gliding motion of the talus during plié

is an important prerequisite motion, as is incorporating the heel in pointing the foot. Other foot motions necessary to dance are often lacking and may require corrective health care consultation in order to establish normal ankle motion. Doing heel clocks while standing on a flat foot will train the joint to work well. **Heel clocks** are special weight-bearing exercises to mobilize the subtalar joint; imagine the face of a clock under your heel, and move the heel around the clock. Figures 9.2*a* and 9.2*b* show the heel clocks exercise. Male dancers do not plantar flex their ankles as much as females, especially females who dance en pointe; thus, they may not experience posterior impingement symptoms.

Anterior Impingement Syndrome

Anterior ankle impingement syndrome is similar to the posterior type of impingement, except it happens in the front of the ankle. Repeatedly going into demi-plié forces the front edge of the tibia near the ankle to hit against the talus (a bone at the top of the foot). Over time, this impact can create additional bone deposits that become painful

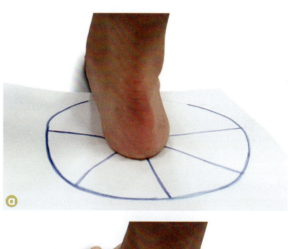

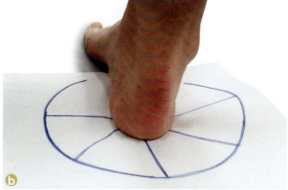

Figure 9.2 Heel clocks exercises showing foot eversion (a) and inversion (b) are helpful in training the joints of the foot.

© Brenda Critchfield

and limit the ankle's dorsiflexion range of motion. Soft tissues can be caught between these two bony landmarks as well. This type of impingement may lead to inflammation of the tissue.

Correct alignment of the foot and ankle when doing a demi- or grand plié is essential for prevention of anterior ankle impingement, as is proper form when landing from jumps. The knee should come down directly over the foot at the second metatarsal. If the knee is allowed to move inward, foot pronation and unnecessary stress on knee ligaments may occur. Also, landing in too deep a plié over time may cause an increased impingement between the front edge of the tibia and the talus.

Flexor Hallucis Longus Tendinopathy

Flexor hallucis longus (FHL) tendinopathy is also known as dancer's tendinopathy; it is rare in nondancers. The flexor hallucis longus muscle is a major flexor of the great toe. Its tendon runs through a tunnel on the medial portion of the ankle. When restricted in this tunnel or when overused, the tendon can become irritated, swollen, and painful. Often a person can feel crepitus, caused by a swollen tendon trying to move, when placing a hand over the area of the tendon on the medial ankle and flexing and extending the great toe.

Unfortunately, many dancers use their FHL to point their ankle and foot, which adds to the load on the FHL tendon, and it can quickly develop an overuse syndrome. Dancers should learn to elevate their heels by using their gastrocnemius-soleus muscle group (calf muscles) that inserts into their heel via the Achilles tendon before they activate their FHL. The role of the FHL should be to push through the big toe to attain a fully pointed foot. In addition, discouraging foot pronation in technique class is essential because pronation puts excessive tension on the FHL and the posterior tibialis tendons, which may lead to tendinopathy.

Achilles Tendinopathy

Achilles tendinopathy is a painful condition of the Achilles tendon, and it is caused by overuse. Classical ballet can cause Achilles tendinopathy because of the pressure placed on the tendon by pointe shoe ribbons. Also, the rigid collar of character shoes can rub on the tendon to cause tendinopathy. Even when working in bare feet, dancers can develop tendinopathy from overuse. When this injury progresses to a more serious state where degeneration of the tendon occurs, it becomes tendinosis.

The best preventive methods for this injury are a flexibility program for the calf muscles followed by a strengthening program for the anterior leg muscles that dorsiflex the foot. This program will help balance the strength and flexibility in the lower leg. Whereas much of dance, especially ballet, requires significant plantar flexion, the Achilles tendon has a tendency to shorten unless it is purposefully stretched. Pronation of the feet should be discouraged because it places the medial Achilles tendon under excessive tension. Sewing elastics into the pointe shoe ribbons will accommodate the widening and narrowing of the lower leg and reduce the friction on the Achilles tendon.

Hallux Limitus and Hallux Rigidus

Hallux limitus is the medical name for a big toe that is unable to move through its full range of motion at the first metatarsophalangeal joint. If it progresses to the point where the joint becomes immobile, the condition is called hallux rigidus. These conditions can be debilitating for many dancers because they limit the first metatarsophalangeal joint's hyperextension of the great toe, which prevents proper relevé and demi-pointe. The two types of hallux limitus or rigidus are structural and functional. The structural type is caused by arthritis or other abnormality of the joint or bones that blocks first metatarsophalangeal hyperextension. Functional hallux limitus occurs during weight bearing; the positioning of the forward portion of the foot causes a restriction in the metatarsophalangeal hyperextension that is not seen when the foot is not bearing weight.

Hallux Valgus

Hallux valgus is a big toe that points out toward the other four toes, and it is commonly experienced by dancers (figure 9.3). It may in some instances be congenital (determined at birth), but it also can be caused by excessive pronation, especially from forcing turnout. When a dancer forces turnout, the big toe is repeatedly forced in that direction. Over time, a bunion may develop on the inner portion of the foot at the first metatarsophalangeal joint. As discussed earlier, this condition can also result from ill-fitting pointe shoes.

You can prevent problems with the big toe and the first metatarsophalangeal joint by wearing correctly sized shoes—not too narrow or too small in the forefoot and toe box area. Proper fit will allow the hallux to have normal joint motion. High-heeled shoes can be a culprit, as well as hard dance footwear such as pointe shoes and character shoes. Gentle range of motion exercises specific to the first metatarsophalangeal joint should be part

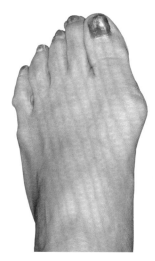

Figure 9.3 This dancer's foot shows the outward angle of the big toe compared to the foot that is characteristic of hallux valgus.

© Jeffrey A. Russell.

of your daily routine. Such exercises are especially important when coming out of shoes that restrict motion of the toes.

Morton's Neuroma

Morton's neuroma is an overuse condition affecting the nerves that travel to the toes between the distal ends of the metatarsals. Often caused by wearing shoes (especially pointe shoes or character shoes) with an overly narrow toe box, adjacent metatarsal heads squeeze the nerve between them. The nerve responds by becoming thickened and painful, followed by tingling and numbness. These sensations are felt on the facing surfaces of two adjacent toes. The second and third toes are the most commonly affected pair, followed by the third and fourth toes.

Spine

The spine is complex because it comprises multiple joints and encases the spinal cord. Therefore, injuries to the spine can be debilitating and difficult to heal. Injuries include spondylolysis and spondylolisthesis, articular facet syndrome, discogenic back pain, lordosis, strains, and ligament sprains.

Spondylolysis and Spondylolisthesis

Spondylolysis is essentially a stress fracture of a location in one or more lumbar vertebrae known as the pars interarticularis. It typically starts from a congenital weakness in this location. Lumbar vertebra 4 is the most commonly affected, followed by lumbar vertebra 5. Repeated hyperextension, or hyperextension with rotation of the spine (seen

in many dance maneuvers such as an exaggerated arabesque) and anterior tilting of the pelvis are the usual causes of an increase in symptoms. As the condition worsens, the stress fracture may become a fracture through the pars interarticularis. When this fracture occurs, one or more of the lumbar vertebrae may slip forward. This aggravated situation is called spondylolisthesis.

A major key to reducing the chance of spondylolysis and spondylolisthesis is limiting the amount of repetitive lumbar flexion and extension that is performed during a dancer's growth spurt. Daily flexibility exercises to loosen the tight muscles of the spine, pelvis, hips, and legs will reduce the stresses placed on the bones. Follow flexibility exercises with muscle strengthening, stabilization training, and endurance training. Conscious breathing, by inhaling to expand the posterior rib cage and exhaling with assistance from the abdominal muscles, is a good internal warm-up and will relax the tension on the spinal joints.

Articular Facet Syndrome

The vertebral column's individual pieces fit together with pairs of bladelike bony structures called articular facets. They are covered with smooth joint cartilage and help control the spine's stability. Articular facet syndrome is a condition of pain and inflammation in these joints, and it can also refer to the facets' surfaces being slightly dislodged. In older people, the facet joints may be affected by arthritis that creates pain and limits mobility.

Changes in joint biomechanics in the spine can be caused by changes in spinal alignment brought about by muscular tightness in the lumbar extensors, hamstrings, tensor fasciae latae, and quadratus lumborum. Minimizing movements of hyperflexion with rotation and hyperextension will reduce the stresses on the facet joints. A stability program for the segmental lumbar spinal joints that includes deep abdominal control will maximize the chance that the spinal segments remain healthy.

Discogenic Back Pain

Discogenic back pain (back pain caused by an intervertebral disc problem) is one of the most difficult low-back conditions to treat. Pairs of vertebrae in the spinal column are separated by intervertebral discs. A disc has a gelatinous middle surrounded by a fibrous outer portion. In instances where excessive compressive force is placed on a disc or when the discs are less resilient because of aging, the inner soft part of the disc can protrude through the fibrous part. When this protrusion (called a herniation) pushes against a nerve root running from the spinal cord, pain, tingling, and numbness can occur, both at the location of the herniation and downward along the area where the nerve travels into the lower extremity. When this happens to one or more nerve roots that converge into the sciatic nerve, the condition is called sciatica. The common name for a disc herniation is a slipped disc. However, the disc does not actually slip from its location between the vertebrae; the protruding herniation generates the symptoms.

The best prevention for discogenic pain is to minimize forward flexion in sitting and standing positions, which will reduce the possibility of disc injury. In addition, decrease compression from high vertical jumps by not repeating such jumps excessively and by learning good landing technique. Developing strength and endurance of the stabilizer and mobilizer muscles of the trunk and pelvic girdle will allow better motor control and proprioception throughout dance activities that, in turn, will decrease the demands on the vertebral discs.

Strains

Muscle strains in the back are usually a result of improper lifting techniques, such as in partnering or when moving equipment during theater load-in and strike. Contracting muscles when they are in an overly stretched position can also cause strains. Strains may occur more readily when a dancer is not sufficiently warmed up. Several layers of muscle exist in the trunk and along the spine. These muscles must work in coordination as well as be equipped with the strength and endurance required for the demands placed on them. Prevention of these injuries requires good strength and flexibility programs for all of the muscles in the spine.

Ligament Sprains

Ligament sprains occur in the spine relatively infrequently, and they result from trauma. The spine has many supporting ligaments, most of which are quite strong. Therefore, it takes a fair amount of force and adverse movement to cause a spinal sprain. As with muscle strains, adequate strength and endurance in the muscles of the spine can assist in prevention.

First Aid: Treating Common Dance Injuries

Despite all of the preventive measures to avoid injury, most dancers have or will experience an injury of one form or another in their career. Knowing how to properly care for an injury will reduce pain, frustration, and time away from dancing. Once an injury has occurred, immediate steps can be taken to care for the injury and reduce time away from dance. These immediate steps are known as first aid, and they are explained in this section.

Use PRICED: Protection, Rest, Ice, Compression, Elevation, and Diagnosis

You may be able to drastically reduce pain and limit the time away from activity due to an acute injury if you take care of the injury promptly and accurately. Remember the acronym PRICED, and use it as a guide for immediate treatment of injuries. Using PRICED within the first minutes and hours following an injury helps control the inflammation, which therefore reduces pain. The acronym is summarized as follows:

› **P**rotection: Remove additional danger or risk from injured area.
› **R**est: Stop dancing, and stop moving the injured area.
› **I**ce: Apply ice to the injured area for 20 minutes every 2 hours.
› **C**ompression: Apply an elastic compression wrap to the injured area.
› **E**levation: Raise the injured area above the heart.
› **D**iagnosis: Have a health care professional evaluate an acute injury.

Avoid HARM: Heat, Alcohol, Running, Massage

In the first few days following an acute injury, remember the acronym HARM. The acronym summarizes what to avoid, as follows:

› **H**eat: Any kind of heat will speed up circulation, resulting in more swelling and a longer recovery. Heat includes long hot showers, hot tubs, sauna, heating pads, and topical treatments that create heat on the skin.
› **A**lcohol: Alcoholic beverages can increase swelling and cause a longer recovery time.
› **R**unning or excessive exercise: Exercising too early can cause more damage to the injured body part, because the structures have been damaged and are not strong enough to prevent further injury. Exercise also increases circulation and temperature, which results in more swelling and a longer recovery.

> **M**assage: Massage increases swelling and bleeding into the tissue, resulting in more pain and a prolonged recovery.

Control the Inflammatory Process

When an injury is sustained, the cells within the injured tissue are damaged. The body tries to limit the damage by releasing a variety of chemicals that create the inflammatory process. Redness, swelling, increase in temperature, loss of function, and pain are all symptoms of the body's inflammatory process. At first, the body cannot determine the difference between a rolled ankle and a cut on the foot from stepping on something; it reacts the same way. The inflammation brings white blood cells to the area to defend against foreign substances, dispose of damaged tissue, and promote new cell growth. The inflammatory process is necessary for the healing of the tissue; however, too much can be problematic. With an acute injury, the goal is to control the inflammatory process but not eliminate it. Controlling inflammation will help reduce pain and increase function to the injured body part. Figure 9.4 shows the inflammatory process.

The inflammatory process also occurs in chronic injuries, but usually the symptoms are not as prevalent as in an acute injury. Chronic injuries are usually the result of microtrauma to tissue, and the body is able to heal it initially. Microtrauma refers to minute damage within tissues, usually from repetitive overuse. If the source of the microtrauma is removed, you probably won't even know that the tissue was injured. However, if the microtrauma happens repeatedly, then the inflammatory response is recurring, and eventually you notice symptoms. You should treat chronic injuries as early as you notice symptoms so that they do not result in a more serious or permanent condition. Many times dancers ignore tendinopathy in its early stages. After a while, the body starts to make adaptations to protect the injured area. Sometimes these adaptations can lead to long-term injury. An example would be Achilles tendinopathy. If it is ignored and the source of the problem that is causing the chronic inflammation is not fixed, the body will start to adapt to the stresses. This adaptation sometimes leads to a thickening of the Achilles tendon, loss of movement, and the dancer being more susceptible to a total tendon rupture. At this stage it is called tendinosis.

Here are some tips to help prevent and treat chronic injuries:

> Don't ignore pain, especially if it has been more than 3 days and doesn't go away even after icing and resting.

> Develop and maintain an overall body conditioning and strength training program that reduces muscular imbalances and increases overall strength. Use cross-training to work on weaknesses. See chapter 3 for more information on how to achieve this goal.

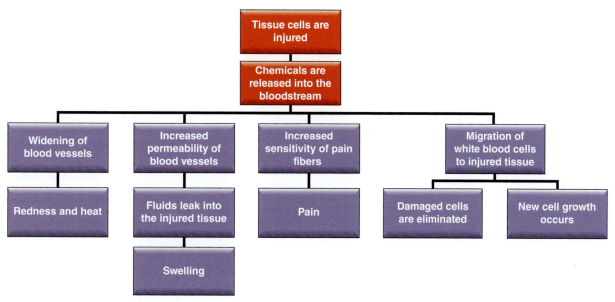

Figure 9.4   Inflammatory process.

Reprinted, by permission, from N. Sefcovic and B. Critchfield, 2010, *Resource paper: First aid for dancers.* © International Association for Dance Medicine & Science, 2010. Available: http://www.iadms.org/?290

> Be aware of movement in classes. Count how many repetitions of a certain movement you do on the right side, and make sure you do the same amount on the left to prevent imbalances.

> Concentrate on posture during the hours you are not dancing. Check to see if you are standing in turnout, if your shoulders are rounded, and if your neck is in a forward position. Notice whether you are looking down at your phone, computer, or tablet. If so, make an effort to correct those postural habits.

> Use a foam roller, lacrosse ball, tennis ball, or golf ball for self-massage work, which helps release tense muscles. However, do not use one of these objects or techniques on an acute muscle strain; it will worsen that acute injury. Remember the M in HARM.

> Be willing to make changes if you notice lingering pain.

> If you have a chronic injury, follow the advice of your medical professional, which may include resting, rehabilitation, strength training, and conditioning.

> You can avoid many chronic injuries if you take care of pain early, perform cross-training and conditioning correctly to strengthen the whole body and prevent imbalances, and follow proper technique and body mechanics.

Dancers can develop awareness of their technique and habits, and help to reduce the number and severity of the injuries that will occur during their careers. However, it is important for dancers to know how to deal with injuries early and when to seek medical advice. First aid is the initial step in dealing with an injury. Always remember to use PRICED and to avoid HARM. This knowledge can empower all dancers to care for their bodies and enjoy a long, satisfying career.

Summary

Injuries are common in dance. To prepare for them you should understand how to prevent them and also how to recognize and deal with them when they do occur. Key prevention strategies include examining your alignment, your movement habits, and your muscle imbalances. Once you are injured, know how and when to apply first aid. Finally, because injuries can be serious and affect your long-term goals, seek out the appropriate medical attention if needed.

Application Activity: **Assess Your Body**

Assess your body in the order that the chapter uses for injury descriptions. Start with your upper extremities (arms, shoulder joints, and shoulder blades), then your hips and pelvis, knees, feet and ankles, and finish with the spine. For each area, determine where you have muscle imbalances. For example, is the front of your chest too tight, and are the muscles in the upper back weak? Are your quadriceps tight and your hamstrings too weak? With each muscle imbalance that you describe, see if you can design one or two exercises that might correct the imbalance. With this activity, you will be on your way to fulfilling your goals of preventing injuries while you improve your technique.

Review Questions

1. What is the difference between acute and chronic injuries?

2. What are some of the genetic factors, bad habits, and muscle imbalances that can lead to chronic injuries?

3. How can you prevent dance injuries in your training practice?

4. What are the most common dance injuries to the upper extremities, hip and pelvis, knee, foot and ankle, and spine?

5. What is the purpose of first aid, and when should it be applied it to an immediate injury?

 For chapter-specific supplemental learning activities, study aids, suggested readings, web links, and more, visit the web resource at www.HumanKinetics.com/DancerWellness.

Part IV

Assessments for Dancer Wellness

The final part of the book describes methods of assessing dancer wellness and creating a personalized dancer wellness plan. Screening (chapter 10) is an excellent tool for learning more about enhancing technique and preventing injuries. Your dancer wellness plan (chapter 11) gives you step-by-step guidelines for developing your plan and tracking it over time.

A dance screening collects information regarding your unique state of health. Screenings may include physical assessments and questions that gather information about nutrition and psychological wellness. Screenings work best for improving wellness when followed by educational programs. Information from a screening can assist in designing training programs outside of class to achieve greater fitness. Injury prevention strategies may also be added to your practices. Education about nutrition, stress reduction, performance anxiety, or confidence issues may be addressed in response to screening results.

In chapter 11, you can design your dancer wellness plan using the sidebars from all of the previous chapters. You examined self-awareness,

empowerment, goal setting, and diversity through the topics in chapters 1 through 10. In each chapter, you completed questions and activities related to the topics of study. In this final chapter, you can use these insights and strategies to design your individualized wellness plan, and use it over time to continue enhancing your training and well-being.

In summary, keeping the body healthy requires attention to many parts of your daily life as a dancer. Your body and mind make up the instrument you use in dance, and you must take care of that instrument. You must carefully consider what you eat and when. You might reduce the risk of injury through proper alignment, sound technique, and conditioning that enhances the strength, flexibility, and stamina of the body. If you do get injured, you must break the pattern of ignoring or hiding injuries, and seek proper medical attention. Facing and treating an injury can eventually reduce time away from dance and limit the risk of reinjury. Dancer screenings can assist in all of these areas of education. As you empower yourself in the development and care of your instrument, you can approach your life's passion with joy and full energy.

Dancer Screening Programs

Marijeanne Liederbach, PhD, PT, and Gary Galbraith, MFA

Gary Galbraith in Martha Graham's "Night Journey." Photo: John Deane

LEARNING OBJECTIVES

After reading this chapter, you will be able to do the following:

❯ Understand the screening process.

❯ Describe the purpose, types, and components of screenings.

❯ Know how to use information from screenings to prevent injuries and improve technique.

❯ Understand the factors that determine the type of screening or evaluation.

❯ Explain the various outcomes from screenings.

One of the best ways for you to become the most outstanding dancer you can possibly be is to participate in a dancer screening. Like all athletes, dancers want to be successful in their activity, and they must have above average strength, flexibility, coordination, endurance, concentration, and discipline. Dancers are subjected to rigorous physical training and aesthetic demands, such as the need to have extreme joint mobility, powerful jumping skills, supernormal balance ability, and depending on the dance genre, a specific body type. This chapter describes what dancer screenings are and why they can be so helpful for you in the pursuit of your goals as a dancer.

As many as 97 percent of dancers will get injured each year, and they will have to take time away from what they love to do because of those injuries. This chapter examines how a dancer screening can help you lower your chance of getting injured by being better prepared for all of the demands of dance that you will encounter. The chapter also discusses how your individual participation in a dancer screening can not only help you excel personally, it can also help to revolutionize the entire profession of dance by adding information to a large scientific database of information about dancer health. When dance medicine scientists and researchers have a high volume of health information to combine and analyze, they are able to see how dancers can train and perform better with fewer injuries.

Understanding the Screening Process

The **dancer screening process** involves a collection of uniform information by a team of experts including dance educators and dance medicine specialists. This team will gather the information from individual dancers about their personal history and their training environment. Screenings also include a selection of physical measurements related to dance activities, such as measurements of muscle strength, joint motion, flexibility, and cardiovascular fitness.

These variables are obtained through tests that yield objective scores. For example, a dancer's external and internal hip rotation can be quantified in stance or prone using low-friction rotational discs or a goniometer, respectively, each of which provides a numeric value. **Rotational discs** are small platforms placed on ball bearings that can rotate in either direction. A **goniometer** is a tool used to measure the angle of a joint between two limbs. Another example could be measuring left versus right leg jump height, which can be given a numeric score when measured using measuring tapes or other instruments. Figure 10.1a and 10.1b illustrate the rotational discs and the goniometer.

Purpose of Screening

The purpose of dancer screenings is twofold. First, they assist individual dancers in identifying factors in their physical and psychological makeup that can be improved in order to enhance their dancing. Second, it is to assist the dance community in better identifying the boundaries of functional capacity that dancers need in order to perform within the largest window of safety and wellness.

The ability to dance well and to dance safely is influenced by many variables, including those intrinsic to the dancer such as muscle strength, age, years of training, general health habits, past injury history, coping style, muscular flexibility, as well as variables in the environment that are extrinsic to the dancer such as shoe wear, floor surface, and teacher or school policies about rest. One method of determining the relative importance of each of

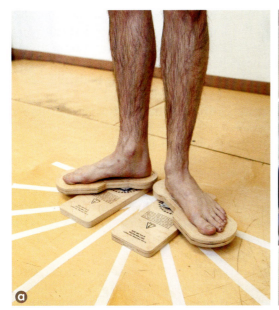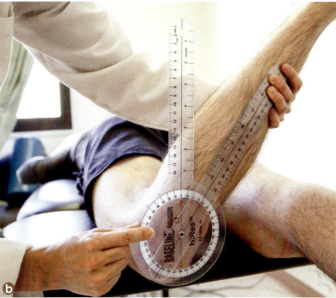

Figure 10.1 Methods of measuring turnout: *(a)* Rotational discs measure functional turnout; *(b)* the goniometer measures passive turnout.

Photos courtesy of Colleen Hahn.

these stand-alone variables to a dancer's health is to compare individual dancer findings to the average values of each of those factors from a very large sample—a group of dancers. With a large number of data points, dance medicine experts can calculate anonymous dancer norms, also called normative values. **Normative values** are expected values for a given population of people based on previously measured values from people in that same population. One of the most successful ways to frame answers about optimal health for each dancer is to obtain normative screening data on large groups of healthy dancers within a given dance form.

When the range of capacities of injury-free, elite dancers from a particular form are known, clinicians are equipped with normative values to which individual patient measures can be compared. This information assists in identifying whether an individual dancer possesses the attributes necessary to participate safely in his or her form of dance. Having this data is also helpful at the time of an injury occurrence and over the course of the dancer's rehabilitation, in order to evaluate how that dancer is progressing toward restoration of preinjury level of health.

Averaged group screening data can be a valuable guide to health care professionals in anticipating clinical problems. It can help teachers develop training programs that maximize performance while avoiding injury. For dancers, it may serve as a basis for comparison of their personal fitness levels with that of elite dancers and as a guide for what to focus on in their personal training to attain their peak performance.

Even though large group normative data is used for individual comparison, dance medicine specialists understand the aim is not to develop average dancers. Each dancer has a unique set of attributes that should be optimized during dance performance. A dance medicine specialist can assess whether risk factors, relative to the larger group normative values, are present that predispose a dancer or group of dancers to health problems so that a personal best health program can be put into place. Success in dance does not rely solely on any one variable. Rather, a combination of many skills forms a dancer's talent and determines success. What one dancer may excel at, another may not. A dancer who may be considered deficient in one area should be encouraged to improve in that area when possible or make up for it in another. Identifying an individual dancer's attributes and concerns is the first step toward providing the dancer with a specific counseling, treatment, or training regimen aimed at preventing injury and maximizing performance potential. Screenings provide dancers with guidance for how to progress to a successful life in dance.

For normative data to be useful, it must be **valid**, meaning that it has to capture accurately the information that each researcher or practitioner intended to capture, in an equally careful manner. Collecting data using validated measures in a standardized or uniform way between dance medicine and dance education professionals is necessary in order for the combined data to be trustworthy. With trustworthy information gathered, dance medicine and dance education professionals can confidently associate causes of injuries and observe their trends in order to more effectively work with dancers and dance organizations to prevent them.

Types and Components of Screening

Dancer screenings can have a number of components, starting with an appointment that entails an individual dancer interview conducted by a licensed health care professional to obtain a thorough medical history. The second component is a brief battery of functional movement tests by a medical practitioner or a dance educator, designed to assess some of the functional skills of the dancer, such as the turnout and jump tests. The third component is a confidential discussion between each dancer and the specialist who conducted the screening. In this discussion, the professional will summarize all of the information and provide appropriate individualized exercise and referral recommendations that aim to help that dancer with his or her health, lifestyle, and training concerns and needs. At the end of this screening, the professional will also provide the dancer with information on health care resources in the event that further workup in any area is needed. Figures 10.2a and 10.2b show a typical screening environment, doing both interviews and physical tests.

Other types of dancer health visits can sometimes be considered screenings. For example, some facilities offer free wellness visits during which a dancer may not go through a physical exam of various systems, such as the cardiovascular system and the musculoskeletal system, or a battery of measured functional tests; rather, the dancer may opt to spend the session learning about social support groups for dancers with work stress, psychosocial concerns, disordered eating, or depression.

Another type of health visit a dancer may participate in may be a more formal full office evaluation, typically with a medical doctor, for routine tests of human health. Such tests include laboratory tests that review blood work, periodic mammograms as appropriate, or radiographic studies to diagnose complaints of bone, joint, or other types of pain.

It is also possible to have longer, more comprehensive annual screenings with periodic follow-up screenings conducted on dancers in professional companies who have the resources to do so. Often these organizations have a line of research questions in place that may involve more complex physical and psychological testing and a recording of injury occurrence.

 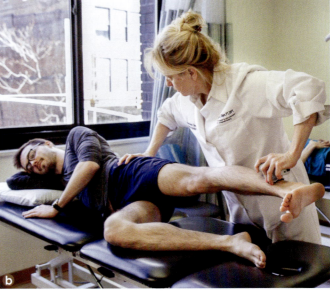

Figure 10.2 Dancer screening in progress: *(a)* the interview process; *(b)* muscle assessment.

Photos courtesy of Colleen Hahn.

Goals of Screening

First and foremost, dancer screenings are meant to help dancers improve their personal awareness about their general health and to direct them to a primary care physician, and then to specialists in cardiology, nutrition, podiatry, gynecology, psychology, as well as to sleep specialists, conditioning or somatic education teachers, or other complementary care professionals as needed. In addition, screenings aim to help dancers determine whether they possess any conditions that may predispose them to injury during their training, such as a significant weakness or lack of control in the musculature of the trunk. Screenings are intended to introduce dancers to qualified health professionals who can guide them into the whole health system as necessary for their health needs. Once a dancer establishes a rapport with a health professional, it is easier to know where to turn when a health need arises.

In addition to helping individual dancers, dancer screenings are also meant for the larger purpose of transforming how everyone in the profession of dance, including teachers, choreographers, dancers, studio owners, and artistic directors, thinks about dancer health in order to improve the well-being, career span, and performance of all dancers worldwide. The best way to make changes to the profession is to employ prevention behaviors. These behaviors include first reviewing the existing research that has been collected in a validated manner on large numbers of dancers. This information will show the frequency and type of injuries that occur among them. The next stage is to improve the quality of clinical research studies going forward that aim to improve dancer health, using a strong scientific basis for detecting a change in the count of injury. The last stage is to make positive changes in the training of dancers and, using this valuable information, assess whether fewer injuries happen. If the number of injuries experienced by dancers is reduced, one can conclude that the effect on dancer health is positive.

A common understanding among professionals is that screenings are to be used for health promotion, dancer education, and research. Most screenings are not used to determine whether a dancer should be admitted into a school or company, whether a dancer should be given a role, or whether a dancer should be promoted to a more advanced technique class. Such a practice could be viewed as discriminatory, and many countries have laws that prohibit such bias. In addition, using screenings to show preference toward particular dancers contradicts most educational goals. Screenings are used to promote healthy practices for dancers, promote effective and efficient dance training, help in creating a unique and personalized profile for the dancer, identify risk factors that may impact the dancer, help in developing a personal training program, and help advocate for health-minded learning and working environments.

Limitations of Screening

Limitations exist in screening. A dance screening is a snapshot of the dancer's condition at the time of the screening. It is almost as if a picture of the dancer is taken to assess the conditions when the screening is administered. Some conditions assessed, such as an adult dancer's height, may not change very much over time. Other conditions, such as a dancer's strength or fitness levels, may vary over time.

For example, if a dancer is screened at the beginning of a company's season or at the beginning of an academic school year, it is possible that some strength characteristics may be lower at this point than during the peak performance period. By contrast, the level of fatigue may be higher during the time of peak performance than it was at the beginning of the season or school year. This finding does not mean that the dancer has failed or is weak, but rather the screening has helped identify areas that may need attention at that point in time. With appropriate training and conditioning, most likely strength will improve over time.

Several factors contribute to the type of screening designed and administered for a group of dancers. These factors include goals of the screening initiative, which types of experts are part of the screening team, and the types of dancers being assessed, as well as what conditions exist for these dancers. Available resources can also impact the type of screening. Remember that screenings serve as a way to look at several factors quickly at a given point in time, whereas an evaluation is a means to provide a more in-depth analysis. Screenings are also used as a way to help promote dancer health and education.

What Screening Research Demonstrates About Patterns of Dance Injury

More than 30 years of research in dance indicates that injuries of the lower extremities are by far the most common, as seen in figure 10.3. To better understand why dance injury patterns emerge and which preventive programs should be used, you need to understand the conditions associated with the occurrence of each dance injury. Data from

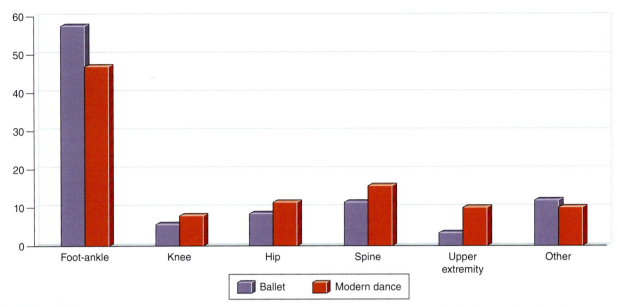

Figure 10.3 Percent of time-lost injuries by anatomic region over 5 years among elite ballet and modern dancers.
Designed by Marijeanne Liederbach.

dancer health screenings help to accomplish this goal. For example, published screening-related research has provided these conclusions:

> Dancers who have substantial complaints of physical discomfort go on to sustain an injury that results in time lost from dance.

> Strong statistical associations exist between insufficient ankle and hip joint control and injuries in traditional classical dance.

> Dancers who worry, who have low social support, experience negative life events, and have a low sense of control in their training environment are at increased risk for injury.

> Dancers are at higher risk for injury when they are in a state of fatigue from lack of adequate rest periods and fueling (balanced and timely nutrition and hydration). They might also experience fatigue from the long-term monotony in training. For more about nutrition and hydration, review chapter 8.

> Personality traits associated with the drive necessary to achieve elite levels of physical skill in dance have also been associated with occurrence of injuries. Dancers with the greatest number of total injuries throughout their careers were found to be significantly more enterprising than those with fewer injuries, and dancers with stress fractures and other overuse injuries were those with the personality type of overachiever, or perfectionist.

Chapter 5 provides information about personality traits that can create problems for dancers.

SAFETY TIP

Warning Signs

Be aware of the warning signs of injury. If you are having pain or discomfort for an extended period of time, seek medical advice. Build a good social support system of people you trust and who are qualified to talk about the issues that stress you. Be sure you are getting adequate rest and nutrition. Finally, be in the best possible physical condition that you can in terms of stamina, strength, and flexibility.

Traditional dance technique training alone does not sufficiently prepare dancers for the workloads they encounter during rehearsal and performance. For example, a screening study done by Liederbach et al. in 2000 looked at data collected from 800 healthy, noninjured, advanced dancers. They found that 68 percent of them had both abnormal calf muscle tightness and poor calf muscle endurance; 63 percent had abnormal hip flexor tightness; 50 percent were not able to maintain their lower-extremity alignment during functional tasks such as stepping off of a bench; 40 percent were unable to balance on a single leg with their eyes closed for 30 seconds; and 38 percent had abnormally weak strength (trunk stability). This information illuminates in part why the number of injuries seen in dancers is so high. Dancers must perform many demanding movements each day, such as partnering, high kicking, and jumping for maximal height more than 200 times per class. From these types of studies it is clear that the ideal level of preparedness for these tasks is lacking, leaving dancers vulnerable to injuries.

Interpreting Data from Screenings

Whenever a person trains for an activity, his or her body adapts in various ways to meet the demands of that training. Regular participation in dance over time will elicit certain training responses in each dancer's body. The data obtained from dance screenings can then be used in several ways:

> To help guide a person to an appropriate form and level of dance

> To prescribe adjunct activities to reduce injury risk

> To design modifying equipment, such as special shoes, padding, or taping

> To identify those in need of referral to specialists for further evaluation

> To predict performance

It is known that dance training results in muscle group imbalances that may lead to injuries. Screenings are used to detect the training responses each dancer's body has gone through. By so doing, clinicians and educators are better equipped to empower each dancer with information about how they can rebalance where necessary. In this way they can achieve their best potential and avoid downfalls, such as physical injury from training in a suboptimal way. Many past research studies have demonstrated that dancers have adaptive shortening or lengthening of calf and hip muscles, which often lead to compensatory positions and motions of neighboring joints and associated movement impairments. **Compensatory movements** are adjustments made for injury or weakness, such as when one muscle works harder than it normally would in order to make up for a different injured muscle.

In addition, dancers lack strength in certain muscle groups, which can be problematic because dance can be such an intense, highly repetitive, and high-impact activity. Given the physical demands of dance, muscular strength and endurance are important attributes for optimal joint and postural stability, shock absorption, motor control, and performance stamina. Relative imbalances and deficits in strength can pose significant risks for injury,

particularly when a dancer becomes fatigued. A cyclical pattern of injuries among dancers coincides with increased volume in training, suggesting an effect of fatigue. **Cyclical** patterns are repetitive and repeating, such as the passing of the seasons each year. This information can be understood more precisely from participation in a dancer screening and put to healthful purposes.

Once screening data are available, it is possible to design strategies to move forward with improving dancer health research. One of the reasons for the high number of injuries is that dance training has traditionally been dictated by artistic traditions and not the scientific principles used by Olympic and professional athletes. Through a dancer screening, dancers can learn about these scientific principles and incorporate them into the way they train. In this way, they are better prepared for the specific stresses and strains they will encounter during rehearsal and performance. They can also learn a lot about their own anatomy and when an ache or pain is a normal training response or the start of an injury. The physical and mental challenges that dancers face can be very high, so having well-informed training guidelines will make a big difference in terms of their ability to reduce their own risk for injuries and other health problems.

Using Data From Screenings to Prevent Injuries

In 2004, the International Association for Dance Medicine & Science (IADMS) assembled a research subcommittee, known as the Standard Measures Consensus Initiative (SMCI), to look into ways to improve the community's work on injury reduction. At that time, IADMS realized that dance educators, scientists, administrators, and health professionals did not have an agreed upon and universally used set of definitions within dance injury research and reporting. For example, researchers in dance were not uniformly defining the term "injury" in the same way as each other, therefore they were getting unreasonably different counts of injury between the different groups of dancers they were studying. For example, some authors conveyed in their work, directly or indirectly, that an ache or pain of any magnitude or duration recalled by a dancer constituted one injury. Other authors applied different criteria for their count of injury. In those studies, for an injury to be counted it had to have been defined as being severe enough to cause the dancer to be unable to dance for one or more days beyond the date of the injury onset itself, and to see a licensed health care professional for a formal diagnosis. This inconsistency made it very difficult for the dance science community to examine, understand, and even use injury research and reporting information in order to amass large amounts of data and advance the discipline of dance medicine and science.

As a result, the members of IADMS resolved to designate a project specifically to solve this problem, and this is how the formation of the SMCI came into being. SMCI's purpose was to develop evidence-based recommendations and standards to assess dancer function, measure injury risk factors and report injuries, as well as help the dance community widely apply these recommendations. Scientists refer to information obtained through scientific study or repeated practice with rigorous standards as **evidence based**. Ultimately, these recommendations will assist the dance community in identifying the most meaningful ways to reduce injury.

The SMCI developed these six recommendations:

1. Conduct injury surveillance.
2. Define injury.
3. Define exposure.
4. Use dance-specific screenings.
5. Use known risk reduction strategies.
6. Collaborate.

Each of these six recommendations examines an aspect of understanding injury prevention and care that can be useful to medical practitioners, dance educators, and dancers.

Conduct Injury Surveillance

Injury surveillance, or injury reporting, means observing and keeping track of injury occurrence and other factors associated with the injury such as injury type; affected body part; and information about when, where, and how the injury happened. If you know how often, when, how, and other factors about injuries, then you can have a high level of confidence in the injury count and implement changes to do something about reducing the risks associated with them. If you pay attention to counting injuries and documenting the factors associated with them in a uniform and careful way, then it is much easier to make a positive change. The SMCI recommends that injury surveillance be mandatory for all dancers in a given dance organization, that a licensed health care professional be the one to diagnose the injuries, and that a standardized format be used to document the injury information.

Define Injury

The term **injury** is used much more loosely in everyday language than it is in the medical world. The SMCI recommends following the well-established path of sports medicine using the following definition: a physical impairment that requires the dancer to take at least one day off from dance activity beyond the day of the injury onset itself. The phrase "dance activity" means participation in a class, rehearsal, or performance. Any ailment that does not meet this specific definition of injury is called a musculoskeletal complaint.

Define Exposure

Any participation in a dance event can put a dancer at risk for injury. Injury risk is calculated by looking at how much exposure a dancer has to dance activity. Just as with the term injury, we have to be very specific in medicine and science to define exactly what we mean by exposure to dance activities. **Exposure** can be measured by the number of dance events a dancer participates in, such as classes, rehearsals, and performances. The SCMI recommends that each one of these events counts as one exposure, regardless of duration. This means that a 2-hour rehearsal and a 4-hour rehearsal each count as one rehearsal exposure. This method is in agreement with decades of sports medicine and research. Some researchers use actual time (the number of hours of dance activity) as the measure of exposure. This count can be a rough count of time, such as average number of hours scheduled for a group of dancers over a 1-year period. Other researchers use a very sophisticated count of time, such as the exact number of hours and minutes danced by each dancer each day. The rough count of time is not encouraged because it does not verify actual activity for each dancer. Rather, it roughly guestimates how much time each dancer did over that yearlong period, such as 40 hours per week. The very sophisticated count of time exposure is the most accurate, but it is also very difficult to do, practically speaking, because it requires the constant attention of a person to do it correctly. Many dance researchers and dance organizations do not have people trained and able to do this in a very careful way each day.

Use Dance-Specific Screenings

Athletes perform specialized, high-functioning movement, and dancers are athletes who also perform specialized movement. Thus, when dancers are being screened, it is useful for the screening's test battery to be more specialized than one that might be used for a sedentary person or for an athlete in a different kind of activity such as baseball. The SMCI recommends that dance medicine screeners who have adequate medical teams in place for post-screen referrals use, as their health history basis, the widely accepted screening instrument for athletes known as the preparticipation physical evaluation (PPE), and complement it with tests that are validated for dancers.

Employ Risk Reduction Strategies

As part of its charge, the SMCI looked to other leading organizations to understand how they had learned historically to best reduce risk among the people for whom they care. One such organization, the World Health Organization (WHO), has a very well thought out model of health, which is biopsychosocial in nature, meaning that it takes biological, psychological, behavioral, and environmental factors into account when assessing health. The SMCI recommends using this model, which takes into account the interaction of many types of factors when assessing risk, to help the dance community predict and avoid injuries and other ailments.

Collaborate

It is critically important for everyone in the dance community to work together and share information so that society can do its best possible work for everyone to benefit. The SMCI recommends that researchers work together, follow best practices, including the previous recommendations. **Best practices** are a set of guidelines that a clinician follows to provide the best possible patient care. This is based on a review of scientific and experiential evidence. Nowadays, thanks to the Internet when it is used in a secure and privacy-protected way, it is possible to accelerate the aims for creating a healthier dance environment and, by extension, healthier dancers, through coordinated efforts of researchers from around the world and from many different disciplines who wish to collaborate with one another.

Strategies for Implementing a Screening Program

Screenings are used to enlighten individual dancers about their strengths and weaknesses, and about various types of training methods available outside of technique class. These training methods can help you to become fully ready for safe dancing. Screenings can also educate you about various types of healing services available when they are needed after an injury occurs.

If you are involved in a typical dancer screening, it will probably include gathering facts such as how many hours and what kind of training you do each week; information pertaining to your personal medical history and your injury experiences; questions about your nutrition, footwear, physical aches and pains, or worries; and then some special fitness-type tests that assess variables such as muscular strength, flexibility, cardiac performance, balance, and functional coordination. In a nutshell, a dancer screening will determine your current level of ability in relation to the requirements of the particular type of dance being studied to make sure that you are as well prepared as you can be.

A dancer screening report provides you with an overall picture of practical activities you can do in your training to improve your performance and health. The screening process can also provide an opportunity for you to develop a trusting relationship with trained medical practitioners who can help you solve problems and who can shed scientific light on the best options for achieving your goals. Ultimately, a dance screening can provide you with knowledge about mental and physical health pitfalls, and you can use the information to avoid problems and gain an edge with regard to training effectiveness.

It is generally understood that participation in dance training is physically and psychologically demanding and that injuries are an expected outcome. Injuries are a part of life as a dancer, just as they are for other athletes. It is important for you to understand your responsibility and role in your own health in order to lessen the frequency and impact of injury. Many dance injuries are preventable with the incorporation of scheduled rest periods between hard work and demanding performance cycles. You need to learn how to work with your training and performance schedules in order to fuel for sustained energy, peak performance, and long-term health. You can learn to identify practitioners of quality and integrity that you can trust. You need to acquire a wide variety of skills and physical assets through supplemental training programs. You can also learn the many self-care techniques that will separate you from dancers who fail to thrive, including management of anxiety, depression and fatigue; proper foot hygiene; core conditioning; and proper fueling. You need to build social support networks and community resources to draw upon when necessary. You also need to be assured to seek medical attention early when symptoms of injury or illness first arise.

Some organizations around the world offer resources for dancer screening on their websites. You should use the Internet to link to legitimate dance medicine health care organizations that can help you find strong dancer screening opportunities in your community. Two examples are the International Performing Arts Injury Reporting System (IPAIRS), sponsored by Harkness Center for Dance Injuries, and the Dancer Wellness Project (DWP), described later in this chapter. IPAIRS was created in 1981 for use with the Joffrey Ballet and, because of its usefulness, it was subsequently expanded into a large, electronic global database. IPAIRS is the first injury reporting system created for dance medicine, modeled after best practice systems used in sports medicine and occupational medicine. These two Internet sources, as well as other legitimate online resources, are careful to protect each person's privacy. A dancer screening should always protect the privacy of each dancer while gathering facts about such things as how many hours and what kinds of training each dancer does per week, and about noteworthy information pertaining to dancers' personal medical history and their injury experiences. In summary, a dancer screening should determine your current level of ability in relation to the requirements of the particular type of dance being studied to make sure you are as well prepared as you can to be.

Factors and Outcomes Related to Screening

A screening initiative is often part of a larger wellness-based program typically associated with professional dance companies, schools, and clinics. Over the past couple of decades there has been a growth in the number of wellness programs and screening initiatives in various schools and dance companies. This growth has been the result of a number of factors, including the following:

> A focus on injury prevention in contemporary health care practices

> Dancers and dance professionals becoming more aware of the various benefits of screenings

> Dancers in general becoming more interested in knowing more about their bodies

> The number of emerging models and resources to help schools and dance companies develop and administer screenings

Factors That Influence Type of Screening

As mentioned previously, there are many parts to being a dancer. They include age, years of dancing, and physical and psychological characteristics. Equally, several factors exist that are a part of a dancer's life and what dancers do, including the type of dance, where they work or train, and how often they are dancing. Because of this variety, there is no singular one-size-fits-all screening that can be used for all dancers. As a result, a number of different types of screenings have been developed for use with dancers. A number of factors can influence the type of screening used, but the three big categories are goals/objectives of the screening, the people who are on the screening/wellness team, and the intended population of dancers and their working/training environments.

"Why do we want to screen, and what do we hope to achieve with the dancers?" is a guiding question when it comes to identifying goals and objectives. Different answers exist for different settings, influencing what type of screening is administered. Goals and objectives not only guide why and how a screening is developed but also how it is administered and how the information is used in the post-screen follow-up.

Each school or company that has a screening program, or those that are developing such a program, will have different experts as part of the team. Such individuals may be dance teachers and dance-friendly medical professionals such as physicians, physical therapists, athletic trainers, mental health professionals, and nutritionists, all of whom will affect the type of screening that is administered. This expertise pool will also influence the goals and objectives of the screening and the type of screening. By being aware of the team members performing your screening, you can have a better idea of what outcomes you can expect and how to proceed with the results.

SELF AWARENESS

Use Your Screening to Understand Your Body

Set a time to speak with the members of your screening team. Ask them what your screening results say about your body and your technique, and ask for ways that you can improve. A screening is a great opportunity to become aware of areas that need development outside the dance class, and you can devise your own program, with help from the team, to work on these areas.

Another consideration that influences the type of screenings is the population of dancers for whom the screening is intended. In some ways, each set of dancers may have different needs and different issues to address. Young dancers have different factors that need to be assessed because their bodies are still growing and changing as compared to older dancers. Because student dancers are also in learning environments, some screening goals may include educational objectives. Within an education setting, the screening team may elect to screen only incoming dancers who may have a different set of situations as opposed to returning students. However, other schools may want to screen returning students as well in order to track changes over time.

A fourth factor is the available resources to aid in the screening initiative. These resources typically involve facilities and equipment. Many screenings are conducted in a dance studio or a medical treatment or examination room. If the available space is small and the number of dancers is large, then the limited space would affect the length of the entire screening thus limiting the size or type of assessments used in the screening.

Common tools found in physical therapists' clinics and offices are often used in screenings. These tools may include goniometers, watches (used to take heart rate) or heart rate monitors, blood pressure cuffs, rotational discs, and ballet barres. While these tools are easily available and inexpensive, if an institution has more sophisticated equipment then they may be able to be more detailed in their data collection. However, screenings are typically designed to be a quick peek and not a complete medical evaluation. Therefore, more complicated or robust screenings are not as common. During your screening, you will see how the various tools provide information that will help you learn ways to improve your training.

In almost all screenings, the assessments administered are quick and easy for the team to do and rarely cause discomfort. If the screening has a technique portion or a functional component (it includes assessments that look at how certain movements are executed), then they will most likely be things that the dancer usually does or can easily do. Consider whether or not the dance movements you are asked to do relate directly to the dance forms you are studying or are interested in.

How the Setting Influences the Type of Screening

The type of setting may impact the type of screening designed and how it is administered. A screening could be given in an educational setting or in a professional setting.

A school may elect to implement a screening for educational purposes. In this setting, the goals would be to collect information about the dancers to promote enhanced educational and training outcomes. The dance teachers who know how to administer the assessments they implement may be part of the screening team along with a health care professional. The screening would consist of assessments that focus on issues that could be addressed within the context of regular dance classes and other training or educational classes.

A screening in a professional dance company may be focused on health factors that may impact a dancer's functional capacity. Such a screening may include assessments to help identify medical conditions, such as past injuries, that may be of a concern for the dancer in the future. This screening would typically be administered in a health clinic or perhaps in a professional company setting by medical professionals whose responsibility it is to help keep the dancers healthy and performing. Assessments that help the medical team working with the company better understand the physical condition of the dancers may also be included.

Screenings Versus Evaluations

A screening is a tool designed to examine several factors quickly. An evaluation is a more detailed examination and exploration of any particular finding that can possibly provide more information. In other words, the screening provides you with the big picture, whereas the evaluation provides the close-up on a particular situation with the hopes of gaining more specific information.

For example, a screening assessment might yield that some muscle imbalances exist in a dancer's body. This information could then be used to help a screening team target a more in-depth evaluation to better understand what is involved and, if applicable, what muscles are involved and what might be at the source or sources of the imbalance. Whether you are having a screening or an evaluation, pay close attention to what the team is discovering and be proactive in designing exercises to correct any weaknesses or imbalances that are discovered.

Potential Outcomes of Screenings

Administering screenings can be a time and labor-intensive activity for the screening team; however, screenings have a number of valuable outcomes. The types of outcomes are closely associated with the goals and objectives of the screening and the personnel involved with the screening. Screenings provide important outcomes for the individual dancer, the entire group of dancers, as well as for the teachers and screening/wellness team members.

Individual Dancer's Profile

The information collected from you can be used to help create a unique profile. A profile is a dancer-at-a-glance view that not only highlights your strengths but also identifies areas that may need attention or further evaluation. Such information can provide feedback to you, helping you to become more aware of your body, a factor that can be important for a long and healthy career. Your individual profile can also be used to help target goals for advancement and improvement.

If you have been screened before, then the profiles can be compared to identify differences between screenings over time. Such comparison or tracking can be helpful if a medical professional is monitoring a health issue, or a dance professional is monitoring technical or functional growth and changes, or you are tracking the effectiveness of your personal conditioning program.

Summary Profiles

Not only can screening data be used to help create an individual dancer's profile, they can also be summarized for all the dancers involved in a particular dance school or professional company. Such a summary creates a profile

A dance screening can help you achieve the high levels of technique needed in performance.

Gary Galbraith in Martha Graham's "Night Journey." Photo by John Deane.

about the entire group of dancers, which may help in describing the commonalities among the dancers and averages for a group of dancers.

Averages across many dancers are helpful for you to know. A great deal of research has been done to identify certain kinds of averages for different groups of people. For example, a wide range of heights are possible for a certain group of people; however, averages exist for particular age groups. It is sometimes helpful to have the averages for different kinds of people for the same age group. People of the same age group in one country may be taller than people in the same age group in a different country.

Currently not a lot of averages are known about dancers. Because dancers have unique conditions and are unique artistic athletes, having more information that describes different kinds of dancers can not only aid teachers, medical professionals, and researchers who work with dancers, it can also give you a clear idea of where you stand in relation to other dancers. For example, the requirements of a musical theater dancer are very different than that of a ballet dancer. Therefore, the average amount of turnout for these two different groups may very well be different. Because of the inherent differences between male dancers and female dancers, different averages for these different groups will exist. On average, male dancers may be taller than female dancers, and they may have more upper-body strength. Because so many different kinds of dance and dancers exist, having summary information about these different groups would be beneficial.

Trust and Perceptions

Dancers are sometimes reluctant to talk about pain, injuries, or other personal factors. This reluctance often comes from the fact that dancers are concerned that if they do talk about these kinds of issues that it may prevent them from participating in dance, being cast to dance certain roles, being advanced to more advance classes, or being perceived as not working correctly or hard enough, or even having failed.

Over the years that screenings have been implemented, a large body of personal observations and some preliminary research data suggest that when dancers see a number of professionals go to the extent of implementing a screening program, it means to them that these professionals care about them. If you participate in a screening, you can begin to develop a trust with the teachers and medical team. This trust factor is extremely valuable on many fronts in that you establish a healthy working relationship with the medical team and teachers,

which could mean better communication about potential health issues in the future or other factors that may affect your dancing. Given this well-placed trust, you may be more comfortable talking about feelings, concerns, or other matters of psychological or nutritional health, which are just as important as musculoskeletal issues.

Many outcomes from a screening can benefit the dancer. Profiles for each dancer are often the result of a screening. An individual profile can help you better understand your own body and, when working with your screening team, can help identify options for improvement. When you participate in a screening, you can build healthy relationships with teachers and screening team members that will have long-term effects, and repeated screenings can help track changes over time, which can be helpful in assessing self-improvement. Group profiles can help teachers and screening team members identify issues for groups of dancers. The occasional use of screenings in research can also be used to help better understand dancers and their unique conditions and situations. Such research can benefit dancers by giving them more information for self-improvement.

Getting the Most Out of Your Screening

Screenings provide a wealth of information about a dancer and, through the development of an individual profile and working with teachers and health care professionals, a wealth of possibilities exist for the dancer. However, you should keep some key points in mind when working with screening information. These points include, but are not limited to, implementation and follow-up, working with the screening team, and progress evaluation.

SETTING GOALS

Work Toward Self-Improvement

After your initial screening, work with your teachers or screening team to help you set specific goals for self-improvement. These goals might be certain areas in which you wish to gain strength or flexibility, or perhaps you need to work on balance. You may wish to make changes to your nutrition or your sleep patterns. If you are fortunate to have follow-up screenings, notice what changes have occurred and whether you are meeting your goals. If so, set new goals that can take your progress even further.

Implement Changes and Follow Up

Screening profiles are used to help build a cross-training program customized for each dancer to help address any areas that were identified in the screening as needing attention. In some cases, the program may include components suggested by the health care professional or a dance teacher to help the dancer in addressing training or other health issues.

Working with the appropriate expert, the program can also include areas that help you achieve your own personal goals. This personal goal setting allows you to feel empowered in the process and that you are part of your own development and action plan. This kind of orientation usually leads to greater success, because you have been a part of the process all along.

Most dance technique classes are designed to address technical and artistic growth for the dancer and are not designed to correct issues found in a screening. Therefore, it may be necessary for you to address the cited issues identified in your profile. You can use your own resources learned in various classes and from experts, and with proper guidance from a teacher or medical professional, you can design conditioning exercises that can address issues not being covered in the dance class.

EMPOWERMENT

Take Control of Your Progress

By working with your teachers and your screening team you can take control of your progress as a dancer. You do not need to wait for an injury to recognize that you need to address certain issues, or wait for a difficult piece of choreography to realize you need more strength and stamina. You can be empowered to address your personal issues in your training, and enjoy the changes and progress you make.

Using the example referenced earlier about strength, a cross-training program may include a combination of strengthening exercises combined with cardiovascular fitness exercises. You can do these exercises at the gym or at the studio before or after class. If dancers work together or do their respective cross-training and conditioning exercises at the studio at the same time, they can create a positive support structure and a means of encouragement and acceptance in doing the additional work. In the context of a wellness program, you could have check-in meetings with members of your wellness team to help keep you on track and help you make modifications to the program as you develop and grow.

Given that various ways exist to address commonly cited issues in a dancer's profile, the suggested exercises may reflect the expertise of the screening/wellness team members. For example, if a physical therapist is part of the wellness team, they may recommend appropriate physical therapy exercises, whereas a dance teacher who is part of the wellness team may recommend exercises from a wide range of dance-specific conditioning systems. These systems are described in chapter 3.

In the case where referrals are recommended or you seek additional assistance, the screening/wellness team members will help identify resources for you. These kinds of resources may include access to other types of education, your primary care physician, a nutritionist or registered dietitian, or a mental health professional.

Work With a Team

Some screenings can produce a lot of information in the resulting profile. It is best if you work with your teachers and health team to better understand what the information means and how to make the best use of the profile. This is important because not all of the information may make sense to you, and the experts can help. Also, the profile may include data that, if taken out of context or not considered with regard to the entire profile, may be misinterpreted. Qualified dance teachers or health care professionals are good resources to help guide you in understanding all of the information.

Some dancers are prone to perfectionism or may take the screening information too personally. Therefore, it is important to work with a teacher or health care professional to help put the information into a healthy perspective so as not to misinterpret it or try to make unrealistic changes based on numbers. No dancer is perfect, and using screening profiles as a means to self-validate is not healthy.

Evaluate Your Progress

It is possible to use screening data to assess progress; however, you can do this only if you have been screened more than once. By comparing the results between screenings, the changes in particular conditions or situations can be better assessed. This progress evaluation can be helpful not only for you but also for the teachers and health care professionals working with you. These evaluations can be used to reassess specific goals for you and to update them as needed.

For example, if you have been working on improving strength in certain areas, a repeated screening could help determine whether the efforts have been working. This comparison is helpful in knowing if the exercises that you have been doing are the right ones, if they are being done correctly, or if the timing of the exercises has been effective. While reviewing the changes between the screenings, you could consider the continuance of these exercises in your training program, modifying the way or the frequency they are done, or finding new ones to help keep you interested.

However, you should not try and assess or evaluate your progress by solely comparing screening results. Again, stay in communication with teachers and other screening team members in assessing total growth, change, and developmental progress.

Screenings provide many opportunities for you to learn about yourself, find ways to improve your health and dancing, and adopt healthy attitudes that will serve you long into your dancing career. The screening profiles can help you create strategies that you can implement yourself to advance toward your goals or address issues that may have been plaguing you for a while. Dancers working together on common goals can help shape the environment of the studio and promote a healthy attitude among all the dancers. Working with your teachers and screening team members can build productive and healthy relationships. Such relationships can be very helpful if you need more information in understanding your profiles or are prone to unhealthy overachieving behaviors. When multiple screenings for you are compared, changes over time can be identified. This comparison can be helpful in promoting goal setting and providing affirmation about changes in the way you may feel.

Collect and Analyze Data

Conducting a screening for dancers involves a great deal of data about dancers. The data make the creation of the dancer profiles possible. Conducting a screening involves information that some people consider sensitive or personal. Many organizations have developed mechanisms on how such information is collected, stored, and managed. In many countries laws exist that govern how such information is to be protected. You may want to check that your team has set up the screening process in a manner that ensures your confidentiality, has sound methods, and is consistent with well-established protocols. The online Dancer Wellness Project offers information for dancers about screening methods.

Confidentiality

When you participate in a dance screening, you will be measured, assessed, and examined. You may feel that this information is too personal, especially when it relates to your body or how you think and feel. You may feel uncomfortable if your teachers or artistic directors know certain kinds of personal information. Many good teachers care and are compassionate about dancers and their health and growth. However, you may still fear that such information will affect your standing in class or the company, whether or not you are cast for certain roles, or the teachers' or directors' perception of you in class and their evaluation of your performance. You may think that if teachers or directors knew about certain issues about your body or how you think or feel, it could impact being advanced to a higher-level technique class or future educational or employment opportunities. Therefore, screening initiatives place a great priority on confidentiality of information and protection of data.

Many screenings include a disclosure of what the screening is about, what the goals of the screening are, what assessments are going to be done, what is expected of you, how the information is to be used, who will have access to the information, how the data are to be kept secure, and what you can do if you have questions or concerns. Having this information up front before participating in a screening will help you better understand the total scope of the screening project.

In many professional company settings, screening profiles are not accessible by the artistic director or any member of the artistic or teaching staff but only to the health care professional. In educational settings, not all teachers may have access to all information, but it will depend on the setup of the wellness program. You need to feel secure about questions of confidentiality and disclosure before participating in a screening so that you can have a positive and safe experience with the screening. For dancers who are still considered minors, parents will need to be informed of all these issues as well and consulted before a dancer can participate in the screening process.

Methods

Historically, screening data have been collected on paper forms. Each of these forms is the same for each dancer and has blanks where data for each test can be filled in. However, despite the ease of filling in blanks, paper forms must then be securely stored in a place where confidentiality can be assured.

Also, the teacher or the person on the screening team will need to go through the entire paper form to assess the data and help the dancer understand the results. Additionally, it is difficult to go through all the forms to collect summary information about all the dancers involved in the screening as well as sort through the various parts of the data to ensure that authorized people of the screening and wellness team have appropriate access.

Systems

With advancements in technology and various Internet resources, many schools and companies are turning to these options to help with their screening programs. A commonly used online resource is the Dancer Wellness Project. According to the project's website, "The Dancer Wellness Project (DWP) is a consortium of organizations (professional dance organizations, universities, schools, and medical clinics) that promote dancer health, wellness, education, and research through the implementation of dancer screening, exposure tracking, and injury surveillance. The goal is to promote injury prevention, career longevity, effective and efficient training, and assist dancers, dance educators, and medical care practitioners who interface with dancers. The DWP provides technological infrastructures and other resources needed to facilitate and support the myriad projects of participating organizations/affiliates." This online resource has been in existence for many years and now supports its many institutional partners around the world that have dancer wellness programs and screening initiatives. Go online to www.DancerWellnessProject.com to explore many of the aspects of screening described in this chapter.

The DWP is organized into five main modules as outlined here:

> **Screening:** One of the most popular modules is the screening module. This module allows schools, studios, and companies to build their own screening tools and utilize the data collection tools available online to manage all the information.

> **Surveys:** This allows affiliates to ask questions from the dancers and let them provide self-reported information safely, securely, and confidentially. These survey questions may ask about health history, injury history, or activities such as how often they are involved in dance.

> **Injuries:** Injuries are a reality of dancing, and this module helps affiliates track injuries that dancers encounter. Unlike screenings, injuries have a time frame for recovery; therefore, tracking injuries

over time is helpful for the schools and companies needing to keep track of dancers and their health.

> **Exposures:** This module helps affiliates monitor how much time that dancers are involved with dance activities. This is helpful for teachers and managers in planning classes and rehearsals, and for medical experts to understand how often a dancer is active. Having this kind of exposure information can also be extremely valuable in certain research projects and for better understanding injury patterns.

> **Profile:** The profile module is where all the previous information is put together to create a big picture of the dancer, their history, their current physical conditions, their training schedule, and other essential information. These profiles are only accessible to authorized people within the dancer's school or company as well as the dancer through secured password-protected login.

Depending on how the access levels have been designed on the DWP for each affiliate, authorized teachers and medical team members will only be able to view the portions of the profile that they have been granted access to. The ability for dancers to review their profiles and to work with their screening team and teachers helps empower their investment in their own development. As stated earlier, dancers are also able to review past profiles to better understand what changes have occurred over time, which areas may have improved, and which areas may still need attention.

The DWP does maintain very high standards when it comes to protecting information about dancers. The issues of confidentiality discussed earlier are at the cornerstone of the DWP. Through the use of a common website, the DWP affiliates are also able to work together to help build a better understanding of how to implement screenings and other aspects of dancer health. A great deal of data exist that are associated with screenings, and several factors are involved when collecting and working with data that pertain to a person. Respecting each person's unique conditions and protecting personal information are at the heart of the confidentiality of screening data. A screening team understands these issues, and dancers should feel comfortable in knowing what information is collected and how it will be used before participating in a dance screening. In addition, screening data have historically been collected through paper forms, which then need to be securely stored. However, online services exist such as the Dancer Wellness Project and the Harkness Center for Dance Injuries Project

(IPAIRS) that many professional dance companies and schools use to help support their screening and wellness programs.

Summary

Screenings are an important tool for dancers in that they can provide valuable information about dancers and their current conditions. Although screenings themselves do not necessarily prevent injury, they do provide insights into which attributes of a dancer might need attention to help their dancing. Through taking the extra steps as a result of the screening, the dancer may help avoid pain or injury associated with dance.

Because of the complexity of a screening, you should not try to screen yourself or your fellow dancers unless you are under the guidance of a teacher or other screening expert. Screenings have many challenges, and it is best that teachers or other professionals with anatomical or screening knowledge perform them. From screenings, you can learn a great deal about your body and mind and learn tools and actions that you can take to help you become better, stronger, and healthier. Such self-empowerment can help you long into your dancing career. Likewise, you should not try to design or institute conditioning, rehabilitative, or injury prevention programs on your own. Seek guidance from professionals working with dancers to address specific goals or questions. Your job is to dance; the skills needed to develop such programs are best left to those who have this kind of expertise. A screening team will be able to help you get connected with such experts. The establishment of healthy practices of self-care and proactive participation in one's own training can serve you well throughout your career.

Application Activity: **Your Personal Screening**

If your school or medical center provides a screening, make a list of the various components you would like to explore, based on your personal interests. What physical or technical aspects included in your screening would you want to understand more fully? Are there lifestyle issues you wish to examine? If a psychological profile is included, what additional information would you like to know more about? Would you be interested in talking to someone else who can help you with your questions, thoughts, or concerns? Simply thinking about the components of your screening that you want to understand can assist you in working with your wellness team and help you to move forward in your training.

Review Questions

1. What is the screening process?

2. What are the purposes, types, and components of screenings?

3. How can you use information from screenings to prevent injuries and improve technique?

4. What are the various factors that determine the type of screening?

5. What are the various outcomes from screenings?

 For chapter-specific supplemental learning activities, study aids, suggested readings, web links, and more, visit the web resource at www.HumanKinetics.com/DancerWellness.

11

Your Dancer Wellness Plan

Donna H. Krasnow, PhD, and M. Virginia Wilmerding, PhD

Photo courtesy of Jake Pett.

Key Terms

diversity
empowerment
goal setting
self-awareness

LEARNING OBJECTIVES

After reading this chapter, you will be able to do the following:

》 Identify the various aspects of self-awareness and how to enhance this aspect of your training.

》 Understand empowerment and its importance to your wellness plan.

》 Discover how to set goals that are unique and important to your development.

》 Recognize the value of diversity in the dance community and how to address it in your personal training environment.

Now that you have read chapters 1 through 10 of this book, you are ready to develop your personal dancer wellness plan. Throughout the book there were recurring sidebars titled Self-Awareness, Empowerment, Goal Setting, and Diversity. These sidebars provided questions and activities for you to assist you in developing a personal plan for enhancing your health and wellness as a dancer. Each of these areas forms a different aspect of how you as an individual dancer can be active in your progress and your well-being. By going through each of these concepts and the sidebars in the chapters, you will be able to design your dancer wellness plan and continue to develop it for many years.

Self-Awareness

Self-awareness is the ability for introspection and the skill to recognize oneself as an individual separate from other individuals. Your self-awareness falls under the self-knowledge part of self. Self-awareness is about understanding your own needs, desires, failings, habits, motivations, and everything else that makes you tick.

Foundations of Dancer Wellness

Self-awareness can take many paths in the various aspects of your training and development. Start with the basics, the foundations of dancer wellness. In dealing with the dance environment (chapter 1), you answered questions about your dance floors and surfaces in your studio, aspects of the space such as temperature, ventilation, lighting, and sound, and how you use mirrors and barres. In terms of dance training and technique (chapter 2), by learning anatomy you discovered how all of the various muscles in your body contribute to your dancing. Regarding your alignment, you explored how it differs in stance and in locomotion. Did you work with a partner from your dance class, and take turns assessing each other from the side to determine if your bony landmarks line up in the plumb line? Did you also look at each other in demi-plié and assess your hip–knee–foot alignment? For your cross-training and conditioning needs (chapter 3), you were asked to think about what your greatest challenges are, such as leg extensions or jumps or falls or partnering work. You can consider what areas of conditioning work you probably need to give the most focus, which can broaden your ability to make choices about supplementary training.

Mental Components of Dancer Wellness

Next, you moved on to thinking about the mental components of wellness. In terms of your mental training (chapter 4), you became more aware of how much you rely on the mirror, and you focused on the sensations of your body while dancing and how you hear and use corrections. Psychology (chapter 5) plays a crucial role in your training and self-awareness. You thought about the reasons you dance and how your motives change over time. You focused more on your intrinsic reasons for dancing, rather than the extrinsic rewards. Rest and recovery (chapter 6) are perhaps the most overlooked aspects of wellness for dancers. You became aware of your needs for rest and recovery by starting a journal that evaluates how you feel during your dancing, especially in the intense time before performances. You gained awareness of your sleep habits and whether or not you are getting enough rest and recovery time. You also considered issues of stress, anxiety, and other mental states that could interfere with your dancing, and how to cope with these mental barriers to your optimal performance.

Physical Components of Dancer Wellness

For the physical components of wellness, you started by examining your nutrition (chapter 7). You added to your journal important information about your daily intake of food and beverages. You became aware of whether or not you are getting all of the necessary nutrients. You were asked to make adjustments, if needed; then you made note of how you felt and whether these adjustments to your food intake changed your energy or other aspects of your health. While related to nutrition, bone health (chapter 8) has other issues of which you should be aware. You examined your family history of osteoporosis, your personal menstrual patterns if applicable, and any early incidents of bone fractures to find signs of possible bone-related health concerns. Injury prevention (chapter 9) is something dancers often don't want to think about, but awareness is the key to prevention. You considered your alignment and your technical habits, and any patterns that could lead to injury. You also thought about how you use your core, how you jump, and how your technique protects you. Finally, screening (chapter 10) provides some of the best opportunities for developing self-awareness. A screening is a great opportunity to become aware of areas that need development outside the dance class. With help from your screening team, you can devise your own program to address these conditioning needs.

In each of these areas—foundations, mental components, and physical components of wellness—you can develop your self-awareness step by step. Once you have examined all the ways that you can become self-aware, it is time to develop strategies to empower yourself.

Empowerment

Empowerment refers to measures designed to increase the degree of independence and motivation in your life in order to enable you to support your interests in a responsible and self-determined way. The term empowerment is also used to denote taking responsibility for your life and your actions.

Foundations of Dancer Wellness

You may think that the environment (chapter 1) where you dance is out of your control. However, you were encouraged to speak up when certain factors in your studio were not supporting your wellness. You took responsibility to alter the lighting or ventilation by changing the curtains or windows, and you became proactive in helping to keep your studio clean and free of clutter. As part of dance training and technique (chapter 2), anatomy helped you to understand the planes of movement and movement terms, which give you a clear insight into what is happening in dance movement, and provide tools for learning clarity in line and action. You thought about giving yourself clear images of how you want to achieve dance movements. In this way you can empower yourself as a dancer to be an active participant in your training and artistry. Cross-training and conditioning (chapter 3) provided many ways to empower yourself in your dancing. You considered adding a cardiorespiratory endurance program (if you are dealing with fatigue on a regular basis). You may well have begun to feel more energetic and less fatigued as time goes on. This increased endurance can increase your confidence as you approach performances.

Mental Components of Dancer Wellness

Mental aspects of your dancing are particularly important for your empowerment. Regarding your mental training (chapter 4), you were encouraged to think about what you feel best about in your dancing. You then created three images that you can use to help you feel more powerful while you are dancing. Can these images assist in movements that are not in your strongest style? In terms of psychology (chapter 5), you can develop a strong sense of self by recognizing your strengths and your weaknesses. Once you have realized that mistakes are part of the learning process, you are free to try new things. You now understand that you deal with a wide range of views about yourself, including self-concept, self-awareness, self-esteem, self-confidence, self-efficacy, and self-compassion. You created a journal about your habits of rest and recovery (chapter 6). If you made adjustments to your rest and recovery patterns, did you observe any changes, especially in the stress patterns? Now that you know what you are actually doing, you can make choices to do what you want. This concept is a key to empowerment.

Physical Components of Dancer Wellness

Moving to physical components of wellness, you thought about ways that you might improve your levels of performance through better nutrition (chapter 7). Perhaps you needed to add more carbohydrates to give your body more energy when dancing. Or you may have needed to add more protein to enhance muscle repair, or to increase your hydration for better muscle function. You are now empowered with new knowledge that you can use to enhance your dancing simply by what you eat and when you eat it. You then took charge of your bone health (chapter 8) through some simple and practical strategies. You considered how you would stay physically active during the times you are not dancing, such as summer breaks. If you smoke, you thought about looking for a program that will assist you in quitting. The practices you develop today will have a huge impact on your bone health later in life. Next, you considered what you know about injury prevention (chapter 9) and your specific physical capabilities. What you learned previously about conditioning and methods of gaining strength, flexibility, and core support gave you the knowledge you need to prevent injuries and sustain long hours of dancing and rehearsing. If you were able to work with your teachers and your screening team (chapter 10), you were able to take control of your progress as a dancer. You do not need to wait for an injury to recognize that you need to address certain issues, or wait for a difficult piece of choreography to realize you need more strength and stamina. You are now empowered to address your personal issues in your training and enjoy the changes and progress you can make.

In each of these areas—foundations, mental components, and physical components of wellness—you can become empowered by examining all the ways that you can take control of your training, your lifestyle, and your progress. Now, it is time to set specific short-term and long-term goals.

Goal Setting

Goal setting is an important method of deciding what you want to achieve in your life, determining what is important versus what is a distraction, and learning how to motivate yourself. Goal setting is a process that begins with careful consideration of what you want to achieve and ends with a lot of hard work. Goal setting also involves the development of an action plan designed to motivate and guide you toward a goal.

Foundations of Dancer Wellness

To begin setting your goals, you considered what could be done about your dance environment (chapter 1). Did you discover ways that you can prepare to dance in the dance studio or other performance areas that accommodate your needs, such as bringing along water or a snack, or taking your allergy pill before you come to the dance studio or outdoor performance area? Perhaps you decided that you need a journal to keep track of your daily needs in the studio. Understanding different aspects of dance training and technique (chapter 2) allowed you to establish short-term and long-term goals. For example, if you decided that some of your muscles are too weak or too tight for optimal function, you set goals to correct any imbalances. You wrote a journal stating what you would like to achieve in 1 month or 1 year, and then designed a plan to accomplish these goals. Setting goals is an excellent way for you to motivate yourself and not become overwhelmed with what you hope to change. Making use of cross-training and conditioning (chapter 3) required understanding what type of dancer you are. You considered how you might broaden your best features and what areas of conditioning could make you a stronger dancer in ways that are not typically your favorite dance movements. Set some reasonable goals for improvement in those areas.

Mental Components of Dancer Wellness

You also set goals in terms of the mental components of wellness (chapter 4). You took time to think about how you approach your movement goals, such as examining whether your focus is on how you look or whether you compare yourself to others. Then you spent some time thinking about and experiencing how the movement feels, and you tried to find a way of doing the movement that is pleasurable and enjoyable. Make it a goal in every class to spend at least some of the time focusing on sensation to accomplish the task. In terms of psychology (chapter 5), goal setting can help you to manage your tasks and reduce stress levels, because it enhances feelings of autonomy, competence, and control by enabling you to become more self-directed. You were encouraged to set SMART (**S**pecific, **M**easurable, **A**ction-oriented, **R**ealistic, and **T**imed) goals so that you can achieve your goals in an effective and timely way. Finally, you were invited to set goals involving rest and recovery (chapter 6). You reflected on the nature of what you do in dance practice, and you thought about taking opportunities to rest between classes or rehearsals. You developed strategies that you might use to alternate activity and rest, such as taking time for mentally practicing choreography that you are just learning or even prior to performances, or cutting back activities as rehearsals become more frequent or intense.

Physical Components of Dancer Wellness

Setting goals involving your nutritional needs (chapter 7) is essential for your energy and health. Once you took a look at your daily food intake, you thought about how you might improve your nutrition. You set some short-term goals, such as eating more fruits and vegetables. In the long term, have you started to reduce the foods you eat that are less nutritious, and replace them with healthier choices? Be patient; making changes can at first be difficult, but with time you can arrive at a healthy, nutritious diet. Next, are you getting the necessary nutrients for bone health (chapter 8)? For example, did you consider adding to your diet to ensure enough calcium and vitamin D? If you are not doing enough weight-bearing exercise, particularly for the upper extremities, make it one of your goals to add these exercises to your conditioning plan. Setting goals for injury prevention (chapter 9) is one of the most important strategies you can do as a dancer. You thought about what aspects of your physical capabilities or technique might predispose you to any of the dance injuries described in this book. To prevent these injuries, you were encouraged to set specific goals in terms of conditioning and realignment that will make you less susceptible. Be proactive, and set goals that will lead to a healthy approach to injury prevention. If you were fortunate enough to participate in a screening (chapter 10), you were able to set some specific goals for self-improvement. These goals might be certain areas in which you wish to gain strength or flexibility, or perhaps you need to work on balance. If you are able to have follow-up screenings, find out what changes have occurred and whether you are meeting your goals.

In each of these areas—foundations, mental components, and physical components of wellness—you can set both short-term and long-term goals by examining aspects of your training, your lifestyle, and your progress, and thinking about what you can do to make specific changes. Finally, you considered aspects of diversity and individuality.

Diversity

Diversity in the simplest definition means the quality or state of having many different forms, types, ideas, and even personalities. The concept of diversity includes acceptance and respect. It means understanding that each person is unique and that we need to recognize everyone's individual differences.

Foundations of Dancer Wellness

Clothing is part of the dance environment (chapter 1), and each style of dance has particular clothing demands. You thought about how to accommodate style differences in your dancing. For example, if you know particular clothing elements are worn in a certain dance style, such as the wrapped skirts in African dance classes, or the baggy pants in street dance, you tried to become familiar with these items as early as possible so that moving in them became familiar to you. Regarding your dance training and technique (chapter 2), motor learning is an important aspect in which every person differs. You examined your learning strategies to determine whether you are a visual learner, a kinesthetic learner, or a verbal/analytic learner. Then you thought about how you might expand your learning strategies. If you can be diverse in your learning strategies, you can work easily with a larger group of teachers and choreographers. Cross-training and conditioning (chapter 3) also require understanding individual and stylistic differences. You considered all of the dance forms that you currently study and thought about what their different conditioning needs are. You thought about each of your classes (ballet, modern, tap, jazz, African, hip-hop, etc.) and determined what conditioning you may wish to consider to make you a better dancer in that form.

Mental Components of Dancer Wellness

In terms of your mental training (chapter 4) and your psychology (chapter 5), you considered what kinds of feedback work best for you. Did you realize that you rely on the visual feedback of watching the teacher and other dancers demonstrate the movement? Or did you discover that verbal corrections work best, or do you prefer kinesthetic or tactile corrections? Now that you understand your preferred feedback, find out if you can diversify your strategies in class and rehearsal. Thinking about rest and recovery (chapter 6), each technique makes different demands on the body, and even though you are used to many hours of training in your chosen form, you may have realized that you still lack the strength and knowledge to tackle a new technique. The wide range and diversity of techniques is remarkable, but you need to make sure you are getting the rest you need.

Physical Components of Dancer Wellness

Even nutrition (chapter 7) and issues of bone health (chapter 8) can vary from person to person. You may have a varied or restricted diet for medical or personal reasons. For example, you may now realize that if you embrace a vegetarian or vegan lifestyle, you need to be particularly aware of the sources you can use to make sure you are getting enough protein. If you discovered that you are lactose intolerant, and you have no dairy in your diet, you know that you need to find out how to get the right amounts of calcium and vitamin D. It is best to speak directly to a registered dietitian to find out what to add or change in your daily food intake to make sure you have a complete and healthy diet.

In terms of injury prevention (chapter 9), you thought about the various dance forms and styles that you do. If you are taking many ballet classes each week, check that you are not walking and standing in turnout in your daily life. If your dance form involves doing repetitions of lumbar hyperextension, make sure that you stretch your low back and walk and stand in good alignment during the day. If you are a ballroom dancer and work in high heels, be sure to stretch out your calf muscles and work on rolling through the feet in ordinary walking. In addition, if you participated in a dancer screening (chapter 10), you know specific areas you need to target to prevent injuries. Each form has its own potential injuries and you can take preventive measures related to your form.

In each of these areas—foundations, mental components, and physical components of wellness—you can understand how diversity of dance forms and your unique needs can direct you to develop your own personal dance wellness plan. It is the final component of your full health and wellness design.

Completing Your Dancer Wellness Plan

Now that you have an overview of dancer wellness and each of the four categories (self-awareness, empowerment, setting goals, and diversity), you can design your personal wellness plan. By now you should know two or three concrete goals in each area that you can begin working to achieve. You can visit this chapter on the web resource for a fill-in chart that will assist you in specifying your goals. In 3 to 6 months, go back and revisit your chart. Are you on track to meet your goals? Do they need to be adjusted? Have you met some of these goals, and can you now establish new goals? By completing this process a few times each year, you will see progress that will encourage you to continue this journey.

Summary

By thinking about self-awareness, empowerment, goal setting, and diversity, you now have a wealth of information and strategies to progress in each of these four areas. Self-awareness gives you the introspective knowledge. Empowerment gives you the courage to take control of your training. Goal setting gives you a progressive way to develop and not feel overwhelmed by what you need to achieve. Diversity allows you to embrace your unique gifts and needs. These four components can help you create your path through a lifetime in dance.

 For chapter-specific supplemental learning activities, study aids, suggested readings, web links, and more, visit the web resource at www.HumanKinetics.com/DancerWellness.

Glossary

acute injuries—Injuries that occur essentially in an instant.

adaptation—Changes that occur as a result of training.

alignment—How the parts of the body organize in stance and movement.

amino acids—The building blocks of protein, which are compounds that contain carbon, hydrogen, oxygen, nitrogen, and sometimes sulfur.

anaerobic capacity—The body's ability to generate energy during very high, intense bouts of physical activity without the use of oxygen.

anatomy—The branch of science dealing with the structures of plants and animals; human anatomy looks at body structures such as bones and muscles in humans.

anorexia nervosa—A complex eating disorder characterized by excessive dieting that results in an abnormal low body weight.

approach-avoidance coping—A coping strategy in which a person either addresses the stress head on, or largely ignores it.

area deformation—The area of floor surrounding a dancer that moves up and down during dance landings and jumps.

articular cartilage—A thin, slippery layer of specialized connective tissue that covers the ends of the bones allowing them to glide smoothly as they move.

autonomy—Having a sense of choice and a say over what one does.

avulsion—Injury where tissue pulls away from its attachment to a bone.

basic needs—A term from self-determination theory, these are the psychological needs for autonomy, competence, and relatedness which, when met, enhance psychological growth and well-being.

best practices—A set of guidelines that a clinician follows to provide the best possible patient care.

This is based on a review of scientific and experiential evidence.

bite—A term used by dancers meaning that the outside edge of the toe box can dig into the vinyl, which increases the resistance of the vinyl and stops the shoe slipping along the floor.

body image—How dancers feel about their bodies, including height, shape, size, and weight.

body–mind—The connection between the physical and mental activities that shows unified function by both.

bone marrow—Soft, fatty tissue important for red blood cell formation and fat cell storage.

burnout—A psychological and physical state characterized by poor dancing, tiredness, or lack of interest due to prolonged overwork.

calorie—A unit that scientist use to measure the energy stored in foods. In practice the energy in food is measured in kcal (kilocalories; 1,000 calories).

cancellous bone—Also called trabecular bone; the spongy tissue inside most bones.

carbohydrate—A macronutrient that contains a rich source of energy, and is broken down in the body to provide us with a quick energy source to the muscles.

cardiorespiratory endurance—The body's ability to supply oxygen to the working muscles during physical activity; sometimes called aerobic fitness.

cartilage—A hard, slippery layer of tissue that allows the bones to glide smoothly over one another.

cartilaginous joints—Joints that act as shock absorbers.

center of gravity (COG)—That point where the downward force of gravity appears to act on the body as a whole.

chronic injuries—Injuries that occur over a period of time.

cognitive anxiety—Psychological symptoms of performance anxiety, such as negative thoughts, worries, self-criticism, distractibility, and negative images.

collagen—A type of connective tissue that holds the internal structure of the bone together.

compact bone—Also called cortical bone; the dense, hard layer on the outer shell of most bones.

compensation—When dancers use muscles and alignment other than what is efficient or optimal because of fatigue or injury.

compensatory movements—Adjustments made for injury or weakness, such as when one muscle works harder than it usually would in order to make up for a different injured muscle.

competence—Knowing you are capable of success.

concentric contraction—Occurs when muscles creating a movement shorten, such as dancers pushing off for a jump.

coping—The deliberate effort to solve personal and interpersonal problems and seeking to minimize or adjust to stressful or challenging experiences.

cross-training—Any form of training other than the targeted activity, which aims to assist the targeted activity.

cyclical—Repetitive and repeating, such as the passing of the seasons each year.

dancer screening process—A series of tests carried out before the start of a season or before any injuries have occurred, to examine various health aspects that may pertain to dance performance and injury occurrence.

decibels (dB)—The measurement of sound intensity.

disaccharides—Two sugar molecules linked together, such as lactose, sucrose, and maltose.

diversity—The quality or state of having many different forms, types, ideas, and even personalities.

doming exercises—Involve contracting the muscles of the arch and the flexors of the proximal phalanges.

duration—How long an exercise or set of exercises lasts.

eccentric contraction—Muscle contraction in which muscles need to elongate even though they continue working, such as dancers landing from a jump.

emotion-focused coping—A strategy in which a person becomes upset, angry, anxious, or uncomfortable about the problem; energy is not invested in solving the problem.

empowerment—Measures designed to increase the degree of independence and self-determination in your life in order to enable you to support your interests in a responsible and self-determined way.

endosteum—A thin layer of cells lining the medullary cavity of the bone.

energy return—A property of a dance floor that assists jumps by releasing stored energy in a floor to the dancer.

epiphyseal plate—Where bone growth takes place separating the two regions of epiphysis and diaphysis.

epiphyses—The enlarged ends of a long bone made up of cancellous bone.

essential amino acids—Those amino acids that humans cannot synthesize but must get from the foods eaten.

essential fatty acids—Those fatty acids that humans need to eat because the human body cannot make them from other fats; a subgroup of unsaturated fats.

evidence based—Based on information obtained through scientific study or repeated practice with rigorous standards.

exposure—An event that puts a dancer at risk for injury, such as participation in a technique class, rehearsal, or performance.

extrinsically motivated—Participating in dance for reasons external to the activity such as praise or punishment.

fascia—Like ligaments, made of tough connective tissue; adds additional stability to the area it covers.

fat—A macronutrient that contains a rich source of energy found in nature in animals and also in certain plants; they provide an abundant source of fuel for energy often in times when the body is doing very little.

fat soluble—Refers to vitamins that dissolve in fats and can be stored in the liver, so they do not need to be consumed daily.

feedback—Messages about the body's position and movement that are sent to the brain.

fibrocartilage—Spacers and shock absorbers, most notably in the spine and knee.

fibrous joints—Joints that allow little or no movement and hold together the bones of the skull; they serve to connect, reinforce, and strengthen bones.

flat bones—Thin, flat bones that protect organs; examples include the skull and the ribs.

flexibility—Range of motion in a joint and the length in the muscles that cross the joint.

flow—Total harmony between your mind and your body, so that your body moves as you imagine without any apparent effort.

force reduction—The property of a dance floor that absorbs energy during the landing impacts of a dancer.

frequency—How often or how many times an exercise is carried out.

friction—The horizontal force between a dancer's body and the floor that prevents slipping.

frontal (coronal) plane—The vertical plane that divides the body into front and back portions, sometimes called the Door Plane.

glycemic index (GI)—A ranking of foods based on their overall effect on blood sugar levels.

glycemic load (GL)—A way of estimating how much a certain food will raise a person's blood glucose level, or the amount of single sugar molecules in the blood.

glycogen—Storage of an energy source in the muscles and liver.

glycogen synthesis—The process where dietary carbohydrates are converted into the human storage form, namely glycogen.

goal setting—Important method of deciding what you want to achieve in your life, determining what is important versus what is a distraction, and learning how to motivate yourself.

goniometer—A tool used to measure the angle of a joint between two limbs.

heel clocks—Special weight-bearing exercises to mobilize the subtalar joint; imagine the face of a clock under your heel, and move the heel around the clock.

high-intensity interval training (HIIT)—Training characterized by movement phrases performed at short intervals of high-intensity close to maximum heart rate followed by low intensity or complete rest.

HRmax—Abbreviation for maximum heart rate.

hyaline cartilage—Lines all of the ends of bones where they come together to form joints.

hydration—Increasing the amount of water in the body.

hyperextended knees—The back of the knee is bowed due to long ligaments.

hypermobility—A condition of greater than typical extensibility of the connective tissues.

imagery—Involves sounds, tastes, smells, and kinesthetic and tactile (touch) sensations.

individuality—Refers to training that is designed to take account of individual skill, previous experience, physical condition, gender, age, and so on.

injury—A physical impairment that requires the dancer to take at least one day off from dance activity beyond the day of the injury onset itself.

injury signs—The outward evidence of a limitation from an injury.

injury surveillance—Also called injury reporting, observing and keeping track of injury occurrence and other factors associated with the injury such as injury type, affected body part and information about when, where, and how the injury happened.

injury symptoms—The sensations that one feels from an injury.

insole—The layer of the sole of the shoe that is in contact with the bottom the foot.

insoluble fiber—Indigestible matter that passes through the digestive system almost unchanged.

intensity—Level of exercise with regard to how hard it is.

interosseous membrane—A specialized fibrous joint, such as the one that holds together the two bones of the forearm.

interval training—A form of training that considers the intensity of exercise and recommends a specific rest interval for optimizing recovery for the activity.

intrinsically motivated—Participating in dance for reasons inherent in the activity such as fun, curiosity, and to learn new skills.

irregular bones—Bones with complex shapes specialized for specific purposes.

isometric contraction—A contraction of a muscle with no change in length.

isotonic drink—Drink with a similar composition per liter as body fluids.

joint—The articulation of two or more bones, that is, where they come together.

joint cavity—A small space surrounded by a synovial membrane that is filled with fluid to lubricate and nourish the joint.

joint hypermobility—A joint that can be extended beyond normal range, such as hyperextended knees; sometimes called swayback legs.

joint mobility—Moving a joint through its range of movement.

joint range of motion—Amount of motion allowed at a joint based on its bones and ligaments.

joint stability—The ability to control joint range of motion or position.

kinesthetic—Related to sensations in your muscles, joints, and tendons that inform you about your body's position and movement.

kinesthetic imagery—Imagery that involves physical sensations.

kinetic chains—A combination of a number of joints that are arranged in a sequence and form a complex motor pattern.

ligaments—Structures that tie bones together at the joint.

long bones—Bones that are longer than they are wide allowing for movement; examples include the bones of the legs, arms, fingers, and toes.

macronutrients—Nutrients that provide energy. Large ("macro") nutrients contained in food form the building blocks needed for growth, repair, and energy of many bodily functions.

marking—Dancing in a way that conserves physical energy in the execution of the movement while at the same time focuses on qualitative aspects of the movement.

mastery oriented—A term from achievement goal theory, this means judging competence in relation to personal progress. It is also known as a task orientation in some literature.

medullary cavity—Cavity located in the diaphysis that contains bone marrow.

meniscus (plural: menisci)—A circular piece of cartilage that forms a spacer pad in the knee joint.

mental practice—Performing movements in your mind instead of doing them physically.

mental rehearsal—Imagining every aspect of a dance class, examination, audition, rehearsal, or performance, as if it were really happening.

metabolism—All biochemical transformations in the body necessary for sustaining life.

metaphorical imagery—Imagery based on words or phrases to communicate an idea or sensation that is not actually occurring.

micronutrients—Vitamins and minerals needed in very small amounts by the body.

midsole—The layer of the sole of the shoe that lies between the outsole and insole.

mindfulness—Being deeply absorbed in what you are doing at the present time.

minerals—Nonliving natural substances of definite chemical composition.

mirror system—The system that enables your brain to share the sensation of another person's movement.

monosaccharides—Single sugar molecules, include glucose, fructose (fruit sugar), and galactose, found in milk products.

motor learning—Changes that occur with practice or experience that determine a person's capability for producing a motor skill; these changes are relatively permanent, and are associated with repetition of motor skills.

motor plan—A series of motor commands (electrical signals) that will occur in a particular order.

motor system—The way the brain and other parts of the nervous system control movement.

movement planner—The brain process that translates a goal into a set of motor commands and sends them to your muscles.

muscular endurance—Ability to exert force for a prolonged period of time.

muscular power—Ability to generate as much force as possible as quickly as possible.

muscular strength—Ability to exert a maximal amount of force.

myofascial pain—A type of pain rooted in overuse of the muscles and the connective tissue (fascia) that surrounds and runs through the muscles.

neurological system—The brain and its pathways to the body.

neutral pelvis—An organization of the pelvis and spine in which the ASIS bones (anterior superior iliac spine—the two projections on the front of the pelvis called the hip bones) are vertically aligned over the pubic bone.

non-doing activities—Activities that ask you to stop (refrain from) your habitual way of doing things.

normative values—Expected values for a given population of people based on previously measured values from people in that population.

nutrients—Substances taken into the body in food or drink that supply energy or building material or contribute to body functions.

ossification—The process by which new bone is formed.

osteoblasts—Bone-building cells.

osteoporosis—A skeletal disorder characterized by compromised bone strength predisposing a person to an increased risk of fracture.

outsole—The layer of the sole of the shoe that is in contact with the ground.

overtraining—A physical, behavioral, and emotional condition that occurs when the volume and intensity of a person's exercise exceeds capacity for recovery.

overuse—Using a muscle or muscle group excessively or in actions being too repetitive and invariable.

pacing—Determining a set level of energy expenditure and keeping a balance of energy expenditure and recuperation.

perceptual skills—Those skills related to perception that are inherited rather than learned but can be enhanced by training.

performance anxiety—A perceived imbalance between the demands placed upon a person and that person's ability to meet those demands.

performance oriented—A term from achievement goal theory, this means judging competence in relation to others. This is also known as an ego orientation in some literature.

periodization—The gradual buildup of intensity in physical training through skillful timing and scheduling of workouts.

periosteum—A thin membrane of specialized cells that create new bone; it covers the compact bone.

plumb line—Imaginary line that can be drawn through the top of the head, center of the ears, bodies of the central cervical vertebrae, acromia of the shoulder girdles, bodies of the central lumbar vertebrae, heads of the femur, centers of the knee joints, and centers of the ankle joints.

plyometrics—A form of jump training exerting maximal force in short intervals.

postural reflex—A series of muscle reflexes that automatically maintain your body posture throughout all movement.

primary motor cortex—Part of your motor cortex that sends nerve signals to control movement.

proactive—Taking charge to control a situation by making things happen or by preparing for possible future problems.

problem-focused coping—A strategy in which a person puts in the energy needed to solve a problem.

progressive overload—Gradual increase of stress placed on the body during exercise as the body adapts.

proprioception—Sense of where the body is in space and in relation to itself; created when specialized tissues (nerve cells) in the bones, muscles, tendons, ligaments, joints, and skin receive information during stance and movement, and send this information to the brain.

proprioceptive neuromuscular facilitation (PNF)—A form of stretching using muscle reflexes and responses to aid in flexibility gains.

protein—Macronutrient that is the building block of many tissues in the body such as hair, muscle, nails, in bone, and even our tears.

reflex arc—A nerve pathway that carries messages to the spinal cord to create a quick, automatic reaction to a stimulus.

relatedness—Psychological need to feel connected to others in the social environment.

remodeling—The process by which old bone tissue is replaced by new bone tissue in the adult skeleton influencing bone strength.

replication—Attempting to do an observed task.

rest—A period of no activity, a true break from the current tasks, either physical or mental.

reversibility—Principle stating that if you are not consistent in your conditioning program, a detraining in performance can occur.

rosin—a sticky material that can be crushed up under the soles of shoes to increase the friction when dancing on a slippery floor, minimizing the risk of falls and slips.

rotational discs—Small platforms placed on ball bearings that can rotate in either direction. Someone can stand with one foot on a disc to rotate the whole leg from the hip without friction from the floor.

sagittal plane—The vertical plane that divides the body into right and left sides; sometimes called the wheel plane.

saturated fat—Contains as many atoms of oxygen as possible in the fat molecule, which makes this form of fat highly solid at room temperature, such as butter, lard, meat fat, and cheese.

self-awareness—The ability for introspection and the skill to recognize oneself as an individual separate from other individuals.

self-compassion—Being kind to yourself.

self-concept—A set of stable beliefs about qualities and characteristics.

self-confidence—The extent to which you feel capable of doing something well.

self-efficacy—The belief that you are capable of accomplishing a specific task.

self-esteem—How you value yourself.

sensorimotor system—Brain areas that use information from your senses to produce movement.

sensory awareness—Being conscious of the sensations coming from the sensory nerves throughout your body.

sensory feedback—Messages to your brain from any of your sensory nerves.

sesamoid bones—Round bones embedded within tendons, such as the kneecap.

short bones—Bones that are shaped like small dice; present in the wrists and ankles allowing for complex and detailed movements.

soluble fiber—Turns to a gel during the digestive process and helps regulate blood glucose levels.

somatic anxiety—Physical symptoms of performance anxiety, such as stiff or shaky muscles, needing to go to the toilet often, "butterflies" in the stomach, increased heart rate, and a dry mouth.

somatic practices or **somatic education**—Learning methods that focus on sensation and awareness to make changes in the body's habitual movements and alignment.

specificity—Principle of training; related to dance, you exercise a muscle group through the same range of motion, speed, and duration as the dance activity in order for the conditioning exercises to transfer adequately to dance.

sprain—An injury to a ligament.

sprung floor—A floor that absorbs shock, improves performance, and may prevent dance injuries.

starches—Hugely varied structures of glucose molecules linked together in various ways, and found in less nutrient rich foods, such as white bread, cakes, and many snack foods, or more nutrient rich foods such as whole-grain bread, brown rice, whole-grain couscous and pasta, and whole-grain oats.

stress—An emotional experience created by a physical or psychological event that can result in physiological and psychological responses in the body.

stress fractures—Small fractures caused by excessive repetitive impact of bones such as the metatarsals.

stressor—A stimulus or event that triggers stress symptoms which can be positive or negative.

subjective imagery—Imagery of personal sensations such as sleepiness, fear, and pain.

synovial fluid—The fluid in the synovial membrane that lubricates and nourishes the joint.

synovial joints—Also known as movable joints; joints with the greatest range of motion.

synovial membrane—Structure in the joint that secretes fluid to lubricate the joint for smooth action.

tapering—Slowly reducing the time or intensity or work.

technique—A broad term that can cover any aspect of dancers' training from functional body elements (e.g., core support and turnout) to specific dance skills (e.g., turning, elevation steps, balancing).

tendinopathy—Injury to a tendon; sometimes incorrectly called tendinitis.

tendons—Attach muscles to bones; they are made of similar tissue as ligaments.

tibial torsion—A condition in which the tibia spirals or twists as it goes down the leg.

torque—A force that causes an object to rotate; used in performing turns.

transfer of training—The effect or influence that skill or knowledge acquired in one circumstance has on learning skills and problem solving in another circumstance.

transverse plane—The horizontal plane that divides the body into upper and lower portions; sometimes called the table plane.

under-recovery—Inability to meet or exceed performance in a particular activity, occurring when the dancer is not attaining sufficient rest and nutrition, and when training variables (intensity, frequency, and duration) are out of balance.

unsaturated fat—Contains one or more spare spaces on the fat molecule, and are liquid at room temperature, such as olive oil and other vegetable oils, and fatty fish such as salmon.

upper—All the material in a shoe that lies on the top and sides of the foot.

valid—Describes when something does what it claims to do, such as when a test or a piece of equipment accurately measures what it claims to measure.

variables—Those characteristics or aspects of the movement that can be changed while still keeping the essence of the movement.

vertical deformation—The up-and-down movement of a dance floor that occurs during dancing.

visual imagery—Imagery that involves seeing objects and abstract shapes in the mind.

vitamins—Organic substances essential to normal metabolism, found in small quantities in natural foodstuffs and sometimes produced synthetically.

volume—How much exercise or how many repetitions one does.

water soluble—Vitamins that are dissolved in water, and are excreted in urine; excess cannot be stored, so they need to be consumed regularly.

References and Resources

Chapter 1

Chockley, C. (2008). Ground reaction force comparison between jumps landing on the full foot and jumps landing en pointe in ballet dancers. *Journal of Dance Medicine & Science, 12*(1), 5-8.

Conti, S.F., & Wong, Y.S. (2001). Foot and ankle injuries in the dancer. *Journal of Dance Medicine & Science, 5*(2), 43-50.

Dance Consortium. (2013). Dancers as athletes. www.danceconsortium.com/features/article/dancers-as-athletes [October 12, 2013].

Dearborn, K., & Ross, R. (2006). Dance learning and the mirror. *Journal of Dance Education, 6*(4), 109-115.

Fong Yan, A., Hiller, C., Sinclair, P.J., & Smith, R.M. (2014). Kinematic analysis of sautés in barefoot and shod conditions. *Journal of Dance Medicine & Science, 18*(4), 149-158.

Fong Yan, A., Hiller, C., Smith, R., & Vanwanseele, B. (2011). Effect of footwear on dancers: a systematic review. *Journal of Dance Medicine & Science, 15*(2), 86-92.

Fong Yan, A., Smith, R., Hiller, C., & Sinclair, P. (2013). The effect of jazz shoe design on impact attenuation. *Footwear Science, 5*(sup1), S124-S125. doi: http://dx.doi.org/10.1080/19424280.2013.799597

Fong Yan, A., Smith, R.M., Vanwanseele, B., & Hiller, C. (2012). Mechanics of jazz shoes and their effect on pointing in child dancers. *Journal of Applied Biomechanics, 28*(3), 242-248.

Hackney, J., Brummel, S., Jungblut, K., & Edge, C. (2011). The effect of sprung (suspended) floors on leg stiffness during grand jeté landings in ballet. *Journal of Dance Medicine & Science, 15*(3), 128-133.

Hagins, M., Pappas, E., Kremenic, I., Orishimo, K., & Rundle, A. (2007). The effect of an inclined landing surface on biomechanical variables during a jumping task. *Clinical Biomechanics, 22*, 1030-1036.

Hopper, L., Alderson, J., Elliott, B.C., & Ackland, T. (2015). Dance floor force reduction influences ankle loads in dancers during drop landings. *Journal of Science and Medicine in Sport. 18(4)*, 480-485. doi: http://dx.doi.org/10.1016/j.jsams.2014.07.001

Hopper, L., Allen, N., Wyon, M., Alderson, J., Elliott, B., & Ackland, T. (2014). Dance floor mechanical properties and dancer injuries in a touring professional ballet company. *Journal of Science and Medicine in Sport, 17*(1), 29-33. doi: http://dx.doi.org/10.1016/j.jsams.2013.04.013

Hopper, L., Wheeler, T.J., Webster, J.M., Allen, N., Roberts, J.R., & Fleming, P.R. (2014). Dancer perceptions of the force reduction of dance floors used by a professional touring ballet company. *Journal of Dance Medicine & Science, 18*(3), 121-130.

Hutt, K., & Redding, E. (2014). The effect of an eyes-closed dance-specific training program on dynamic balance in elite pre-professional ballet dancers: a randomized controlled pilot study. *Journal of Dance Medicine & Science, 18*(1), 3-11. doi: http://dx.doi.org/10.12678/1089-313X.18.1.3

Laws, K. (2008). *Physics and the art of dance.* 2nd ed. New York: Oxford Uniersity Press.

Liederbach, M., Richardson, M., Rodriguez, M., Compagno, J., Dilgen, F., & Rose, D. (2006). Jump exposures in the dance training environment: A measure of ergonomic demand. *Journal of Athletic Training, 41*(2 Suppl.), S85-86.

McGuiness, D., & Doody, C. (2006). The injuries of competitive Irish dancers. *Journal of Dance Medicine & Science, 10*(1&2), 35-39.

Pedersen, E.M., & Wilmerding, V. (1998). Injury profiles of student and professional flamenco dancers. *Journal of Dance Medicine & Science, 2*(3), 108-114.

Sawyer. Thomas H., editor-in-chief. (2013). *Facility Planning and Design for Health, Physical Activity, Recreation, and Sport.*13th ed. Champaign, IL: Sagamore.

The National Institute for Occupational Safety and Health. (2013). Indoor environmental quality. www.cdc.gov/niosh/topics/indoorenv [April 21, 2015].

The National Institute for Occupational Safety and Health. (2014). Controls for noise exposure. www.cdc.gov/niosh/topics/noisecontrol [April 21, 2015].

Walter, H.L., Docherty, C.L., & Schrader, J. (2011). Ground reaction forces in ballet dancers landing in flat shoes versus pointe shoes. *Journal of Dance Medicine & Science, 15*(2), 61-64.

Wilmerding, V., Gurney, B., & Torres, V. (2003). The effect of positive heel inclination on posture in young children training in flamenco dance. *Journal of Dance Medicine & Science, 7*(3), 85-90.

Chapter 2

Batson, G. (2008). Proprioception. Resource Paper. International Association for Dance Medicine & Science.

www.iadms.org/displaycommon.cfm?an=1&subarti-clenbr=210

Biel, A. (2010). *Trail guide to the body*. 4th ed. Boulder, CO: Books of Discovery.

Clippinger, K. (2006). *Dance anatomy and kinesiology*. Champaign, IL: Human Kinetics.

Education Committee, IADMS. (2000). The challenge of the adolescent dancer. Resource paper. International Association for Dance Medicine & Science. www.iadms.org/displaycommon.cfm?an=1&subarticlenbr=1

Hamilton, N., Weimar, W., & Luttgens, K. (2008). *Kinesiology: Scientific basis of human motion.* 11th ed. Boston: McGraw-Hill.

Krasnow, D., & Deveau, J. (2010). *Conditioning with imagery for dancers.* Toronto: Thompson Educational.

Krasnow, D., Monasterio, R., & Chatfield, S. J. (2001). Emerging concepts of posture and alignment. *Medical Problems of Performing Artists, 16*(1), 8-16.

Krasnow, D., & Wilmerding, V. (2011). Turnout for dancers: Supplemental Training. Resource paper for the International Association for Dance Medicine & Science, peer-reviewed by the Education Committee. www.iadms.org/displaycommon.cfm?an=1&subarti-clenbr=329

Krasnow, D.H., & Wilmerding, M.V. (2015). *Motor learning and control for dance: Principles and practices for teachers and performers*. Champaign, IL: Human Kinetics.

Laws, K. (2011). Storing momentum in ballet movements. *The IADMS Bulletin for Teachers, 3*(1), 5-8.

Laws, K., & Petrie C. (1999). Momentum transfer in dance movement—vertical jumps: A research update. *Medical Problems of Performing Artists, 14*(3), 138-40.

Laws, K., & Sugano, A. (2008). *Physics and the art of dance.* 2nd ed. New York: Oxford University Press.

Magill, R.A. (2011). *Motor learning and control.* 9th ed. New York: McGraw-Hill.

Muscolino, J.E. (2009). *Musculoskeletal anatomy coloring book.* 2nd ed. St. Louis, MO: Mosby Elsevier.

Schmidt, R.A., & Lee, T.D. (2011). *Motor control and learning: A behavioral emphasis.* 5th ed. Champaign, IL: Human Kinetics.

Schmidt, R.A., & Wrisberg, C.A. (2014). *Motor learning and performance: A situation-based learning approach.* 5th ed. Champaign, IL: Human Kinetics.

Shumway-Cook, A., & Woollacott, M. (2001). *Motor control: Theory and practical applications.* 2nd ed. Baltimore: Williams & Wilkins.

Sugano, A., & Laws, K. (2002). Physical analysis as a foundation for pirouette training, *Medical Problems of Performing Artists, 17*(1), 29-32.

Wilmerding, V., & Krasnow, D. (2011). Turnout for danc-ers: Hip anatomy and factors affecting turnout. Resource paper for the International Association for Dance Medicine and Science, peer-reviewed by the Education

Committee. http://www.iadms.org/displaycommon.cfm?an=1&subarticlenbr=323

Wilmerding, V., & Krasnow, D. (2009). Motor learning and teaching dance. Resource Paper. International Association for Dance Medicine & Science. www.iadms.org/displaycommon.cfm?an=1&subarticlenbr=250

Chapter 3

Ambegaonkar, J. (2004). Encouraging dancers to train for upper body fitness. *Bulletin for Dancers and Teacher, 5*(1), International Association for Dance Medicine & Science. www.iadms.org/?page=bulletinv5n1

Calais-Germain, B. (2007). *Anatomy of movement*. Seattle, WA: Eastland Press.

Clippinger, K. (2016). *Dance anatomy and kinesiology.* 2nd ed. Champaign, IL: Human Kinetics.

Clarkson, P.M., & Skrinar, M. (1988). *Science of dance train-ing.* Champaign, IL: Human Kinetics.

Dowd, I. (2005) *Taking root to fly: Articles on Functional anatomy.* Irene Dowd.

Fitt, S. (1996). *Dance kinesiology.* 2nd ed. Independence, KY: Cengage Learning.

Franklin, E. (2012). *Dynamic alignment through imagery.* 2nd ed. Champaign, IL: Human Kinetics.

Franklin, E. (2004). *Conditioning for dance.* Champaign, IL: Human Kinetics.

Koutedakis Y., & Sharp, N. C. C. (1999). *The fit and healthy dancer*. Chichester, UK: Wiley.

Krasnow, D., & Deveau, J. (2010). *Conditioning with imagery for dancers.* Toronto: Thompson Educational.

Laws H. (2005). Fit to Dance 2: Report of the second national inquiry into dancers' health and injury in the UK. London: Dance UK.

Moore, M. (2007). Golgi tendon organs (GTOs): Neu-roscience update with relevance to stretching and proprioception in dancers. *Journal of Dance Medicine & Science, 11*(3), 85-92.

Quin, E., Rafferty, S., & Tomlinson, C. (2015). *Safe dance practice: An applied dance science perspective.* Champaign, IL: Human Kinetics.

Rafferty S. (2010). Considerations for integrating fitness into dance training. *Journal of Dance Medicine & Science, 14*(2), 45-49.

Solomon, R., Minton, S.C., & Solomon, J. (1990). *Preventing dance injuries: An interdisciplinary perspective.* Reston, VA: American Alliance for Health, Physical Education, Recreation and Dance.

Watkins, A., & Clarkson, P.M. (1990). *Dance longer, dancing stronger: A dancer's guide to improving technique and pre-venting injury.* Hightstown, NJ: Princeton Books.

Welsh, T. (2009). *Conditioning for dancers.* Gainseville, FL: University Press of Florida.

Wynn, K., & Lawrence, M.E. (2013). *The anatomy coloring book.* Boston: Addison-Wesley Educational.

Chapter 4

Anema, H.A., & Dijkerman, H.C. (2013). Motor and kinesthetic imagery. In *Multisensory Imagery* (pp. 93-113). New York: Springer.

Barlow, W. (1973). *The Alexander Technique*. New York: Random House Incorporated.

Bartenieff, I., Hackney, P., Jones, B.T., Van Zile, J., & Wolz, C. (1984). The potential of movement analysis as a research tool: A preliminary analysis. *Dance Research Journal, 16*, 3-26.

Batson, G. (2009). Somatic studies and dance. Resource Paper. International Association for Dance Medicine & Science. www.iadms.org/?248

Batson, G. (2008). Proprioception. Resource Paper. International Association for Dance Medicine & Science. www.iadms.org/displaycommon.cfm?an=1&subarticlenbr=210

Batson, G. (2007). Revisiting overuse injuries in dance in view of motor learning and somatic models of distributed practice. *Journal of Dance Medicine & Science, 11*(3), 70-75.

Batson, G., Quin, E., & Wilson, M. (2012). Integrating somatics and science. *Journal of Dance & Somatic Practices, 3*(1-2), 183-193.

Brodie, J., & Lobel, E. (2004). Integrating fundamental principles underlying somatic practices into the dance technique class. *Journal of Dance Education, 4*(3), 80-87.

Calvo-Merino, B., Glaser, D.E., Grèzes, J., Passingham, R.E., & Haggard, P. (2005). Action observation and acquired motor skills: An fMRI study with expert dancers. *Cerebral Cortex, 15*(8), 1243-1249.

Enghauser, R. (2007). The quest for an ecosomatic approach to dance pedagogy. *Journal of Dance Education, 7*(3), 80-90.

Enghauser, R. (2007). Developing listening bodies in the dance technique class. *Journal of Physical Education, Recreation & Dance, 78*(6), 33-38.

Feldenkrais, M. (1972). *Awareness through movement*. New York: Harper and Row.

Franklin, E.N. (2013). *Dance imagery for technique and performance*. Champaign, IL: Human Kinetics.

Geber, P., & Wilson, M. (2010). Teaching at the interface of dance science and somatics. *Journal of Dance Medicine & Science, 14*(2), 50-57.

Green, J. (2002). Somatic knowledge: The body as content and methodology in dance education. *Journal of Dance Education, 2*(4), 114-118.

Ideokinesis. www.ideokinesis.com/pioneers/todd/todd.htm

Kearns, L.W. (2010). Somatics in action: How "I feel three-dimensional and real" improves dance education and training. *Journal of Dance Education, 10*(2), 35-40.

Krasnow, D. H., & Wilmerding, M. V. (2015). *Motor learning and control for dance: Principles and practices for performers and teachers*. Champaign, IL: Human Kinetics.

Mainwaring, L.M., & Krasnow, D.H. (2010). Teaching the dance class: Strategies to enhance skill acquisition, mastery and positive self-image. *Journal of Dance Education, 10*(1), 14-21.

Moyle, G.M. (2014). Mindfulness and dancers. In *The Cambridge Companion to Mindfulness and Performance*, pp. 367-388. Cambridge: Cambridge University Press.

Nordin, S.M., & Cumming, J. (2006). The development of imagery in dance: Part I. Qualitative findings from professional Dancers. *Journal of Dance Medicine & Science, 10*, 21-27.

Nordin, S.M., & Cumming, J. (2006). The development of imagery in dance: Part II. Quantitative findings from a mixed sample of dancers. *Journal of Dance Medicine & Science, 10*, 28-34.

Overby, L.Y., & Dunn, J. (2011). The history and research of dance imagery: Implications for teachers. *IADMS Bulletin for Teachers, 3*(2), 9-11.

Sweigard, L.E. (1988). *Human movement potential: Its ideokinetic facilitation*. Lanham, MD: University Press of America.

Todd, M.E. (1937). *The thinking body*. New York: Princeton Books.

Chapter 5

ACSM. (2011). Information on the female athlete triad. American College of Sports Medicine brochure. http://acsm.org/docs/brochures/the-female-athlete-triad.pdf

Aujla, I.J., Nordin-Bates, S.M., Redding, E., & Jobbins, V. (2014). Developing talent among young people: Findings from the UK Centres for Advanced Training. *Theatre, Dance and Performance Training, 5*(1), 15-30.

Byrne, E., & Mainwaring, L. (2015). Walk it off: Walking to Regulate Negative affect. 14th European Congress on Sport Psychology, Bern, Switzerland.

Clark, T., Nordin-Bates, S.M., & Walker, I.J. (2009). Beyond physical practice: Psychological skills training for enhanced performance. *Foundations for Excellence Fact Sheet*, DSCF. Available to download at www.foundations-for-excellence.org/resources

Cumming, J., & Duda, J.L. (2012). Profiles of perfectionism, body-related concerns, and indicators of psychological health in vocational dance students: An investigation of the 2x2 model of perfectionism. *Psychology of Sport and Exercise, 13*, 727-738.

De Souza, M.J., Nattiv, A., Joy, E., Misra, M., Williams, N.I., Mallinson, R., Gibbs, & Matheson, G. Expert Panel. (2014). Female athlete triad coalition consensus statement on treatment and return to play of the female athlete triad: 1st International Conference held in San Francisco, May 2012 and 2nd International Conference held in Indianapolis, Indiana, May 2013. *British Journal of Sports Medicine, 48*, 289. doi:10.1136/bjsports-2013-093218. http://bjsm.bmj.com/content/48/4/289.short

Dodge, R., Daly, A.P., Huyton, J., & Sanders, L.D. (2012). The challenge of defining wellbeing. *International Journal of Wellbeing, 2*(3), 222-235.

Frost, R., Marten, R., Lahart, C., & Rosenblate, R. (1990). The dimensions of perfectionism. *Cognitive Therapy and Research, 14*, 449-468.

Grove, J.R., Main, L.C., & Sharp, L. (2013). Stressors, recovery processes and manifestations of training distress in dance. *Journal of Dance Medicine & Science, 17*(2), 70. http://dx.doi.org/10.12678/1089-313X.17.2.70

Hamilton, L.H., Hamilton, W.G., Meltzer, J.D., Marshall, P., & Molnar, M. (1989). Personality, stress, and injuries in professional ballet dancers. *The American Journal of Sports Medicine, 17*(2), 263-267.

Krasnow, D., Mainwaring, L., & Kerr, G. (1999). Injury, stress and perfectionism in young dancers and gymnasts. *Journal of Dance Medicine & Science, 3*(2), 51-58.

Lazarus, R., & Folkman, S. (1984). *Stress, appraisal, and coping.* New York: Springer.

Liederbach, M. & Compagno, J.M. (2001). Psychological aspects of fatigue-related injuries in dancers. *Journal of Dance Medicine & Science, 5*(4), 116-120.

Mainwaring, L., Kerr, G., & Krasnow, D. (1993). Psychological correlates of dance injuries. *Medical Problems of Performing Artists, 8*, 3-6.

Mainwaring, L M., & Krasnow, D.H. (2010). Teaching the dance class: Strategies to enhance skill acquisition, mastery and positive self-image. *Journal of Dance Education, 10*(1), 14-21.

Muilli, M., & Nordin-Bates, S.M. (2011). Motivational climates: What they are, and why they matter. *IADMS Bulletin for Teachers, 3*(2), 5-7.

Nordin-Bates, S. (2014). Perfectionism. Resource Paper. International Association for Dance Medicine & Science. http://www.iadms.org/?page=RPperfectionism

Nordin-Bates, S.M., & McGill, A. (2009). Standing on the shoulders of a young giant: How dance teachers can benefit from learning about positive psychology. *IADMS Bulletin for Teachers, 1*(1), 4-6.

Nordin-Bates, S.M., Walker, I.J., Baker, J., Garner, J., Hardy, C., & Irvine, S. (2011). Injury, imagery, and self-esteem in dance: Healthy minds in injured bodies? *Journal of Dance Medicine & Science, 15*(2), 76.

Quested, E., & Duda, J.L. (2009). Setting the stage: Social-environmental and motivational predictors of optimal training engagement. *Performance Research: A Journal of the Performing Arts, 14*,(2), 36-45.

Radell, S.A. (2013). Mirrors in the dance class: Help or hindrance? Resource Paper. International Association for Dance Medicine & Science. www.iadms.org/?400

Ringham, R., Klump, K., Kaye, W., Stone, D., Libman, S., Stowe, S., & Marcus, M. (2006). Eating disorder symptomology among ballet dancers. *International Journal of Eating Disorders, 39*(6), 503-508. doi:10.1002/eat

Sekulic, D., Peric, M., & Rodek, J. (2010). Substance use and misuse among professional ballet dancers. *Substance Use & Misuse, 45*, 1420-1430. doi:10.3109/10826081003682198

Thomas, J.J., Keel, P.K., & Heatherton, T.F. (2011). Disordered eating and injuries among adolescent ballet dancers. *Eating and Weight Disorders, 16*(3), 216-222. doi:10.1007/BF03325136

Walker, I.J., & Nordin-Bates, S.M. (2010). Performance anxiety experiences of professional dancers: The importance of control. *Journal of Dance Medicine and Science, 14*(4), 133-145.

Chapter 6

Batson, G. (2009). The somatic practice of intentional rest in dance education—Preliminary steps towards a method of study. *Journal of Dance & Somatic Practices, 1*(2), 71-97.

Batson, G. (2007). Revisiting overuse injuries in dance in view of motor learning and somatic models of distributed practice. *Journal of Dance Medicine & Science, 11*(3), 70-75.

Batson, G., & Schwartz, R.E. (2007). Revisiting the value of somatic education in dance training through an inquiry into practice schedules. *Journal of Dance Education, 7*(2), 47-56.

Dance UK: www.danceuk.org/events/rest

Fietze, I., Strauch, J., Holzhausen, M., Glos, M., Theobald, C., Lehnkering,H., & Penzel, T. (2009). Sleep quality in professional ballet dancers. *Chronobiology International, 26*(6), 1249-1262.

Liederbach, M., Schanfein, L., & Kremenic, I.J. (2013). What is known about the effect of fatigue on injury occurrence among dancers? *Journal of Dance Medicine & Science, 17*(3), 101-108.

Twitchett, E., Manuela Angioi, M., Koutedakis, Y., & Wyon, M. (2010). The demands of a working day among female professional ballet dancers. *Journal of Dance Medicine & Science, 14*(4), 127-132.

Wyon, M. (2010). Preparing to perform periodization and dance. *Journal of Dance Medicine & Science, 14*(2), 67-72.

Chapter 7

Brown, D., & Wyon, M. (2014). An international study on dietary supplementation use in dancers. *Medical Problems of Performing Artists, 29*(4), 229.

Brown, D., & Wyon, M. (2014). The effect of moderate glycemic energy bar consumption on blood glucose and mood in dancers. *Medical Problems of Performing Artists, 29*(1), 27.

Burke, L. (2007). *Practical sports nutrition.* Human Kinetics.

Challis, J., Stevens, A., & Wilson, M. (2016). IADMS Nutrition Fact Sheet and Resource Paper. www.iadms.org/?page=186

Clarkson, P.M. (1998). An overview of nutrition for female dancers. *Journal of Dance Medicine & Science, 2*(1), 32-39.

Dixon, M. (2001). Eating and dancing: Nutritional advice for dancers from Jasmine Challis. *Ballett International-al-Tanz Aktuell, 5,* 72-73.

Gibney, M.J., Lanham-New, S.A., Cassidy, A., & Vorster, H.H. (Eds.). (2013). *Introduction to human nutrition.* Oxford, UK: John Wiley & Sons.

Lanham-New, S.A., Stear, S., Shirreffs, S., & Collins, A. (Eds.). (2011). *Sport and exercise nutrition.* Oxford, UK: John Wiley & Sons.

Manore, M., Meyer, N.L., & Thompson, J. (2009). *Sport nutrition for health and performance.* Champaign, IL: Human Kinetics.

Maughan, R.J., & Shirreffs, S.M. (2008). Development of individual hydration strategies for athletes. *International Journal of Sport Nutrition, 18*(5), 457.

Sawka, M.N., Burke, L.M., Eichner, E.R., Maughan, R.J., Montain, S.J., & Stachenfeld, N.S. (2007). American College of Sports Medicine position stand. Exercise and fluid replacement. *Medicine and Science in Sports and Exercise, 39*(2), 377-390.

Wilmerding, M.V., Gibson, A., Mermier, C.M., & Bivins, K.A. (2003). Body composition analysis in dancers: Methods and recommendations. *Journal of Dance Medicine & Science, 7*(1), 24-31.

Wilmerding, M.V., McKinnon, M.M., & Mermier, C. (2005). Body composition in dancers: A review. *Journal of Dance Medicine & Science, 9*(1), 18-23.

Chapter 8

Burckhardt, P., Wynn, E., Krieg, M.A., Bagutti, C., & Faouzi, M. (2011). The effects of nutrition, puberty and dancing on bone density in adolescent ballet dancers. *Journal of Dance Medicine & Science, 15*(2), 51-60.

Clippinger, K. (2016). *Dance anatomy and kinesiology.* (2nd ed.). Champaign, IL: Human Kinetics.

Donnelly, E. (1990). *Living anatomy* (2nd ed.). Champaign, IL: Human Kinetics.

Friesen, K.J., Rozenek, R., Clippinger, K., Gunter, K., Russo, A., & Sklar, S.E. (2011). Bone mineral density and body composition of collegiate modern dancers. *Journal of Dance Medicine & Science, 15*(1), 31-36

Koutedakis, Y., & Sharp, C. (1999). *The fit and healthy dancer.* Chichester: WileyMonahan, F.D., Drake, T., & Neighbors, M. (1994). *Nursing care of adults.* Philadelphia: W.B. Saunders.

Nattiv, A., Loucks, A.B., Manore, M.M., Sanborn, C.F., Sundgot-Borgen, J., & Warren, M.P. (2007). The female athlete triad. *Medicine & Science in Sports & Exercise.* Position Stand. American College of Sports Medicine, 39 (10), 1867-82

Olsen, A., & McHose, C. (2004). *BodyStories: A guide to experiential anatomy, 2nd* ed. Lebanon, NH: University Press of New England.

Peer, K.S. (2004). Bone health in athletes: Factors and future considerations. *Orthopaedic Nursing, 23*(3), 174- 179.

Pescatello, L.S. (Ed.). (2014). *ACSM's guidelines for exercise testing and prescription.* (9th ed.) Philadelphia: Wolters Kluwer Health/Lippincott Williams & Wilkins.

Rizzoli, R. (2014). Nutritional aspects of bone health. Best Practice & Research Clinical Endocrinology & Metabolism, 28, 795-808

Robson, B., & Chertoff, A. (2008). Bone health and female dancers: physical and nutritional guidelines. Resource Paper. International Association for Dance Medicine and Science. www.iadms.org/?212

Tenforde, A.S., & Fredericson, M. (2011). Influence of sports participation on bone health in the young athlete: a review of the literature. *American Academy of Physical Medicine and Rehabilitation, 3* (9), 861-867.

U.S Department of Health and Human Services. (2004). Bone health and osteoporosis: A report of the surgeon general. Rockville, MD: Office of the Surgeon General. www.ncbi.nlm.nih.gov/books/NBK45513

Chapter 9

Batson, G. (2008). Proprioception. Resource Paper. International Association for Dance Medicine & Science. www.iadms.org/displaycommon.cfm?an=1&subarticlenbr=210

Clippinger K. (2016). *Dance anatomy and kinesiology.* 2nd ed. Champaign, IL: Human Kinetics.

Critchfield B. (2011). Stretching for dancers. Resource Paper. International Association for Dance Medicine & Science. www.iadms.org/?353

Critchfield B. (2010). First aid for dancers. Resource Paper. International Association for Dance Medicine & Science. www.iadms.org/?290

Hamilton, W.G., Molnar, M., & Sefcovic, N. (2015). Flexor Hallucis Longus Tendinopathy. In B. Reider, M.T. Provencher, & G.J. Davies (Eds.), *Orthopaedic Rehabiliatation of the Athlete* (pp. 1492-1510). Philadelphia: Elsevier Saunders.

Howse J., & McCormack, M. (2009). *Anatomy, dance technique and injury prevention.* (4th ed.) London: Methuen Drama.

IADMS Education Committee. (2000). The challenge of the adolescent dancer. Resource Paper. International Association for Dance Medicine & Science. www.iadms.org/?1

Irvine S., Redding E., & Rafferty, S. (2011). Dance fitness. Resource Paper. International Association for Dance Medicine & Science. www.iadms.org/?303

Richardson M., Liederbach M., & Sandow, E. (2010). Functional criteria for assessing pointe-readiness. *Journal of Dance Medicine & Science, 14*(3), 82-88.

Russell, J.A. (2015). Insights into the position of the ankle and foot in female ballet dancers en pointe. *IADMS Bulletin for Dancers and Teachers, 6*(1), 10-12.

Russell, J.A. (2013). Preventing dance injuries: current perspectives. *Open Access Journal of Sports Medicine, 4,* 199-210.

Russell, J.A. (2012). Breaking pointe: foot and ankle injuries in dance. *Lower Extremity Review, 4*(1), 18-22. http://lermagazine.com/cover_story/breaking-pointe-foot-and-ankle-injuries-in-dance

Russell, J.A. (2010). Acute ankle sprain in dancers. *Journal of Dance Medicine & Science, 14*(3), 89-96.

Sefkovic, N., & Critchfield, B. (2010). First aid for dancers. Resource paper for the International Association for Dance Medicine and Science, peer-reviewed by the Education Committee. www.iadms.org/?290

Weiss, D.S., Rist, R.A., & Grossman, G. (2009). When can I start pointe work? Guidelines for initiating pointe training. *Journal of Dance Medicine & Science, 13*(3): 90-92.

Chapter 10

Chatfield, S. (1998). The health of our dancers: What is it and what is it to be? *Journal of Dance Medicine & Science, 2*(1), 3.

Clippinger, K.S. (1997). Dance screening. *Journal of Dance Medicine & Science, 1*(3), 84.

Gamboa, J.M., Roberts, L.A., Maring, J., & Fergus, A. (2008). Injury patterns in elite preprofessional ballet dancers and the utility of screening programs to identify risk characteristics. *Journal of Orthopaedic & Sports Physical Therapy, 38*(3), 126-136.

Garrick, J.G. (2004). Preparticipation orthopedic screening evaluation. *Clinical Journal of Sports Medicine, 14*(3), 123-126.

Liederbach, M. (2010). Perspectives on dance science rehabilitation understanding whole body mechanics and four key principles of motor control as a basis for healthy movement. *Journal of Dance Medicine & Science, 14*(3), 114-24.

Liederbach, M. (2000). General considerations for guiding dance injury rehabilitation. *Journal of Dance Medicine & Science, 4*(2), 54–65.

Liederbach, M. (1997). Screening for functional capacity in dancers: designing standardized, dance-specific injury prevention screening tools. *Journal of Dance Medicine & Science, 1*(3), 93-106.

Liederbach, M., & Compagno, J. (2001). Psychological aspects of fatigue related injuries in dancers. *Journal of Dance Medicine & Science, 5*(4), 116-120.

Liederbach, M., Gleim, G.W., & Nicholas, J.A. (1994). Psychological and physiological measurements of performance-related stress and injury rate in professional ballet dancers. *Medical Problems of Performing Artists, 9*(1), 10-14.

Liederbach, M., Hagins, M., Gamboa, J.M., & Welsh, T.M. (2012). Assessing and reporting dancer capacities, risk factors, and injuries: recommendations from the IADMS Standard Measures Consensus Initiative. *Journal of Dance Medicine & Science, 16*(4), 139-153.

Liederbach, M., & Richardson, M. (2007). The importance of standardized injury reporting in dance. *Journal of Dance Medicine & Science, 11*(2), 45-48.

Liederbach, M., Schanfein, L., & Kremenic, I.J. (2013). What is known about the effect of fatigue on injury occurrence among dancers? *Journal of Dance Medicine & Science, 17*(3), 101-108.

Molnar, M., & Esterson, J. (1997). Screening students in a pre-professional ballet school. *Journal of Dance Medicine & Science, 1*(3), 118-121.

Plastino, J.G. (1997). Issues encountered in the screening process. *Journal of Dance Medicine & Science, 1*(3), 85-86.

Shah, S., Weiss, D.S., & Burchette, R.J. (2012). Injuries in professional modern dancers: Incidence, risk factors, and management. *Journal of Dance Medicine and Science, 16*(1), 17-25.

Siev-Ner, I., Barak, A., Heim, M., Warshavsky, M., & Azaria, M. (1997). The value of screening. *Journal of Dance Medicine & Science, 1*(3), 87-92.

Solomon, R. (1997). A Pro-active screening program for addressing injury prevention in a professional ballet company. *Journal of Dance Medicine & Science, 1*(3), 113-117.

About the Editors

M. Virginia Wilmerding danced professionally in New York City and is now a Research Professor at the University of New Mexico in Albuquerque, where she teaches for both the exercise science and dance programs. Courses include kinesiology, research design, exercise physiology, exercise prescription, exercise and disease prevention, and conditioning. She also teaches at the Public Academy for Performing Arts, a charter school. Ginny is formerly the Chief Executive Officer of the International Association for Dance Medicine & Science (IADMS). She is past president of IADMS and served on the IADMS Board of Directors from 2001 to 2011. Ginny was the Associate Editor of science for the *Journal of Dance Medicine & Science*. She has published original research in *Journal of Dance Medicine & Science, Medical Problems of Performing Artists, Medicine & Science in Sports & Exercise, Journal of Strength and Conditioning Research*, and *Idea Today*. With Donna Krasnow she has coauthored resource papers for IADMS. Research interests include body composition, training methodologies, injury incidence and prevention, pedagogical considerations in technique class, and the physiological requirements of various dance idioms.

Donna H. Krasnow is a Professor Emerita in the Department of Dance at York University in Toronto, Canada, and was a member of the Special Faculty at California Institute of the Arts in the United States. She specializes in dance science research, concentrating on dance kinesiology, injury prevention and care, conditioning for dancers, and motor learning and motor control, with a special emphasis on the young dancer. Donna has published numerous articles in the *Journal of Dance Medicine & Science* and *Medical Problems of Performing Artists*, as well as resource papers in collaboration with M. Virginia Wilmerding for the International Association for Dance Medicine & Science (IADMS). She was the Conference Director for IADMS from 2004 to 2008 as well as serving on the Board of Directors. Donna was the Associate Editor for dance for *Medical Problems of Performing Artists*. She conducts workshops for dance faculty in alignment and healthy practices for dancers, including the Teachers Day Seminars at York University, and is a nine-time resident guest artist at Victorian College of the Arts and VCA Secondary School, University of Melbourne, Australia. Donna has created a specialized body conditioning system for dancers called C-I Training (conditioning with imagery). She has produced a DVD series of this work, and in 2010 she coauthored the book *Conditioning with Imagery for Dancers* with professional dancer Jordana Deveau. She offers courses for teachers in Limón technique pedagogy and C-I Training.

Ginny and Donna co-authored *Motor Learning and Control for Dance: Principles and Practices for Performers and Teachers*, published by Human Kinetics in 2015.

About the Contributors

Imogen Aujla, PhD, is a senior lecturer in dance and course coordinator of the MSc dance science program at the University of Bedfordshire. She trained as a dancer before specializing in dance science and later dance psychology. She has a particular interest in the psychological factors that drive participation in dance.

Glenna Batson, DSc, PT, is professor emeritus of physical therapy at Winston-Salem State University, research associate professor of health and exercise science at Wake Forest University, and Fulbright senior specialist in dance. For four decades she has honed a multidisciplinary approach to human movement studies as a teacher, researcher, and author.

Derrick D. Brown, MSc, is a researcher and certified sport nutritionist (CISSN). He is program manager and lecturer in dance science at the University of Bern Institute for Sport Science in Switzerland and senior researcher at the National Centre for the Performing Arts in the Netherlands.

Jasmine Challis, BSc, RD, is a registered dietitian and nutritionist on the UK High Performance Sport and Exercise Nutrition Register. She has worked with professional dancers, teachers, and students by giving talks, running workshops, and providing one-on-one sessions for over 25 years. She also presents at national and international conferences.

Julia Christensen, PhD, is a Newton international research fellow by the British Academy in the Cognitive Neuroscience Research Unit at City University London. Her current work explores the neurocognitive mechanisms underlying the emotional expertise of dancers and other artists.

Brenda Critchfield, MS, ATC, is the director of dance medicine and wellness facility at Brigham Young University. Since 2001 she has been a certified athletic trainer working with all levels of athletics and dance. She has traveled worldwide providing medical care to athletes and dancers.

Alycia Fong Yan, PhD, BAppSc, is a biomechanics lecturer at the University of Sydney. A former dancer and dance teacher, Alycia has applied her knowledge in exercise and sport science to dance research. Her main area of interest is dance footwear and its effect on dance performance and injury risk.

Gary Galbraith, MFA, danced with several notable dance companies and is a former principal dancer with the Martha Graham Dance Company. He is the founder and director of the Dancer Wellness Project, an online resource used worldwide by various school, professional companies, and clinics to serve the health and wellness needs of dancers.

Pamela Geber Handman, MFA, BFA, is an associate professor and director of undergraduate studies in modern dance at the University of Utah. She teaches dance kinesiology, contemporary technique, improvisation, composition, and teaching methods and has been the director of Performing Dance Company. Pamela is cofounder of Dance Science and Somatics Educators and a long-time member of IADMS.

Patrick Haggard, PhD, FBA, is a professor at the Institute of Cognitive Neuroscience at University College London. His pioneer work on how dance expertise changes neural activity in the brain while watching dance has inspired scholars from diverse disciplines such as cognitive neuroscience, psychology, art, and dance.

Luke Hopper, PhD, BSc, is a postdoctoral research fellow at the Western Australian Academy of Performing Arts. Luke was the IADMS student research award recipient in 2007 and 2009. He has served on the IADMS student and promotion committees and was elected to the IADMS board of directors in 2015.

Janet Karin, OAM, GradCert, retired as a principal dancer of the Australian Ballet to teach ballet in Canberra. Now at the Australian Ballet School, she applies neuromotor and somatic principles in her coaching. Awards include Order of Australia Medal,

2014 Australian Dance Award, and IADMS 2015 Dance Educator Award. She was IADMS president from 2013 to 2015.

Kenneth Laws, PhD, is professor emeritus of physics at Dickinson College in Pennsylvania. He is the author of the renowned text *Physics of Dance* and has published articles in *American Journal of Physics*, *Dance Research Journal*, and *Kinesiology for Dance*. Dr. Laws has given classes and seminars at universities and private dance schools nationally and internationally.

Marijeanne Liederbach, PhD, PT, is director of the Harkness Center for Dance Medicine at NYU Langone Medical Center Hospital for Joint Diseases. A former dancer and choreographer, she is a physical therapist and certified athletic trainer with a doctorate in biomechanics and ergonomics, providing backstage therapy for hundreds of dancers, dance companies, and Broadway shows.

Lynda Mainwaring, PhD, CPsych, is an associate professor of kinesiology and physical education at the University of Toronto and a registered psychologist. Her interests are in the psychology of dance injuries and performance and rehabilitation psychology. She is a member of the Research Committee for IADMS and cofounder of the Canadian Centre for Performance Psychology.

Marika Molnar, PT, LAc, is a physical therapist, educator, and dance medicine pioneer. In 1980, George Balanchine invited her to be the first onsite physical therapist for New York City Ballet. She is president of Westside Dance Physical Therapy, past president and fellow of IADMS, and developer of the Parasetter, an apparatus for self-help in recovery.

Christina Patsalidou, MFA, BSc, holds an MFA and a BFA in dance and a BSc in nutrition sciences. She is a full-time research faculty member in the dance program of the University of Nicosia, a codirector of 35 33 Dance Company, and an active researcher in the fields of dance medicine and dance education.

Emma Redding, PhD, MSc, is the head of dance science at Trinity Laban Conservatoire of Music and Dance in England. Her projects focus on dancers' health, talent, and performance. Emma is a member of the board of directors and past president of IADMS and partner of the National Institute for Dance Medicine and Science.

Jeffrey A. Russell, PhD, ATC, is assistant professor of athletic training and director of Science and Health in Artistic Performance (SHAPe) at Ohio University, where he leads a multifaceted performing arts medicine initiative he designed for the university's dance, music, theater, and marching band programs. He holds a PhD in dance science.

Shannon Sterne, MS, MA, is a registered dietitian nutritionist (RDN) with master's degrees in nutrition and dance and an assistant professor of dance at Case Western Reserve University. She performed with the San Diego Ballet and Dancing Wheels Company and now researches nutrition issues and dietary behaviors in dancers.

Arleen Sugano, MFA, coauthor of *Physics and the Art of Dance,* is a master ballet teacher having taught for the Joffrey Ballet School and professional companies, universities, and studios. Authoring the TED–Ed (Technology, Entertainment, Design–Education) fouetté video, she is the founder of SuganoSystemBallet, a scientific approach to ballet to reduce injury and promote longevity.

Margaret Wilson, PhD, MS, is a professor in the department of theater and dance at the University of Wyoming, where she teaches modern dance technique, kinesiology, and history and codirects the BFA in dance science. She also teaches, choreographs, performs, and researches rope and harness vertical dance both indoors and outdoors.

About the International Association for Dance Medicine & Science

The International Association for Dance Medicine & Science (IADMS) was formed in 1990 by an international group of dance medicine practitioners, dance educators, dance scientists, and dancers. Membership is drawn equally from the medical and dance professions, and has grown from an initial 48 members in 1991 to over 1,200 members at present world-wide, representing 35 countries.

IADMS was formed to foster several related goals in the field of dance medicine and science; the purposes and objectives of the organization are summarized in this mission statement:

IADMS enhances the health, well-being, training, and performance of dancers by cultivating educational, medical, and scientific excellence.

For information about IADMS activities and how to join, go to www.iadms.org.

Index

Note: The italicized *f* and *t* following page numbers refer to figures and tables, respectively.